THIS SHRINKING LAND

ROBERT DUCK

THIS SHRINKING LAND
CLIMATE CHANGE AND BRITAIN'S COASTS

DUNDEE UNIVERSITY PRESS

First published in Great Britain in 2011 by
Dundee University Press

University of Dundee
Dundee DD1 4HN

www.dup.dundee.ac.uk

ISBN: 978 1 84586 118 6

British Library Cataloguing-in-Publication Data
A catalogue record for this book is available on
request from the British Library

The publishers gratefully acknowledge the support
of the Scotland Inheritance Fund towards the
reproduction of illustrations in this book.

Typeset by Mark Blackadder

Printed and bound in Britain by Bell and Bain Ltd, Glasgow

For Bill Duck

CONTENTS

PREFACE

speak to the Earth, and it shall teach thee

Job 12:8

It is a favourite popular delusion that the scientific inquirer is under a sort of moral obligation to abstain from going beyond that generalisation of observed facts which is absurdly called 'Baconian' induction. But any one who is practically acquainted with scientific work is aware that those who refuse to go beyond fact, rarely get as far as fact; . . .

Thomas Henry Huxley, *On the Advisableness of Improving Natural Knowledge*, 1866

Craggy Island has its charms. The west part of the island was beautiful, until it drifted off of course . . . yes, there was a bit of a storm and it just came loose. Now we don't have a west side, it's just north, south and east. But it was lovely when it was there.

Graham Linehan and Arthur Mathews, *Father Ted*

This is not a textbook about coasts. There are too many good ones written already that I cannot better. Rather, it is a factual account of the shrinking fringes of island Britain that aspires to blend contemporary earth science and societal themes with the historical and cultural records and, for good measure, just a hint of myth and romance for seasoning. The latter are essential – many scientists, me included, need to get real. The book falls within Dundee University Press's theme of 'Science and the Public Understanding of Science' and, in many ways, it is a tribute to the numerous adult education classes that have put up with me and given me enormous satisfaction in what has turned out to be a thirty-year unbroken commitment of making science accessible to the wider public. Some years ago, my own university ran a recruitment advertising campaign under the banner of 'Serious Fun' – it received mixed reactions. I think that 'Serious Fun' is a really appropriate descriptor of what follows – and if I'm criticised for saying so, I shall be unrepentant. This, I hope, turns out to be a fun book but with a very serious message.

I was born and brought up over 60 kilometres from the sea in Easingwold, in the Vale of Mowbray in the North Riding of Yorkshire, and not to be confused with Easington in Holderness that features in subsequent chapters. In British terms, this is quite a long way from the coast and the one hour or rather more by car that the journey entailed seemed like eternity to a small boy in the late 1950s and early 1960s. However, despite the time of travel, it is thanks to wonderful family holidays and day trips with my Dad and late Mum to the likes of Filey, Scarborough, Robin Hood's Bay and Whitby that my passion for the coast and my early interest in geology became kindled and subsequently flourished. At Robin Hood's Bay in 1962, immortalised as Bramblewick in Leo Walmsley's books, I have vivid recollections of seeing a house almost completely undermined and with one corner perched on a plinth of crumbling bricks, precariously hanging over the edge of the cliffs. This was my first taste of the societal consequences of coastal erosion. A few years later, I read of the long history of houses being lost to the sea as their foundations on the cliff slopes gave way beneath them. In 1780 alone, twenty-two houses fell onto the rocky shore. In 1961, the year before my inspirational visit, three seventeenth-century cottages joined together to form the studio of painter and sculptor the late Dame Ethel Walker, collapsed into the sea only an hour or so after its owners made a hasty departure on hearing a loud crack.[1] Even today, despite the hand of man in shoring up Robin Hood's Bay, most notably in the massive sea wall defence scheme of 1975, the still obvious fragility and vulnerability of the place are what make it so enchanting (Plate 1). Walmsley's description of the place is evocative:

> The clay cliff ends abruptly at the village whose foundations are on tougher shale; but as we came in sight of the clustered cottages, we saw a heavy sea smash on to the ramparts of the old coastguard station, and its spray drive among the chimney pots like hail. Behind the rampart of masonry and cliff, however, the village, with its street

lamps already lighted, looked snug and secure, and soon we were moving down towards it, out of the sting of the wind.[2]

At a then little-known or indeed little-visited spot called Stoupe Beck beneath Stoupe Brow, close to Ravenscar and within sight of Robin Hood's Bay, I found my first ammonite on the shore that same year. This was a near-perfect specimen of what I think is *Gagaticeras* (but 'they' keep changing the names), preserved in pyrite that had been eroded by the waves out of the Jurassic sedimentary rocks that comprise the lower parts of the cliffs in this area. Like so many before, I took it for gold at the time and, were it not for wave erosion, I would not have found it. I still have it. Ravenscar is a tiny cliff-top village, but well known for its Raven Hall Hotel, of Bram Stoker fame. Older folks from around these parts know it as the 'Town that Never Was'. A grand plan in the 1890s to develop Ravenscar into a resort to rival nearby Scarborough never came to fruition – a good thing given the natural instability of the local cliffs. Natural instability, augmented by centuries of ironstone mining and alum quarrying, caused the collapse of almost the entire village of Kettleness, along with much mining infrastructure, into the sea in December 1829.[3] The continuous erosion of the friable Jurassic shale and sandstone in this area ensures a plentiful supply of fossils to the beach and rocky platform below the cliffs. At this spectacular locality (Plate 2), north of Whitby, I found a huge ammonite specimen about the size of a tea plate, which now lives in Easingwold as a splendid garden ornament. This and many other finds, in subsequent years, were the initial catalyst for my wanting to study geology at university. Long before I did, however, at the age of seven for a Christmas present, as an aid to identification of my growing collection of specimens, my Aunty Gwen and late Uncle Roy bought me a wonderful book, *British Fossils* by Duncan Forbes[4] – which I also still have. It was a bit too advanced for me at the time; actually it still is. The irony is that I grew to detest palaeontology at university and instead developed interests and perhaps even a bit of expertise in earth surface processes, specialising in the physical sedimentology of lakes, estuaries and, of course, coasts. At secondary school in Easingwold, where *velle est valere* [where there's a will there's a way], in the early years, before I could do things that really excited me like putting pieces of sodium into water, I was fed on a staple diet of Shakespeare, the climate of British Columbia and Marcus throwing his ball into the River Tiber. I found this rather unpalatable at the time. However, some things must have stuck in those dark recesses as I can recall, from *Richard II*, John of Gaunt pointing out to the Duke of York (living very near to York, teachers seemed to be so obsessed with this character) that, 'Small showers last long, but sudden storms are short', an apt reminder of the unevenness of change at the coast and indeed elsewhere in Earth history.

Today I live very much closer to the sea and just a long walk or a short cycle ride from the famous Tentsmuir National Nature Reserve, which has given me so much inspiration over the years. This is a wild area – in medieval times roaming with *diaboli, urses et bos primiginius* [devils, bear and oxen] – of forest, dunes and beaches. Tentsmuir Point is, ironically, the most rapidly accreting part of Britain, but elsewhere to the south the shores are eroding. Moreover, it is apt that its warden, Tom Cunningham, whose energy and enthusiasm are so infectious, always refers to the Reserve as 'Paradise'. It will therefore come as no surprise that Tentsmuir features more than once in the following pages. Anyone who walks the same piece of coast on a regular basis will be able to report change over time and often over quite a short period, if there have been stormy conditions between visits. In some instances, a build up of sediment, or accretion, is noted, but in Britain, nine times out of ten, erosion is observed. I have been walking the Fife coastal path for closer to forty years than thirty but it is since around 2000 that the pace of erosion has really accelerated. For instance, the stretch between Pittenweem and St Monans (Plate 3) has changed enormously since the 1980s, and in the last five years or so has been breached and overtopped repeatedly in several places during storm wave attack resulting in the installation of patchy piecemeal shoring-up defences and realignment inland at locations where the erosion was more severe. Had the old salt pans of the former Newark Coal and Salt Company[5] near St Monans still been operational they would certainly have been 'wronged' (see Chapter 7) in the storms of January 2009. This is mere observation by one individual, not hard science, but I am far from alone in noting that storminess and associated coastal erosion events have become far more commonplace in eastern Scotland in, say, the last decade and a half than perhaps they were previously. That is not to say that we have not had hugely damaging storms over the centuries as this book will explore.

In Britain we no longer have active volcanoes. The last ones to erupt were in the Western Isles of Scotland around forty or so million years ago. However, the country is not immune from the impacts of volcanic activity elsewhere in the world, as the events of April 2010, triggered by the

Eyjafjallajökull eruption, so clearly underlined. Compared with many other parts of the world our seismic activity is relatively minor and results largely from the impacts of past mining activity and uplift of the land following its compression in the last ice age. As an island, Britain's main threat is from the sea and from climate change. My mantra for decades, to the point of boring folks, I suspect, derives from my old geology lecture notes from the 1970s, written in fountain pen and now somewhat yellowing, a legacy of those wonderful 'chalk and talk', pre-laptop, pre-PC and pre-Power Point days. In those from 1973–74 I have recorded within quotation marks, 'the oceans are the graveyards of the lands', but I have no idea where I got this from or who first wrote it, which today is an irritation and a lesson that good referencing is essential. Anyway, whoever penned the words was absolutely right in the geological sense – lands become eroded by the action of the seas and it is no surprise to find that most of the world's shorelines are in a state of erosion.[6] Underpinning what much of this book is about, I had noted the phrase in the context of the Earth undergoing cycles of change as first realised by the father of geology, James Hutton, and articulated in his 1795 tour de force *Theory of the Earth*. It was to take almost another century for other geologists, most notably Sir Charles Lyell, to popularise Hutton's writings and ideas and to expound them. I was, however, many years ago struck by the way in which the then Poet Laureate Alfred Lord Tennyson (whose work also features again) encapsulated culturally the Huttonian theory in a small part of one of the most widely read of all nineteenth-century poems, *In Memoriam A.H.H.*, a rather lengthy requiem written between 1833 and 1849:

> *There rolls the deep where grew the tree.*
> *O earth, what changes hast thou seen!*
> *There where the long street roars, hath been*
> *The stillness of the central sea.*
>
> *The hills are shadows, and they flow*
> *From form to form, and nothing stands;*
> *They melt like mist, the solid lands,*
> *Like clouds they shape themselves and go.*

In understanding contemporary coastal processes, coastal changes through time and enriching the underpinning science, such words are almost as inspirational as a visit to 'Paradise'. This will hopefully provide a starter for the flavour of the main course. On geological timescales, changes can be immense and it is worth reflecting that in Britain and elsewhere the rock record shows that areas now far removed from the sea were once at the coast. For example, I was fascinated as a student by the pictorial reconstruction of the shoreline scenery near Builth Wells, now in mid-Wales, in the early Ordovician period around 480 million years ago (Plate 4).[7] With its vertical cliffs, geos and stacks, this is a vista not dissimilar to that observed today, carved out of the Devonian sedimentary rocks at spectacular Duncansby Head in Caithness (see Chapter 5).

Inspiration has also come from so many people over the past close-on four decades, not least the best geology lecturer I have ever had the pleasure to be spellbound by in my life, Professor Donald Ramsay – but, as a structural geologist, he taught me nothing about coasts. Professor John McManus did, however, in spades (both metaphorically and in reality), and we spent the best part of two decades working together on all manner of coastal and estuarine problems and issues around the world. Those were the days, and I thank John for all his mentoring, his companionship and the good fun we always had together in the field. In later years, it has given me great pleasure to work with two inspirational and justifiably proud Welshmen, Professor Mike Phillips and Professor Allan Williams, two of the finest coastal specialists in Britain, and whose knowledge, enthusiasm and friendship have been more than influential to me. It has been an enormous privilege for me over the last decade or so to be the Chair of the Tay Estuary Forum, one of a network of voluntary Local Coastal Partnerships in Britain. This has given me the opportunity to work with and learn from so many people from different walks of life, but all concerned with and passionate about the wise and sustainable use of the coastal zone. To single out one person is perhaps unfair, but the Forum's current Project Officer, Laura Booth, is, quite simply, the epitome of the individual with a 'can do attitude' and a truly exceptional colleague with whom it has always been a delight to work.

I have supervised many PhD students over the years, but none has given me more pleasure than Dr Derek McGlashan, whose studies of legal issues associated with dynamic coasts led us both into exciting new territory and in so doing has given us both a great deal of satisfaction. I have worked with and learned so much from Professor José Figueiredo da Silva in our studies in Portugal since the mid 1990s – an environmental engineer whose ability to interject with those 'but the Emperor isn't wearing any clothes' comments has often made me pause and think again. All of these folks are not only great colleagues but great friends, and I'm sure that I owe them all several drinks. So too is Professor Chris Whatley, a famous Scottish historian, Vice-Principal and my 'boss' at the University of Dundee; he was the person who encouraged me to write this book and had the faith in me that I could do it. I hope he was right, but even if he wasn't, I thank him for pushing me, quite hard at times. I am also indebted to Hugh Andrew, Managing Director of Birlinn Limited, for his wise words; 'you're an academic', he reminded me, 'so don't be shy of using adjectives!' Thirty years ago when there was time to do such frivolous things, we academic geologists used to compile so-called 'howlers', those nuggets of mirth, misunderstanding and downright mistakes from student examination scripts that kept your stamina for marking going until the bottom of the pile. For instance, 'Great Britain is loosing about ten feet of coast each year with the effect that Blackpool is getting nearer to Skegness.'[8]

At home, Ann has put up with all this nonsense with remarkably good humour by letting me hide away in my untidy study at nights and weekends with piles of books and papers – she's been tolerant over and above the call of duty and I really thank her for that. At work, on the sporadic occasions when I've found time to write any of this stuff, the other ladies in my life, Jaclyn, Jennifer and Pat, have been equally accommodating by knowing when to make me coffee at just the right times, but also knowing instinctively when to keep out of my way and shut my office door. I couldn't have done it without any one of you. I am indebted to Professor Colin Reid of the School of Law in the University of Dundee for drawing to my attention the Culbin Sands legislation from 1695 that features in Chapter 6. Finally, I am most grateful to Tracey Dixon whose expert cartographic skills produced many of the figures for me.

Rob Duck
Tayport, August 2010

1
CLIMATE CHANGE AND SEA LEVEL RISE: IS THERE A PROBLEM IN BRITAIN?

These isles are exposed continually to the uncontrolled violence of the Atlantic, for no land intervenes between their western shores and America. The prevalence, therefore, of strong westerly gales, causes the waves to be sometimes driven with irresistible force upon the coast, while there is also a current setting from the north. The spray of the sea aids the decomposition of the rocks, and prepares them to be breached by the mechanical force of the waves. Steep cliffs are hollowed out into deep caves and lofty arches; and almost every promontory ends in a cluster of rocks, imitating the forms of columns, pinnacles, and obelisks. Modern observations show that the reduction of continuous tracts to such insular masses is a process in which Nature is still actively engaged.

Sir Charles Lyell, *Principles of Geology*,
Vol. 1, 1830, describing the Shetland Islands

ATTACK FROM THE SEA: TSUNAMI AND SURGE

Danger lurks from other quarters in the Shetland Islands. When the huge tsunami waves hit and ripped forcefully, inundating the flat landscape of those far northern Scottish islands, their Mesolithic dwellers would have been obliterated. There would have been nowhere to take refuge, nowhere to run; death by drowning a tragic inevitability for all. The wall of water breaking over and engulfing these lands without warning would have been maybe 25–30 metres in height; death would have been violent, but at least it would not have been lingering.

Around 8,100 years ago, a vast submarine landslide, one of the largest the world has ever known, occurred off the coast of western Norway. An enormous volume of gravel, sand, clay and rock at the edge of Norway's continental shelf, probably around the size of Scotland's landmass today in area, collapsed catastrophically. Possibly caused by an earthquake or perhaps by the escape of methane gas from beneath the seabed, this sudden underwater collapse generated the so-called 'Storegga' tsunami[1] sweeping giant waves across the North Atlantic Ocean and North Sea towards Greenland, the Faroe Islands, Britain, Belgium and the Netherlands; so-called because Storegga is the Old Norse word for the 'Great Edge'. Other parts of the east coast of Britain in Scotland and in England were also affected by the Storegga tsunami, particularly those that were low-lying. Indeed, the devastation in coastal communities would have been immense. This was a massive event no less in scale and effect than the infamous Indian Ocean tsunami that first struck Indonesia, Sri Lanka, India and Thailand on Boxing Day in 2004. Over 250,000 lives across fourteen countries were claimed in that disaster. Many of the bodies were so damaged they were unidentifiable; scenes of sheer devastation were beamed across television screens all over the world. The fragility of life had been highlighted in bold. However, unlike the 2004 disaster, the Storegga tsunami took place long before the advent of the written word, of video footage and of instantaneous digital photographic record. Nor would there have been humanitarian aid to help rebuild homes, communities and lives. In fact, all that remains today as the somewhat inconspicuous, unassuming signature of the devastating event is a buried layer of sand. This is located about 5 or 6 metres above contemporary sea level, washed up with ferocity from the nearby seabed and often preserved sandwiched between layers of peat below and above (Plate 5). Indeed, such sequences of layers from other sites have been dated, and suggest that two further tsunamis hit the Shetland Islands around 5,500 and 1,500 years ago.[2] Their cause, however, is not known. It has even been suggested[3] that the unusual grooves on rocks at Cullen on the Banffshire coast of the Moray Firth, which resemble the cavettos that a stonemason might carve, were formed by the force of the Stroregga event (Plate 6).

The death toll caused by the Storegga tsunami and the two later events in Shetland will always remain a mystery. However, there is far more detail established of the loss of life in what is believed to have been another huge tsunami which struck the south-west of England on the morning of 20 January 1606, which in the modern calendar is 30 January 1607. On this winter forenoon, a massive wave travelled up the Bristol Channel and the Severn Estuary flooding more than 500 square kilometres of coastal lowlands. The tsunami wave's height is believed to have increased from 4 metres to over 6 metres as it was funnelled inland into the Severn Estuary.[4] Possibly triggered by an underwater earthquake, due to movement along a fault beneath the seabed to the south of Ireland, at least 2,000 people and countless animals are believed to have perished. In addition, a 60-ton ship was thrust inland by the wave at Appledore at the mouth of the River Torridge in north Devon.[5] Indeed, this flood event is widely regarded as Britain's worst natural disaster on land. The breaching of an embankment at Burnham-on-Sea in Somerset by the wave led to the human and animal populations of some thirty villages being obliterated.[6] Whatever its cause, since some authorities believe it was not a tsunami but a storm surge,[7] the scale of the devastation was widespread, affecting counties along both shores of the estuary. In the low-lying Somerset Levels on the southern side, between the Quantock and the Mendip Hills, the flood waters intruded about 20 kilometres inland. The flood was documented widely with either commemorative plaques or marks denoting the highest levels reached by its waters being cut into the stone walls of inundated churches in South Wales and Somerset.[8] In the latter county, for instance, the wall plaque in the Church of All Saints, Kingston Seymour, bears the inscription:

> An inundation of the Sea-water by overflowing and breaking down the Sea banks; happened in this Parish of Kingstone-Seamore, and many others adjoining; by reason where-of many Persons were drown'd and much Cattle, and Goods, were lost: the water in the Church was five feet high and the greatest part lay on the ground about ten days.
> William Bower

The publication of a pamphlet in 1607 was important:

> God's warning to his people of England. Wherein is related his most wonderful, and miraculous works, by the late overflowing of the waters, in the Counties of Somerset and Gloucester, the Counties of Monmouth, Glamorgan, Carmarthen, and Cardigan, with diverse other places in South Wales. Wherein is described the great losses, and wonderful damages, that happened thereby: by the drowning of many towns and villages, to the utter undoing of many thousands of people.[9]

A British tempest

In late November 1703, on the 26th and 27th of the month, another massive storm wreaked havoc in Britain. Tracking roughly north-east with low pressure centred along a line from Pembrokeshire to the Wash, this was the climactic culmination of a stormy fortnight;[10] indeed it has been referred to as 'The Greatest Storm'.[11] It claimed some 8,000 lives, ravaging numerous vessels of the Royal Navy, merchant and fishing fleets. The devastation was immense; there was widespread coastal flooding by the surge it created, inundating the coastal lowlands of the Bristol Channel area and elsewhere along the Atlantic coasts of south-west England, Ireland and Brittany.[12] On British Admiral Sir Francis Beaufort's familiar wind scale used by mariners and others, this event would have registered as a Force 12 – or hurricane force. However, this was not the first attempt to categorise wind forces. That honour goes to none other than Daniel Defoe. He witnessed the extensive devastation and destruction of 1703 and in the following year in his famous essay 'The Storm', drawing on the invited observations of numerous correspondents, he 'set down in a table of degrees'[13] the twelve terms that he applied to winds of increasing strength, a century-older precursor to the Beaufort Scale:

- Stark calm
- Calm weather
- Little wind
- A fine breeze
- A small gale
- A fresh gale
- A topsail gale
- Blows fresh
- A hard gale of wind
- A fret of wind
- A storm
- A tempest[14]

The lengthy sub-titles encapsulate the enormity of the event and the inevitable seventeenth-century belief in its wrathful cause.

On Saturday and Sunday, the weekend of the last day of January and the first day of February 1953, what is arguably the greatest peace-time disaster in living memory took hundreds of lives and devastated vast expanses of the British coast and beyond. This was most certainly not the result of a tsunami, but a no less destructive and, indeed, not dissimilar event. The highest tidal surge ever recorded in the North Sea, fuelled by the coincidence of high spring tides and hurricane force winds funnelling from north to south, coupled with low atmospheric pressure centred over the sea, overwhelmed eastern coastal defences extending from Yorkshire through Lincolnshire, the Wash, and East Anglia to the Thames Estuary and Kent (Figure 1.1). Sea level rises by 1 centimetre per millibar drop in normal air pressure; the so-called reverse barometer effect. The deep depression over the North Sea at this time was almost 50 millibars below normal atmospheric conditions, thereby causing a 50 centimetre rise in water levels over and above the effects due to wind forcing and tides. Such a depression would normally have passed to the north-west of Scotland but, on this occasion, it took a more southerly route from the north of Scotland and tracked south-eastwards from Shetland towards Denmark. With the storm force winds driving and piling water up against the shore, the 1953 surge reached almost 3 metres in height above the normal spring high tide level in the south-east of England. As a result of its ferocity, with breaking waves of twice that height and the absence of any warning of the impending threat, over 300 lives were lost and tens of thousands of helpless citizens, young and old, were rendered homeless.[15] The entire 13,000 population of low-lying Canvey Island in the Thames Estuary, an area of Essex (see Chapter 4) claimed from the sea centuries earlier, had to be evacuated from their homes; fifty-eight of the islanders lost their lives.[16] In all, in eastern England, some 24,000 houses were damaged. Sea walls could not withstand the force of the massive waves and were reduced to piles of rubble, earthen embankments and wooden retaining structures were obliterated, promenades were destroyed, vessels were wrecked or grounded and there was widespread flooding affecting nearly 2,000 acres of coastal infrastructure, docks, towns, villages and agricultural land.[17]

The tide in Kent rose in some places as high as eight feet above the predicted level. More than 78 square miles of low-lying ground

Figure 1.1 The extent of the inundation of the east coast of England during the 1953 storm surge and subsequent floods (map reproduced from Steers, J.A. (1953) The east coast floods. *The Geographical Journal*, 119, 280–295, by kind permission of the Royal Geographical Society with the Institute of British Geographers).

were inundated. Industrial undertakings on Thames-side were put out of action. On the Isle of Grain, the British Petroleum Company's refinery was flooded. On the exposed north Kent coast, the promenades of Margate and Herne Bay, and the newly constructed concrete sea wall at Minnis Bay were pounded and broken by waves. The 60-foot-high lighthouse at the end of the jetty at the entrance to Margate Harbour was undermined and fell into the sea. The Isle of Sheppey was cut off, half of it under deep water, and three-quarters of the town of Sheerness, including the Naval Dockyard, was flooded.[18]

Thousands of livestock and pets were also drowned in the carnage caused by the storm surge. Rabbits fled inland from Blakeney Point in North Norfolk to the safety of higher ground. Their concentration on the nearby Beacon Hills was such that, 'their burrowing became so extensive that the ground would often collapse beneath one's feet'.[19] A year later their populations were to be annihilated entirely by the deadly myxomatosis virus that was on the rampage northward from Kent.[20] Blakeney village was another scene of devastation. Wall plaques in the village provide a stark reminder of the height reached by the 1953 surge along with a later, but lesser, event on 11 January 1978 (Plate 7). Although the latter also caused great damage to property on the coasts of Lincolnshire, the Wash and East Anglia, mercifully it claimed no human lives.[21]

Much further to the north, on the opposite shores of the country, the angry sea was poised to claim yet another infamous disaster that would earn a place in the annals of history. The British Railways car ferry, a Clyde-built vessel of only six years of age, was struggling slowly, making little headway on its Saturday morning passage across the Irish Sea. Departing at 7.45 a.m. on 31 January 1953, it would normally have taken the ship no more than two hours to cruise from the port of Stranraer at the head of Loch Ryan in the south-west of Scotland to Larne in Northern Ireland. But this was no ordinary crossing. Once clear of the relative shelter afforded by Loch Ryan, about an hour after departure, the ferocity of the open sea waves driven by the exceptional winter gale ripped open the stern doors to the car deck. Thus stricken and no longer 'under command', the *Princess Victoria* had taken on so great a volume of water that her cargo shifted. She then listed onto her side and within around four hours of keeling over she sank to the bed of the North

One storm, four piers

The 11 January 1978 storm spectacularly claimed four, once proud, structural victims and almost a fifth. The late nineteenth-century Victorian piers at Skegness in Lincolnshire, Hunstanton in Norfolk, and Herne Bay and Margate in Kent were all destroyed in the surge,[22] whilst that at Southwold in Suffolk was also damaged.[23] At Skegness two large sections of the 900-metres-long structure were washed away and the theatre was left marooned by a gap more than 100 metres in width. At Hunstanton,[24] almost the entire structure collapsed and some of its iron supports were later found more than 8 kilometres to the south,[25] shifted by the strong tidal currents. At Herne Bay, the middle section was destroyed by the force of the waves, leaving the head isolated. Similarly, at Margate, most of the pier was washed away and the remainder had to be demolished.[26] It is curious that these structures, symbols of Victorian ingenuity, had survived the 1953 event and other surges in the past. The 1978 storm was clearly the straw that broke these aging camels' backs. In addition to the damage to piers and other coastal infrastructure, it was noted wryly that at Wells-next-the-Sea in Norfolk the beach huts were greatly damaged, 'and readers of the local and national press were made aware that a 300-ton coaster had been quietly left in the car park on Wells quay.'[27]

Channel. One hundred and thirty-three people, comprising nine crew and one hundred and twenty-four passengers, including the Deputy Prime Minister for Northern Ireland, Major Maynard Sinclair, were lost to the Irish Sea in this horrific tragedy. It was and is still the worst ferry disaster ever to have occurred in British coastal waters. There were just forty-four survivors; the captain went down with his ship.[28] Though its impacts were felt to a far lesser degree than south of the border, in Scotland-wide terms, this event was still the most devastating storm to have affected the country over the last five centuries in terms of flooding, coastal erosion and damage to coastal defence structures. Aside from the *Princess Victoria* tragedy, there were a further nineteen fatalities and numerous injuries.[29]

Directly to the east of the coast of East Anglia, on the opposite fringe of the North Sea in the Netherlands, the surge waves were even greater in magnitude, exceeding 3 metres in height. The waves breaking onto the shores were, however, climbing to over 6 metres in elevation. As the country's flood protection dykes and embankments burst due to the force of the water, the extent of the flooding and devastation that ensued, together with the number of fatalities, was even greater than in eastern England. Over six times as many people drowned in that vulnerable, fragile, low-lying country, around twice as many houses were damaged and the area of land engulfed by flood waters was well in excess of 3,000 acres.[30] Worst affected in terms of death toll was the province of Zeeland in the south-west of the country bordering with Belgium, large parts of which are below sea level and had been created by land claim centuries earlier. This was a national catastrophe of unparalleled proportions for the Dutch peoples; as if the centuries-old struggle of the Netherlands against the power of the sea had suddenly and without warning been lost. The North Sea has not been, however, always as we recognise it today.

ANCIENT BRITISH COASTLINES: REALITY AND MYTH

> Myth could be as sustaining as reality – sometimes even more so.
>
> Alexander McCall Smith,
> *The Lost Art of Gratitude*, 2009

If you had by chance been a resident of the Netherlands some 12,000 years before the 1953 disaster you could, if you chose, have walked from Leiden to Lowestoft. You would have arrived at the most easterly town in the British Isles and thus the first place to see the morning sun rise. Were you able to somehow travel back in time to that period of 10 000 BC, you could have strolled on your return journey from Felixstowe to Flevoland (Figure 1.2). At that time the southern North Sea between Britain, Belgium, The Netherlands and Germany was dry land;[31] Britain was not at that time an island nation but attached firmly to the European mainland (Figure 1.2). While travelling on your 200 kilometre walking expedition you would have been greeted by the Mesolithic hunter-gatherers that occupied the vast dry, undulating plain that is today completely submerged. Thanks to the identification of animal bones caught up in the nets of North Sea trawlers, you might also have met with bear, bison, wolf, horse, hyena,

Figure 1.2 Britain, Doggerland, the North Sea and neighbouring lands during the Mesolithic age prior to Britain's isolation from the European mainland (drawing by T. Dixon; based on Moffat, A. (2005) *Before Scotland.* Thames and Hudson, London).

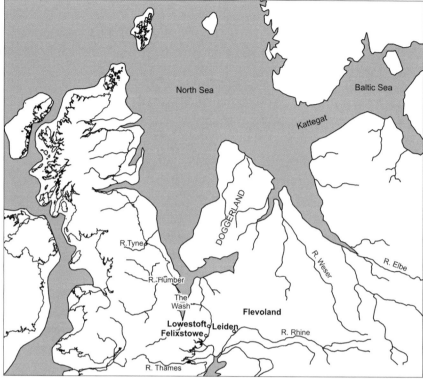

woolly rhinoceros, Irish elk, reindeer, mammoth, red deer, beaver, walrus and wild ox.

The Mesolithic people lived in what archaeologists have called Doggerland, one of the largest and best preserved prehistoric landscapes in Europe, now a world lost beneath the central and southern North Sea.[32] There is little doubt that the Storegga tsunami that engulfed Shetland would also have struck the northern shores of Doggerland[33] and one can speculate that this event may well have exacerbated its depopulation. However, whether or not this was the case is immaterial, as this area was destined for gradual submergence anyway, a dramatic casualty of rising sea levels around 5500 BC. The submergence of this exceptional landscape, taking its name from the vast Dogger Bank 100 kilometres to the east of the Northumberland coast, is a powerful, spectacular example of the consequences of climate change and the historic impact of global warming experienced by Mesolithic peoples. But this is no one-off casualty of sea level rise around island Britain.

At the far opposite, northern end of the country, the dozens of islands

Figure 1.3 The sea level around what are today the Orkney Islands and Caithness in the far north of Scotland around 10,000 years ago as compared with the present day coastline (drawing by T. Dixon; based on Dawson, S. and Wickham-Jones, C.R. (2007) Sea level change and the prehistory of Orkney. *Antiquity*, 312).

that today form the Orkney Islands of Scotland were, about 10,000 years ago, all one continuous landmass, joined together as a single large island (Figure 1.3).[34] Here too, rising sea levels caused problems for the local people, hunter–gatherers who were forced to abandon their homes and regroup further and further from the sea as the islands, both large and small, that we see today gradually and progressively became cut off from one another. Even today, centuries later, the sea continues its relentless attack on those long-abandoned, enigmatic Mesolithic dwellings, as at Skara Brae, that form such an important part of Orkney's rich archaeological heritage (see Chapter 3). Similarly, were the Bronze Age settlers able to return 4,000 or so years later to their homes at Calanais on the north-west coast of the Isle of Lewis in the Outer Hebrides of Scotland, famed for its mysterious stone circle, they would find them all but obliterated. The remnants of the foundations of their dwellings are now submerged beneath the rising sea.

Impressed and sealed: evidence of Mesolithic children at work in the Severn Estuary

> *Lives of great men all remind us*
> *We can make our lives sublime,*
> *And, departing, leave behind us*
> *Footprints on the sands of time;*
>
> *Footprints that perhaps another,*
> *Sailing o'er life's solemn main,*
> *A forlorn and shipwrecked brother,*
> *Seeing, shall take heart again.'*
>
> Henry Wadsworth Longfellow,
> *A Psalm of Life*, 1839

Walk along a sandy beach and the footsteps that you leave behind are a short-lived reminder of your presence; the next rise of the tide will normally obliterate them completely. In exceptionally rare circumstances, however, human and indeed animal footprints can be preserved within sedimentary sequences – sea level rise is not always a destructive force. Though it might be responsible for driving peoples away, it cannot erase completely the evidence of their former occupation. Amongst the great variety of enormously important archaeological remains within the deposits of the Severn Estuary, ranging through the Mesolithic, the Neolithic, the Bronze Age, the Iron Age, the Roman and the Medieval periods, are some jewels – human and animal footprints that are preserved in mud. These have been dated between 6,800 and 7,600 years old and thus from the Mesolithic.[35] Whereas sand grains typically lack interparticle cohesion, mud is characteristically sticky or cohesive and this property is an important prerequisite for footprint preservation.

For every footprint preserved in mud, many millions, similarly impressed, must have been destroyed. In extremely rare circumstances, however – the subsequent deposition of a protective veneer of fresh mud that sticks fast and does not become re-entrained on the rising tide – the usually ephemeral impressions can become sealed in. During the Mesolithic, relative sea level (see Chapter 2) in the Severn Estuary was lower than today. At locations in the Gwent Levels on the Welsh side of the estuary, such as Goldcliff and Uskmouth, the subsequent inundation has preserved a unique archaeological record of footprints in what were, 7,000–8,000 years ago, intertidal mud-flats. Here are not only impressions made by adults, but also children, preserved in the mud below peat deposits;[36] the latter the remains of a submerged forest visible only at very low tide. Detailed examination has revealed what are believed to be annual laminations within the overlying mud sequences; coarser sediments were deposited in the winter months and finer grained sediments during the summer when the water was relatively quiescent. The best-preserved footprints are in the finer grained deposits and this indicates peak activity in the warmest months of the year.[37] Along with human footprints, those of animals include red deer, aurochs (the forebears to our domestic cattle) and wolf, along with bird footprints, in particular those of the crane, which is no longer a native of our shores. At Goldcliff, the impressions made by twenty-one barefoot individuals have been identified.[38] Most of these were children, some believed to be as young as three to five years of age, thought to be out on a hunting trip at low tide – working for their survival. Footprints of children have also been found at Uskmouth, which are thought to record their activities of stalking animals, including fowl, driving aurochs and emptying fish traps.[39] These scarce impressions from the past are a precious window into the Mesolithic, its peoples and their way of life. Many more such footprints are likely to remain hidden in mud, buried further inland beneath the deposits laid down during the post-glacial relative sea level rise, yet these are vulnerable to future erosion.

Rugged outcrops of grey granite fringed by beautiful white sandy beaches form the spectacular cluster of the low-lying Isles of Scilly that break surface some 45 kilometres west of Land's End in Cornwall. Five of the islands, St Mary's, Tresco, St Martin's, St Agnes and Bryher, are inhabited, but the entire archipelago is made up of well over a hundred small rocky islets. Known to have been settled by humans since the Bronze Age, the Romans subsequently referred to the area as *Scillonia Insula*, or the sunny island. Their use of the singular, as opposed to the plural *insulae*, is not insignificant and it suggests that one large island of granite or perhaps one dominantly bigger than all others, existed 2,000 years or so ago. Indeed, this was the case; much in the same manner as the Orkney Islands, the creation of these islands is yet another dramatic and obvious conse-quence of rising sea levels. Once connected to the English mainland as an integral part of the Land's End body of granite, they have become progres-sively submerged and engulfed through time from initially one large *insula* into increasing numbers of smaller and smaller *insulae*. Today, the Isles of Scilly and the small tidal island of St Michael's Mount are all that remain of the lost, sunken land of Lyonnesse (also spelled variously Lyonesse), possibly meaning the 'Island of the Lion' (Figure 1.4). In the early eighteenth century, the causeway to St Michael's Mount was accessible for

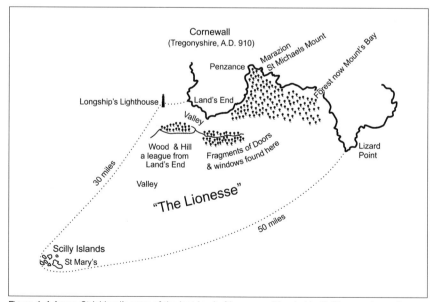

Figure 1.4 Agnes Strickland's map of the lost land of Lyonesse (drawing by T. Dixon; redrawn from Willson, B. 1902. *The Story of Lost England*. George Newnes Ltd, London).

around six hours over low tide. Today it is accessible for just four hours. It is thought that in forty years or so it may be accessible for less than one hour[40] and, eventually, St Michael's Mount could become a true island. As the causeway becomes redundant, the local harbour will increase in importance but, with time, it too will become increasingly vulnerable to flooding as the submergence of this fragment of lost Lyonesse continues.

The sometime importance of Lyonesse was alluded to in the opening paragraph of the 'Survey of the County of Devon and the City and County of Exeter' of 1785 as:

> That region which geographers account the first of all Britain, and which shooteth out farthest into the West, was once reputed the fourth Part of this Island, and supposed to be a Kingdom, before the Sea swallowed up the Land between St. Burian [the parish in which Land's End is located] and the Islands of Scilly.[41]

Poetically it was described as:

> *A land of matchless grace was Lyonesse,*
> *Glorious with rolling hills, rejoicing streams,*
> *Hoar monuments upreared when time was young,*
> *Wide plains of forest, slopes of golden corn,*
> *And stately castles crowning granite peaks.*[42]

A fertile land with many churches, some say no less than 140, it has been suggested that the ultimate demise of Lyonesse was in AD 1099 in which year, according to the Anglo-Saxon Chronicle, 'on the festival of St Martin, the sea-flood sprung up to such a height, and did so much harm, as no man remembered that it ever did before. And this was the first day of the new moon'[43] [so this event was a spring tide]. Of the Islands of Sylley [*sic*] wrote William Borlase in 1753, 'History confirms their former union.' He also described, citing 'The sea is the insatiable monster', their subdivision into smaller and smaller masses: 'But see how the sea has multiplied these islands; there are now reckon'd one hundred and forty: Into so many fragments are they divided, and yet there are but six inhabited.'[44]

This land of Lyonesse was famed in medieval Arthurian legend as the site of the ultimate battle between the notorious traitor Sir Mordred and King Arthur as well as in Cornish and Breton Celtic mythology. Whilst

many myths of sunken lands worldwide have no more than tenuous links
with reality at best, hereabouts, off the Cornish coast is the epitome of the
convergence of scientific evidence and centuries-old legend. The latter
was encapsulated unintentionally, one must suppose, to perfection and
with some quite remarkable, but coincidental, scientific accuracy by the
then Poet Laureate Alfred Lord Tennyson in his epic poem *Idylls of the
King*, published in 1859:

> *Then rose the King and moved his host by night,*
> *And ever push'd Sir Modred, league by league.*
> *Back to the sunset bound of Lyonnesse –*
> *A land of old upheaven from the abyss*
> *By fire, to sink into the abyss again;*
> *Where fragments of forgotten peoples dwelt,*
> *And the long mountains ended in a coast*
> *Of ever-shifting sand, and far away*
> *The phantom circle of a moaning sea.*

Almost a century later, in Evelyn Waugh's classic 1945 nostalgic novel,
Brideshead Revisited: the Sacred and Profane Memories of Captain Charles Ryder,
the now middle-aged narrator reflects on the Oxford of his university
undergraduate days, of his languid youth, as being, 'submerged now and
obliterated, irrecoverable as Lyonnesse, so quickly have the waters come
flooding in – Oxford in those days, was still a city of aquatint'. In his
mourning of Oxford, Charles Ryder is also lamenting the passage of his
youth for evermore beneath the rising sea of modern times – 'this
shrinking youth'. In this way, his elegy personifies the haunting effect that
the submerged land has on the human mind. Indeed, such is the awesome
magnitude of the influence of this lost land on some people that a strange
sect, living near Land's End for two years virtually hidden, was discovered
in 1993 by the under-cover investigations of author William Shaw.[45] Living
in primitive shelters of rock, its members were awaiting patiently the
emergence of the goddess Lyonesse, whom they believed would bring
forth a new civilisation, rising up, as if by isostatic uplift (see Chapter 2),
from beneath the waves.

British expatriate and sometime Professor of Geology at the University
of Saskatchewan in Canada, the late William Sarjeant, under the pen name
of Antony Swithin (his 'middle names'), even wrote a fantasy quartet of

novels each accorded the subtitle: *The Perilous Quest for Lyonesse*. This series is clearly influenced by Tolkien's *The Lord of the Rings*, and was set on a large fictional island known as the Republic of Rockall, a 'sea-girt realm' of magical places and beings.[46] Complete, not surprisingly given the profession of the author, with its own exquisitely fabricated geological map and geological succession, this mythical land was based very loosely on the tiny authentic island of the same name that today breaks surface in the middle of the North Atlantic Ocean. The real Rockall is, in fact, a very small part of an almost completely submerged igneous centre of 'fire-derived' rocks, eruptive lavas and intrusive rocks such as granite, of the same age and origin as those exposed on land in Scotland in the Isle of Skye, the 'Small Isles' of Rum, Eigg, Muck and Canna and the Ardnamurchan peninsula, along with the Isles of Mull and Arran. The perennial, ongoing subject of ownership dispute, claim and counter-claim, this rocky islet of Rockall, remote and pounded by some of the largest and most powerful storm waves in the world, is itself fabled in Gaelic folklore and indeed held by some people as all that remains visible today of the lost continent of Atlantis.

Such curious, complex intertwines of geology and fantasy, of science and legend, abound in this North Atlantic area. Hereabouts, the British Geological Survey, following their extensive offshore geophysical survey investigations, has discovered numerous igneous centres for which dominant features in Swithin's quartet of novels have provided their names.[47] Thus, the Lyonesse igneous centre, as if transported magically to the bed of the north Atlantic, from beneath the waters between the Isles of Scilly and Land's End, is now juxtaposed close to the Owlsgard, Sandarro and Sandastre centres. To square the circle of fact and fantasy, if that is indeed possible, Swithin the perpetrator of myth, even has a submerged igneous centre named after him, one of the largest in the area. There is thus an interesting irony here that is epitomised in the North Atlantic Ocean; mythical places and indeed the pseudonym of their very architect have together become cemented for evermore in offshore geological and site nomenclature.

When the Roman legions made their invasive crossing of the Menai Straits to Ynys Môn or Mam Cymru, the 'Mother of Wales', Anglesey as she is also known, was already an island. The Welsh know these straits as *Yr Afon Fenai*, or River Menai, which indicates the presence of a lesser body of water in the past, and they were certainly very much narrower and

Lyonnesse claims the *Torrey Canyon*

Speaking in the House of Commons on 4 April 1967, the then Prime Minister Harold Wilson asserted, 'This was a national disaster which could have imperilled all our beaches, not merely in the West Country but further afield.'[48] He was referring to the vast spillage of crude oil from the first of the large super tankers, the *Torrey Canyon* that struck Pollard's Rock in the Seven Stones Reef, marked by a lightship, between the Isles of Scilly and Land's End on 18 March 1967. As a result of the captain's navigational error, the entire cargo of 120,000 tons of oil escaped from the stricken vessel leading to the largest oil pollution incident recorded up to that day. Around 15,000 seabirds were killed along with untold numbers of marine organisms between Cornwall and the shores of Normandy. The oil slick covered around 700 square kilometres and nearly 200 kilometres of the Cornish coasts were contaminated. An official enquiry, held in Liberia where the vessel was registered, found that the captain had taken a short cut en route to Milford Haven in Pembrokeshire. He had steered the ship on a course between the Isles of Scilly and Land's End, rather than make safe but rather longer passage to the west of the archipelago. This attempt to save time brought the vessel into a collision course with the reef, a tiny but tough exposure of the lost land of Lyonnesse. On that day, it claimed its biggest ever victim of the hundreds over the years, the *Torrey Canyon*, and in so doing resulted in a major environmental disaster for which this country was not prepared.[49]

shallower than they are today when chronicled by the Roman writer Tacitus who recorded:

He [Suetonius Paulinus, Roman general and Governor of Britain] prepared accordingly to attack the island of Mona, which had a considerable population of its own, while serving as a haven for refugees; and, in view of the shallow and variable channel, constructed a flotilla of boats with flat bottoms. By this method the infantry crossed; the cavalry, who followed, did so by fording or, in deeper water, by swimming at the side of their horses.[50]

Such a manner of crossing would be impossible today, even on a very low spring tide when the shallowest part of the Menai Straits is some 3 metres in depth. The invasion of this Druid stronghold in the year AD 61 is alleged to have wiped out the last of these priests of the Celtic tribes in Britain, effectively destroying Druidism as a religious force.[51] Not surprisingly, the shallow, fordable conditions of the Menai Straits were similar a few years later when the Romans turned their attention on Anglesey again in AD 78. The new Governor of Britain, Gnaeus Julius Agricola, who had served previously under Paulinus, invaded again; on this occasion, the target was the Celtic tribe, the Ordovices:

> He almost exterminated the whole tribe . . . His plans had been hastily formed and so, as was natural, he had no ships on the spot; yet the resourcefulness and determination of the general bridged the straits. For after unloading all the baggage he picked up a body of native auxiliaries who knew the fords, and had the facility in swimming which belongs to their nation, and by means of which they can control simultaneously their own movements, their weapons, and their horses: he then launched them upon the enemy so suddenly that the astonished islanders, who looked for fleets of ships upon the sea, promptly came to the conclusion that nothing was hard and nothing invincible to men who fought in this fashion. Accordingly they petitioned for peace and surrendered the island . . . [52]

Thus, the lower sea level than today in the Menai Straits during the first century AD helped to shape the course of military history. At the end of the Pleistocene glaciation (see Chapter 2), however, Ynys Môn was an integral part of north Wales. As sea level rose when the ice melted, the straits are thought to have been breached around 8,400 years ago, initiating the tidal causeway[53] that the Roman legions would have crossed much later. Ultimate submergence was probably complete by between 5,600 and 4,800 years ago, by which time the 'Mother of Wales' had become isolated – and her country shrank a little.

To the east of Anglesey, where the Menai Straits broaden out into the sweeps of Conwy (Conway) Bay, are the Lavan Sands, a large intertidal area of sand bars and mud flats, famous for its mussel beds, with intercutting channels and creeks that are a refuge for sea birds. At low water, some parts are passable on foot with care, but other areas are more muddy and treacherous. On very low spring tides, the roots of trees, now distant from the land, can be seen *in situ*. The ancient name, *Traeth Lafan*, means 'the place of weeping', which is supposedly a reference to the inundation of what was once dry land (Figure 1.5) and the loss of its former inhabitants who were forced from their formerly fertile farms as sea levels rose. It is thought that the ultimate demise of this part of Wales to the sea took place between the years AD 634 and AD 664.[54] The underwater archaeological evidence for former occupation, in the form of walls and roadways crossing this now intertidal and subtidal area to the south-eastern tip of Anglesey, is compelling.[55] Tradition has it, that a royal palace or court, known as Llys Helig, once stood proud in Conwy Bay prior to the inundation of Tyno Helig or Helig's Vale. This is long held in folklore to be the residence of the Prince Helig ap Glannawg, who lived there in the sixth century.[56] It is said that he was the father of three Welsh saints; Boda, Gwynin and Brothen.[57]

A Mr Charlton R. Hall set out from Llandudno by boat on 19 August 1864, in the company of five others, in an attempt to locate the ruins. As geologist William Ashton, reported, the search was for long a vain one, and

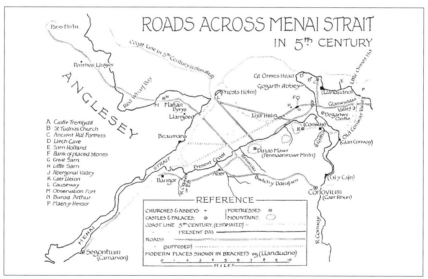

Figure 1.5 Map of the Lavan Sands and Llys Helig showing the routes of supposed fifth century roadways between the mainland of North Wales and Anglesey (reproduced from Ashton, W. (1920) *The Evolution of a Coast-line: Barrow to Aberystwyth and the Isle of Man, with notes on Lost Towns, Submarine Discoveries etc.* Edward Stanford Ltd, London).

was about to be abandoned when some black seaweed on the surface of the sea came into sight. This seaweed was found to be growing 'upon the top of what appeared to have been a wall. It became evident that the stones ran in straight lines.' Although this evidence was slight, it prompted Ashton to plan a visit to the site himself and he, 'resolved to take advantage of the first very low tide which coincided with sufficiently calm weather for an independent search to be made'.[58] On 13 September 1908, the conditions proved favourable and Ashton set out on his search with boatman Richard Thomas from Penmaenmawr to a place about midway between Penmaenmawr Mountain and the ruins of Gogarth Abbey on the Great Orme's Head. This was a spot known amongst the local boatmen as 'rocky ground' and therefore hazardous at low tide. Mounting a stone that projected from a bank of boulders, which was nearly submerged and offered the minimum of standing room, Ashton was able to 'take a steady view of the entire area.' For this point of vantage he was able to observe:

> Three sides of a large square, with a large rectangular recess at the south-west side, were seen to be well defined by straight and almost continuous lines of wall, for the most part covered by a tall, ribbon-like seaweed. Where the stones did not project 3 or 4 inches above the surface they were discernible through the water. These stones did not vary 6 inches from a straight line. They seemed to form the apex of a base of thrown-down stones, forming projecting supports, which would account for the walls enduring over many centuries. One could not confidently say that the stones had ever been masoned, nor that they had been mortared together, though they may have been so. The longest wall, that on the east or Deganwy side, was 130 yards in length. A stone stood up prominently some 70 yards from the eastern corner. This proved to have a counterpart another large stone about 7 feet away, just below the surface, as if they had formed two pillars of a gateway. A causeway of stones with perpendicular sides connected these two stones with the eastern corner. This causeway ran out directly towards the nearest land at Penmaenbach, more than a mile away. On the north or open-sea side the force of the waves would appear to have demolished the wall, as no straight line could be traced, but only odd stones jutting out irregularly. The walls appeared to stand in about three to four feet of water.[59]

Figure 1.6 Sketch
map of the layout of
Llys Helig (repro-
duced from Ashton,
*The Evolution
of a Coast-line*).

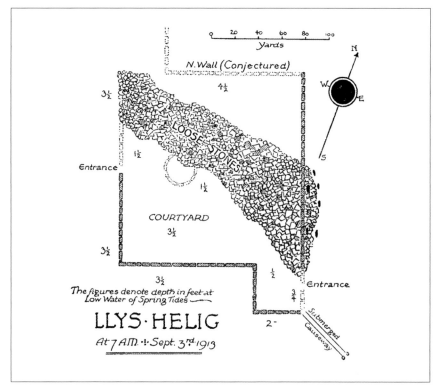

The latter reference to the depth of water over the site is a measure of the degree of inundation that has taken place in the area since the fifth century or so. Ashton believed that the walls probably formed the boundaries of a courtyard surrounding Helig's abode (Figure 1.6), rather than the perimeter of the palace building itself. These would have formed a defence against enemy attack and also facilitated the herding of cattle.

In 1940, geologist Dr F.J. North wrote a pamphlet 'The legend of Llys Helig, its origin and its significance', which was published as a Supplement to the *Proceedings of the Llandudno, Colwyn Bay and District Field Club*. In the company of archaeologist Mr W.F. Grimes, North examined the stone walls, previously described by Ashton, in August 1939. Noting that the original basis for the legend is a manuscript attributed to Sir John Wynn, dating from the early seventeenth century, North suggests that this is a piece of folklore that had been translocated from Cardigan Bay in west Wales (see below) and that Wynn's 'An ancient survey of Penmaenmawr' had been 'invented' on the basis of little or no historical evidence. Moreover, his colleague, Grimes, in an appendix to the pamphlet on archaeological aspects, concludes that the stones recorded in such detail by Ashton are of no archaeological significance.[60] North concluded that the patch of stones, in all probability, represented the debris of a denuded hillock of boulder clay (a deposit laid down by a glacier or ice sheet), the result of subsidence completed by the end of the Neolithic period.[61] This raises the question of whether sea level has risen in the area, or the land level has subsided – issues that will be explored in Chapter 2. The detailed description of Llys Helig provided by Ashton is certainly no flight of the imagination, nor is it a castle in the air. Moreover, the last words on the subject rightly deserve to be his: 'It is quite impossible for anyone to view these 350 or more yards of strictly rectangular remains and to entertain the slightest doubt as to their having been human handiwork.'[62]

Shrinkage of the country was to occur, however, on a scale even greater than that of the Lavan Sands elsewhere in the west of Wales, as has been so hauntingly and vividly described by Susan Cooper:

> Though they tried, they never found the road again. There was no sign anywhere of the golden horses; panic had taken them away. So Will and Bran turned their faces towards the shining tower and tramped over the rough reedy grass of the pastureland, through clumps of gorse on the firm ground and soggy patches of marsh on lower land where the water still lay. All the Lost Land was low: a coastal plain, with the sweep of Cardigan Bay at their left hand and the mountains rising hazily purple-brown far inland, to the right. Somewhere ahead, Will realized, the River Dyfi must run, towards a mouth considerably further out to sea than the one he had known before. It was as though all the coast of their own time had been given an extra half-mile stretch on its seaward side. 'Or rather,' he said aloud, 'given back the land it lost.' Bran looked at him with a half smile of understanding. 'Except that it hasn't been lost yet, has it?' he said. 'Because we've gone back in time.' Will said pensively, 'Have we?' 'Well of course we have!'[63]

The loss of the fabled Cantref y Gwaelod, or the Lowland Hundred, beneath the waters of Cardigan Bay (Figure 1.7)[64] is attributed in legend to a water gate in one of the sea walls that protected it having been left open in the sixth century by a drunken gate master called Sicthenym or Seithenyn:[65]

Figure 1.7 The lost
land of Cantref y
Gwaelod – specu-
lative map comparing
the twentieth-century
and fifth-century
coastlines of mid-
Cardigan Bay (repro-
duced from Ashton,
*The Evolution
of a Coast-line*).

> Seithenyn, buried now in sleep,
> The floodgates opened in his wine;
> And on them rushed the angry deep,
> Commissioned by the wrath divine.
>
> The torrent deluged wide the land,
> And to the cities forced its way;
> The palaces were filled with sand,
> And thousands in their ruins lay.[66]

This large fertile tract of pastureland, the Welsh Atlantis, nearly as large as
Lyonesse, is believed to have extended from Ramsey Island off the coast of
the St David's peninsula in Pembrokeshire to Bardsey Island off the Llŷn
Peninsula.

The ocean rolled his mountain wave,
Where lofty towers reached the sky;
And turned the palace to a grave –
Now vessels sail where cities lie!

Where grazed the cattle, now the whale
Is rolling down the boiling deep;
Where flowers drank the morning gale,
The monsters of the ocean creep.[67]

Legend holds that Cantref y Gwaelod hosted some sixteen townships and the main sea wall or dyke that protected it was called Sarn Badrig or St Patrick's Causeway. This bank of glacial deposits, a hazard to shipping that is exposed at low water on a spring tide, extends south-westwards from Shell Island near Harlech parallel to the Llŷn Peninsula for over 20 kilometres. Four main roads, believed by some to be continuations of mainland thoroughfares, are held to have traversed this land, also visible at low tide as causeways; Sarn y Bwch (the Goat's Causeway), Sarn Cyngelyn (Cymbeline's Causeway), Sarn Ddewi (St David's Causeway) and Sarn Cadwgan (Cadogan's Causeway).[68] These too are made of coarse deposits laid down by glaciers. Whilst the Lowland Hundred, without doubt, once extended the area of Wales westwards, its demise was just like that of Lyonesse to the south; a consequence of rising sea levels and not, though a wonderful rascally tale it is, the foolish act of an incapacitated drunkard.

In the sixteenth edition of *The New Seaman's Guide and Coaster's Companion* for 1809, navigation directions are provided for the 'North Side of the British Channel', one of which relates to Selsey in Sussex:

After you are past the East Barrow-head, the leading mark into the Park is a tuft of trees, at Pagham, and Chichester church in one, bearing nearly north. This mark will carry you safe into the Park, where you may anchor between the Barrow-head and Selsey Bill in 4½ or 5 fathoms of water [27–30 feet], good ground for 2 miles from shore. This is by far a better place for anchoring with southerly winds than the Downs, for the east end of the East Barrow is nearly dry at low water, spring tides.[69]

Noah's Woods: Britain's submerged forests

That Britain, or more specifically England and Wales, is indeed shrinking is encapsulated by Clement Reid's splendid 1913 account of *Submerged Forests*. This detailed tour of the fringes of the two southern countries of Britain shows that submerged forests quite literally have been found almost everywhere around the intertidal zones, often being revealed by excavations for docks and harbours, but also by widespread coastal erosion. It is this work that gives a first indication of the former existence and potential significance of Doggerland, and introduces the trawler man's word 'moorlog', a term that today is often more widely used to describe remains of a submerged forest caught up in trawl nets, composed of a tangled mass of brushwood and tree trunks and forming a 1 to over 2 metres thick layer. Over Dogger Bank, 'the masses of moorlog are usually dredged on the slopes at a depth of twenty two or twenty three fathoms'.[70]

> When trawlers first visited the Dogger Bank its surface seems to have been strewn with large bones of land animals and loose masses of peat, known to the fishermen as 'moorlog,' and there were also many erratic blocks in the neighbourhood. As all this refuse did much damage to the trawls, and bruised the fish, the erratics and bones were thrown into deeper water, and the large cakes of moorlog were broken in pieces.[71]

Close to the village of Cresswell on the southern edge of Druridge Bay on the Northumberland coast, the stumps of oak and alder trees protrude from peat in the partially submerged forest of Blakemoor Links. Here, Neolithic materials[72] and evidence of forest clearance by humans[73] have been discovered in the intertidal zone, indicating a considerable rise in sea level since that period. Elsewhere on the east coast, submerged forests are to be found off the shores of Cleveland, near to Hartlepool; Yorkshire, close to Withernsea;[74] Lincolnshire; Norfolk, such as the Cromer Forest Bed; Suffolk, as at

Southwold; and Essex at, among other localities, Clacton-on-Sea, Grays and Tilbury. Along the English Channel, similar beds have been found off Dover, Southsea and Poole Harbour. More recently, in the latter part of the twentieth century, a submerged forest has been located by divers in the western part of the Solent in a depth of 11 metres of water. This is situated off the north-east coast of the Isle of Wight near Yarmouth and the drowned landscape contains human-worked and burnt flint tools which have been dated to the Mesolithic.[75] Continuing this clockwise coastal tour, around the Cornish peninsula alone some thirty-seven submerged forest sites have been identified,[76] including potential remnants of Lyonesse off St Michael's Mount. Indeed there is no reason to suspect that the latter was an island at the time of the *Domesday Book* of 1086. Similar sites also occur in the Bristol Channel and Severn Estuary. In more or less the centre of the west Wales coast of Cardigan Bay lies the small village of Borth where, thanks to the now exposed remains of the submerged forest protruding through the beach, the legend of lost Cantref y Gwaelod becomes spectacular reality. In north Wales too, such forest remains are to be found at Rhyl and Abergele, with other examples in eastern England at localities along the estuaries of the Rivers Dee, Mersey and Ribble (Figure 1.8).[77] The very name of Birkenhead on the west bank of the Mersey facing Liverpool evokes the birchen wood, the stumps of which are exposed offshore on low tides. Indeed Beckles Willson[78] cites an old Cheshire rhyme:

From Birchen Haven to Hilbre
A squirrel might hop from tree to tree.

Hilbre (or Helbre) refers to the island of that name, once an integral part of the Wirral Peninsula (Figure 1.9), as indeed were the neighbouring islets of Middle Eye and Little Eye, but now reduced to what Willson calls 'a miserable little remnant' off the north-west corner of the promontory.[79]

Although Reid's treatise did not extend into Scotland, submerged forests are also a characteristic of many intertidal areas around the country. It is hardly surprising that they are found in

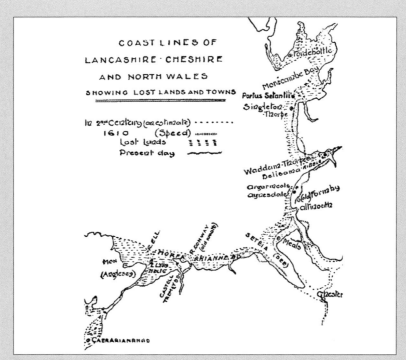

Figure 1.8 The lost lands and towns of Lancashire, Cheshire and North Wales (note the location of Llys Helig) – speculative map comparing the twentieth-century, seventeenth-century (Speed's map of 1610) and estimated second-century coastlines (reproduced from Ashton, *The Evolution of a Coast-line*).

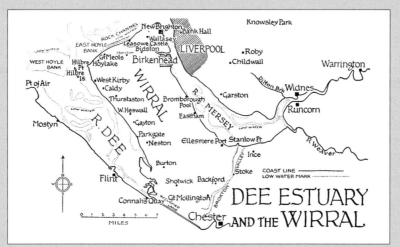

Figure 1.9 The Wirral Peninsula between the Rivers Dee and Mersey. Note the locations of Hilbre Island and Leasowe Castle (reproduced from Ashton, *The Evolution of a Coast-line*).

many places off Orkney, where rising sea levels have been shown to have created innumerable small islets from one large landmass. One of the most famous and extensive in Scotland is on the east coast in the Tay Estuary, which was first recorded by local parish minister, the Reverend John Fleming, in 1822 who wrote:

> The bed of peat to be described, and now dignified by the title of a *Submarine Forest*, occurs on the south bank of the Frith [*sic*] of Tay, and has been observed in detached portions on the west side of Flisk beach, to the extent of nearly 3 miles, and on the east side, upwards of 7 miles.[80]

Fleming went on to discover yet another submarine forest with the remains of tree stumps in their position of growth in Largo Bay on the northern shores of the Frith [*sic*] of Forth,[81] close to the place of birth of Alexander Selkirk, the inspiration for Daniel Defoe's legendary Robinson Crusoe. However, the submerged forest chosen by Reid a century ago to illustrate the phenomenon,[82] that exposed by erosion at Dove Point on the north coast of the Wirral Peninsula in Cheshire and long attributed to inundation by the Scriptural Deluge, cannot be surpassed (Plate 8) as the exemplification of a shrinking land.

It may seem curious to mariners that this deep-water anchorage on the west side of the promontory of Selsey Bill, the most southerly point in West Sussex, should be called 'the Park'.[83] Many sea-goers may never have queried it. However, this reference to what would normally be thought of as a piece of terra firma was at one time just so. In the reign of Henry VIII this was indeed a very large deer park with hundreds of noble stags and does roaming. This is yet another victim of rising sea levels and in the words of Beccles Willson, 'Here truly, is a choice and memorable fragment of Lost England.'[84] Today, the Selsey street names of 'Deer Park Lane', 'Deer Park Drive', 'Park Lane' and 'Park Road' provide modern day reminders. The names of other now submerged features, such as 'Sunk Sand', a large bank in the outer Thames Estuary, also provide indications of a shrinking Britain.

According to popular belief, Anglo-Saxon King Canute the Great failed to hold back the advancing tide, as legend has it, on the northern shores of the curiously rectangular Wirral Peninsula, historically part of Cheshire. As if to emphasise his failure, the submerged forest of Dove Point and the remnant island of Hilbre are but a few kilometres from where, at one time a wooden seat, called 'Canute's Chair' located overlooking the sea at Leasowe Castle (Figure 1.9) bore the inscription, 'Sea come not hither nor wet the sole of my foot.'[85] This peninsula, bounded on its north side by Liverpool's great River Mersey and on the south by the River Dee, has long been a microcosm of this shrinking land. This vulnerable spot would have been an obvious choice for Canute to attempt to show his courtiers that he was only a mere human being and there were limits to even his kingly powers since, quite contrary to folklore, Canute was not trying to hold back the sea. As he leaped backwards to escape inundation he is reputed, as Lord Raglan has documented,[86] to have said, 'Let all men know how empty and worthless is the power of kings, for there is none worthy of the name but He, whom heaven, earth and sea obey by eternal laws'. As long ago as 1612, English poet Michael Drayton, in one of the thirty songs that comprise his topographical epic *Poly-Olbion* that describes the traditions, history and landscape of England and Wales, made reference to the real fragility of the Cheshire Wirral with the words:

> *Until they come at length where Mersey for more state,*
> *Assuming broader banks himself, so proudly bears,*
> *That at his stern approach extended Wirral fears*
> *That what betwixt his floods of Mersey and the Dee,*
> *In very little time devoured he might be.*[87]

Further to the north off Barrow-in-Furness in Lancashire, the Cistercian monks of Furness Abbey were constructing wooden coastal defences in an effort to protect Walney Island as long ago as the thirteenth century. In his description of this low lying and vulnerable island, Drayton noted:

> *To fence her furthest point from that rough Neptune's rage,*
> *The isle of Walney lies, whose longitude doth 'swage*
> *His fury when his waves on Furnesse seem to warre,*
> *Whose crooked back is armed with many a crooked scarre,*
> *Against his boystrous shocks, which this defensive isle*
> *Of Walney still assayle, that shee doth scorn the while.*[88]

Little has changed, it would seem. A rather more contemporary account from the early 1990s relates:

> Walney Island, a long, low hump of grass, boulder clay, sand dunes and sea-borne stones, is shaped like some gigantic, stranded whale. It guards the south-western flank of the Furness peninsula against the perpetual rollers of the Irish Sea; it is a slim land barrier, fatter in the middle, ever under threat from the tides; a battleground in the constant struggle between marine erosion and deposition.[89]

Crossing to the east of England, travel to the Holderness coast of East Yorkshire and try as you might to locate the towns of Northorpe, Southorpe, Great Colden, Monkwell or Owthorne, to name but a few, and you will not succeed. These are just a handful of the dozens of settlements that have been lost without trace to North Sea coastal erosion since Roman times. Rising sea levels may be a contributory factor, but in these areas it is the very power of the sea that is the driver. The once prosperous, twelfth and thirteenth century industrial sea port of Dunwich in Suffolk (see Chapter 3), a former capital of East Anglia and once a cathedral city, has now been reduced to a small village, destroyed by the force of the North Sea. On the English Channel coast of West Sussex, the ancient Saxon cathedral city of Selsey, whose deer park has already been mentioned, is yet another of the numerous British victims of coastal erosion over the centuries. Fast forward in time to the present day, and if you live near the two East Anglian ports of Lowestoft or Felixstowe where this journey began, or along the Holderness coast, or indeed in many other parts of the picturesque but often dangerous edges of island Britain, it is likely that you are becoming increasingly concerned by rising sea levels, perhaps by the possibility of the loss of your own home and grounds to the encroaching sea. Indeed, it would seem that no section of the coastal community is immune to the threat of erosion. Even a paradise for naturists at the village of Corton near Lowestoft, a spot long noted for erosion,[90] one of Britain's first nudist beach enclaves established more than three decades ago, has been under such assault from wave attack that it has had to be de-designated as such by the local Waveney District Council. It has now had to be stripped of its 'clothing optional' status because coastal erosion has so effectively reduced the beach space available for non-naturists in the area.[91] Britain is indeed a shrinking land. But why is it so?

Is it shrinking everywhere around the edges; is it being uniformly eaten away around its coastal fringes? Are we doing anything about it? Are we doing enough about it? Can we do anything about it? Should we be doing anything more about it than we are doing already? Should we abandon vulnerable towns and villages to the sea, as did our forebears, and relocate such coastal settlements inland? These are some of the tricky, thorny and indeed potentially emotive questions that this book explores.

Plate 1 Straddling a stream-cut ravine and still clinging on to the Yorkshire coast south of Whitby, Robin Hood's Bay in 2010 (photo R.W. Duck).

Plate 2 Spoil heaps of burnt shale from the former alum industry give an almost lunar landscape to the top of the unstable cliffs of Jurassic rocks that form the promontory of Kettleness, north of Whitby. The extent of the rocky platform below gives an indication of the amount of land that has been lost by erosion (photo R.W. Duck).

Plate 3 The shored-up Fife coastal path between Pittenweem and St Monans has been breached and overtopped by storm attack many times, but particularly so in the last few years – here is its state in 2010 (photo R.W. Duck).

Plate 4 Reconstruction of the coastal scenery near Builth Wells, mid-Wales, during early Ordovician times around 480 million years ago (reproduced from Jones, O.T. and Pugh, W.J. (1949) An early Ordovician shore-line in Radnorshire, near Builth Wells. *Quarterly Journal of the Geological Society of London*, 105, 65–99, by kind permission of the Geological Society of London).

Plate 5 (left) The signature of a tsunami. Section cut through the deposits at Maryton on the south-west shore of the Montrose Basin of the Angus coast. At the base are laminated clays laid down in marine conditions during the decay of the last ice sheet to have occupied the area, above which is a thin, dark brown layer of peat laid down during the Holocene (see Chapter 2). Above this is part of a laterally persistent layer of uniform, pale grey, silty sand that is believed to have been deposited by the surge of the Storegga tsunami about 8,000 years ago, when the east of Scotland was inundated. Above the latter, another layer of peat has developed (photo R.W. Duck).

Plate 6 (below) Unusual depressions and markings cut into stacks (see Chapter 5) at Cullen on the southern shore of the Moray Firth have been attributed to the force of the Storegga tsunami (photo R.W. Duck).

Plate 7 (right) Wall plaques in Blakeney, north Norfolk, denoting the heights of the 1953 and 1978 storm surges. The former is 3 metres or so above the pavement level. A lower, third plaque, the outline of which can just be made out, has been dislodged. This showed the flood height reached in a surge in 1897 (photo courtesy of L. Booth).

Plate 8 (below) Buried forest seen at low water at Dove Point on the Cheshire coast of the Wirral Peninsula (reproduced from Reid, C. (1913) *Submerged Forests*. Cambridge University Press, Cambridge).

Plate 9 Features of coastal emergence at Gruinard Bay, Wester Ross, in the North West Highlands of Scotland. Sequence of two raised shoreline terraces backed by former cliff lines eroded at higher relative sea levels (photo R.W. Duck).

Plate 10 The village of Collieston on the Aberdeenshire coast is developed on a series of raised shoreline terraces (photo R.W. Duck).

Plate 11 The gently undulating golf links at Elie, Fife, developed on a raised shoreline – but note the signs of erosion along the coastal edge (photo R.W. Duck).

Plate 12 Camas Cuil an t-Saimh or 'The Bay at the Back of the Ocean' on the west coast of the Island of Iona in the Inner Hebrides. Here the raised beach is capped by wind-blown shell sand that forms gently undulating machair land, communally grazed by cattle, sheep and occasionally golfers. As at Elie, erosion is taking place along the coastal edge, but hereabouts it is exposed to waves generated across the entire expanse of the North Atlantic Ocean. This distance is known as the fetch length, the significance of which is discussed in Chapter 3 (photo R.W. Duck).

Plate 13 Ailsa Craig, also known as Paddy's Milestone, in the Firth of Clyde, as seen from Byne Hill in Ayrshire looking across to the Mull of Kintyre. The granite body that comprises this island, projecting some 334 metres above sea level, contains a green amphibole mineral called riebeckite that gives the rock a characteristic hue. Owing to its uniformity and durability, this rock was for decades the traditional source of curling stones in Scotland. Quarrying on the island ceased in 1973, but in 2001 permission was granted for the removal of 1,500 tons of material as a stockpile to manufacture 'new' stones over many years to come. Only fallen blocks of rock were removed; there was no blasting, so as not to disturb the island's numerous sea birds – but another means of shrinking land (photo R.W. Duck).

Plate 14 The Thames Barrier (photo R.W. Duck).

Plate 15 View north over the Tay Estuary to Dundee along the foundations of the piers of the first Tay Railway Bridge. Immediately to the west is its successor (photo R.W. Duck).

Plate 16 Robert Stevenson's lighthouse at Dunnet Head, the most northerly point of the British mainland, stands high above the treacherous waters of the Pentland Firth (photo R.W. Duck).

Plate 17 The rocky ledges and caves of the chalk cliffs of Flamborough Head's North Landing have been friend to seabird and to smuggler over the centuries (photo R.W. Duck).

Plate 18 View northwards along the slender, curving, 'sickle-like' spit of Spurn Head from the top of the High Lighthouse (photo R.W. Duck).

Plate 19 The old Low Light on the west side of Spurn Head with a water tower on top as seen from the top of the High Lighthouse (photo R.W. Duck).

Plate 20 Owthorne church at the edge of the Holderness cliffs in 1797 looking northwards (from Sheppard, T. (1912) *The Lost Towns of the Yorkshire Coast*. A. Brown & Sons, London).

Plate 21 Kilnsea at the northern end of Spurn Point after the winter storms of 2009–10 (photo R.W. Duck).

Plate 22 The end of the 'road to nowhere' at Aldbrough on the rapidly receding Holderness coast of East Yorkshire – its residents are still served by a regular bus service. Erosion and land slipping of the soft till cliffs in this area have been enhanced since the building of rock armour revetment and two rock groynes a few kilometres updrift at Mappleton (photo R.W. Duck).

Plate 23 The parish church in Aldbrough showing water-worn cobbles used in its construction, a legacy of the once important trade in Holderness (photo R.W. Duck).

Plate 24 The gas processing plant at Easington, East Yorkshire, appears to sit precariously close to the edge of the soft eroding and slumping cliffs of Holderness in this aerial photograph taken in 1996; in the background is the Humber Estuary. The plant is now, however, protected from the sea by a large revetment of rock armour at the base of the cliff, which has been regraded to improve stability (photo courtesy of The Lighthouse for Learning, North East Lincolnshire Council).

Plate 25 At Easington, to the south of the gas processing plant, the sea is the curse of the caravanner. Each year pitches have to be abandoned and the relics of the cables and pipes that serviced them protrude eerily from the rapidly receding cliff (photo R.W. Duck).

Plate 26 Crangon Cottages at Birling Gap before (1999 – upper) and after (2001 – lower) the demolition of the most seaward residence owing to recession of the chalk cliffs (photos courtesy of D. McGlashan).

Plate 27(above) Constructive power – high, spectacular, mobile dunes of the Sands of Forvie, Aberdeenshire (photo R.W. Duck).

Plate 28 (left) Erosion threatens the Neolithic village of Skara Brae, a World Heritage Site on the Bay of Skaill, Orkney, Scotland. The erosional bight in the distance (see Chapter 4) is being created by the sea wall (out of view) that is intended to protect the ancient monument (photo R.W. Duck).

Plate 29 Kenfig Pool amid the dunes that have buried Kenfig village (photo R.W. Duck).

Plate 30 Placed at High Water Mark in 1940, the concrete anti-tank blocks at Tentsmuir Point provide a striking timeline against which accretion of land can be measured (photo R.W. Duck).

2
COOLING AND WARMING

I tell you naught for your comfort,
Yea, naught for your desire,
Save that the sky grows darker yet
And the sea rises higher.

G.K. Chesterton, *The Ballad of the White Horse,*
Book I: The Vision of the King, 1911

And Noah he often said to his wife when he sat down to dine,
'I don't care where the water goes if it doesn't get into the wine.'

G.K. Chesterton, 'Wine and Water'
(from *The Flying Inn*), 1914

THE IMPACT OF ICE

Around 2 million years ago, for reasons that are well outside the scope of this book, the Earth entered a lengthy period of climatic deterioration that led to a reduction in the temperature of its surface and its atmosphere. In consequence, polar ice sheets, continental ice masses and glaciers expanded progressively in volume giving rise to what is often referred to as an 'ice age'. Within the northern hemisphere, much of north-west Europe was repeatedly glaciated in at least four periods of ice advance during cold phases, with intermittent retreat during warmer, so-called interglacial periods. This period of geological time, from 2 million or so years ago until 10,000 years ago, is known as the Pleistocene, following which, in what is called the Holocene (that is 'Recent Whole'), from some 10,000 years ago to the present day, the climate ameliorated and glaciers left Britain. The maximum extent of glacier ice in Britain was probably around 18,000–20,000 years ago, the so-called Last Glacial Maximum. The southern extremity of England, however, south of a line drawn approximately from the Severn Estuary in the west to the Thames Estuary in the east, escaped glaciation but experienced extremely cold temperatures characterised by permafrost conditions. An important consequence of the loss of water from the world oceans to form ice masses was a worldwide lowering of sea level that fluctuated according to the glacial–interglacial cycles during the Pleistocene. At the Last Glacial Maximum, it is likely that the sea level around Britain would have been some 100–120 metres lower than at the present day, resulting in a remarkable change in our island's coastline.[1] One such change was indeed the loss of our isolation, with the emergence and subsequent colonisation of Doggerland in the southern North Sea.

Ice masses act as a dead weight, acting vertically downwards upon the brittle rocks that comprise the outer skin of the Earth, known as its crust. Although there were large variations in ice thicknesses over Britain, being thickest in those areas of the highest precipitation, the last ice sheet over the Grampian Highlands of Scotland reached an elevation relative to the modern land surface of over 1,800 metres. This would have covered the highest mountain summits with several hundred metres of ice.[2] As a result, such ice masses caused the crust of the Earth to be compressed under their great weight, pushing it downwards into the plastic part of the underlying upper mantle, known as the asthenosphere, which is not brittle but capable of flow. This phenomenon is called isostatic depression. As this sinking takes place, mantle material becomes deformed and squeezed sideways from below an ice mass; imagine it behaving in much the same way as putty. This sideways movement of plastic mantle material away from below the ice pushes the crust upwards in areas not covered by ice, making the land rise in what is known as a forebulge. It is believed that the land beneath the central part of the North Sea rose upwards substantially by this means,[3] thereby helping to form and to maintain Doggerland. Similarly, southern England south of the Severn and Thames Estuaries, including the lost land of Lyonnesse, rose upwards due to this process of forebulging.

When the climatic conditions eventually improved and the ice masses began to melt at a greater rate than new ice was being formed, so the sea level around Britain began to rise. A major victim was Doggerland and its Mesolithic peoples who were forced to relocate their settlements away from the advancing waters to one side of the North Sea or to the other, as Britain eventually became an island. So too, Lyonnesse and Cantref y Gwaelod were progressively engulfed. The sea did not, however, simply return to its pre-Pleistocene level. Because of isostatic depression of the crust and with large regional variations, vast areas of former coastal lowlands became flooded such that by 5,000 years ago when the population of the country was probably little more than a quarter of a million people, Britain had shrunk very substantially in its surface area. This was a period of widespread marine flooding known as the Flandrian Transgression. At its maximum, in Scotland, for instance, Loch Lomond, today the largest lake in Britain in terms of its surface area, became connected with the rising waters of the Firth of Clyde at its southern end. It was thus, during this marine transgression, no longer a body of fresh water. To the east, the inundation of the Forth Valley and the Carse of Stirling all but isolated the northern part of Scotland from the rest of Britain as the rising sea waters came close to those of Loch Lomond (Figure 2.1). Only a narrow neck of land, between Drymen and the Lake of Menteith in Stirlingshire, remained like a fragile causeway above the sea holding Scotland together. Still further to the north-east the fertile Carse of Gowrie between Perth and Dundee was flooded; so too, in Fife, the famous Mesolithic site at Morton Farm[4] on Tentsmuir that had been occupied by fish and shellfish eating hunter-gatherers from around 9,500 until around 8,400 years ago. By that time, however, the rising sea was beginning to isolate their settlement,[5] forcing the inhabitants to displace, abandoning their pit dwellings, their circular huts made of turf and wattle, and their implements fashioned from stone, wood and bone. Moreover, no trace of an island was evident from the shore by 5,000 years ago; by that time the Flandrian Transgression had engulfed the whole of Tentsmuir, its former settlements inundated completely (Figure 2.1).

We know that today the level of the sea around Britain is nowhere near as high as during the maximum of the Flandrian Transgression, highlighted by the examples given above. So, something dramatic must have happened to Britain in the last 5,000 years; Loch Lomond is now a freshwater loch, the Carse of Gowrie, the Carse of Stirling and Tentsmuir are all dry land, the latter in stark contrast to Doggerland. The compression of the crust into the mantle beneath by the great weight of ice resting upon it had created an unstable situation, and once the weight of ice was removed due to melting the crust began to return to its former level, a process that is called isostatic recovery. It did so by rebounding upwards, moving slowly but discontinuously with periods of uplift and intervening periods of relative stability. In this way, the land rose slowly upwards with the effect

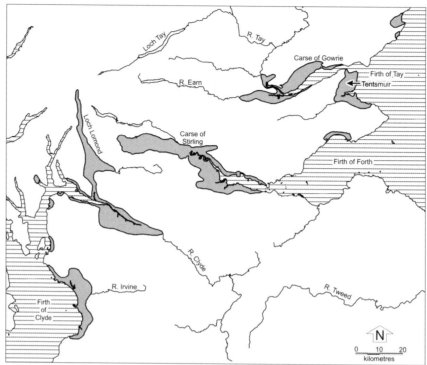

Figure 2.1 Areas inundated by the sea in the Clyde, Forth and Tay Valleys of Central Scotland at the maximum of the Flandrian Transgression around 5,000 years ago. Note Loch Lomond, the Carse of Stirling, Carse of Gowrie and Tentsmuir (drawing by T. Dixon; after Price, R.J. (1983) *Scotland's Environment during the Last 30,000 Years*. Scottish Academic Press, Edinburgh, Figure 5.6).

that sea levels receded. Such rebound was not at the same rate everywhere; those parts of Britain that had been covered with the greatest thicknesses of ice, like the Grampian Highlands of Scotland, had been compressed the most and so uplifted to the greatest extent. Elsewhere, where the ice cover had been thinner, as for example near to the Severn–Thames line, isostatic uplift was to a much lesser degree. In this way, the land areas inundated during the Flandrian became progressively exposed, rising slowly from beneath the sea. We know that the uplift was episodic with intervening periods of stability, since the sea was, in many places around the coast, able to cut and carve cliffs into the uplifted land. In this way, series of raised shorelines can be seen, giving a step and stair, tread and riser-like form to the coastline, the oldest shoreline at the top and the youngest at the bottom, the last to emerge from beneath the sea (Plate 9). In coastal settlements developed in such terrain, the raised terraces provide the horizontal foundations for dwellings at the different levels above the high water mark and the lines of houses themselves often serve to highlight the form of the sequentially raised, step and stair, coastline above (Plate 10). Where raised shorelines are sufficiently extensive they form the ideal topography – especially when capped with undulating dunes – for links golf courses (Plate 11) and for grazing (Plate 12).

Another consequence of ice melting and isostatic recovering of the overlying crust is that the forebulge sinks back to its former level. This process not only contributed to the eventual demise of Cantref y Gwaelod, Lyonnesse and Doggerland to a watery grave but is the principal reason why southern England, the most densely populated part of Britain, is still sinking slowly today; the sinking of the forebulge is not yet complete. To make things even more complicated, beyond local changes in the land level of Britain, we also have to consider the impact of global variations in sea level, so-called eustasy or eustatic changes, arising from increases or decreases in the total volume of water in the Earth's ocean basins. Such changes are largely the result of either increased storage of water as ice or increased melting of the polar ice sheets. The latter is exemplified powerfully by sequential satellite observations of the wastage of the Pine Island glacier, one of the largest ice masses in Antarctica, which reveal that its surface is lowering at the rate of around 16 metres per year. This rate of thinning is four times faster than a decade ago in the 1990s.[6] However, global warming, which is causing these polar ice masses to melt at such accelerated rates, has another much less well known effect, that of thermal expansion of sea water. As the waters of the ocean basins heat up, they expand in volume thereby, along with the melting of polar ice, contributing to a rise in sea level worldwide. It has been estimated, for example, that a temperature increase of as little as 1°C throughout the uppermost 500 metres of the oceans would alone, that is in the absence of any polar ice melting, result in a sea level rise of approximately 100 millimetres.

GLOBAL WARMING

Established in 1988 by the United Nations Environment Programme (UNEP) and the World Meteorological Organization (WMO), the Intergovernmental Panel on Climate Change (IPCC) is the pre-eminent scientific body tasked with the assessment of global climate change and the potential environmental and socioeconomic consequences of such change. The IPCC has estimated that global sea level rose by an average of 1.8 +/− 0.5 millimetres per year from 1961 to 2003, a trend that has been accelerating since the Industrial Revolution began in the late eighteenth century (Figure 2.2). These findings are based on historical information recorded by tidal gauges located around the world and, more recently, from remotely sensed satellite altimetry of sea levels. The latter suggest an increase to 3.1 +/− 0.7 millimetres per year since 1992 (Figure 2.2). Although the present phase of so-called global warming began at the end of the Pleistocene Ice Age, long before the eighteenth century and the development of the internal combustion engine, the Industrial Revolution was one of the most important periods in history. Rooted in Britain, it was to herald profound changes in transport, manufacturing processes, mining methods and agricultural practices that were set to proliferate throughout Europe, thence to North America and ultimately the rest of the world.

The 'revolution' was fuelled by coal; a unique, combustible sedimentary rock. This fossil fuel was derived from plant debris laid down in the Carboniferous Period around 300 million years ago, and was plentiful at or beneath the surface in many parts of mainland Britain, such as the Central

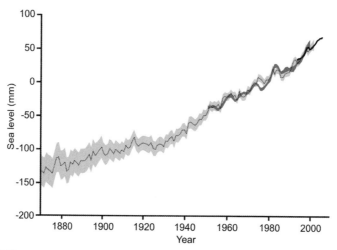

Figure 2.2 Mean global sea level trends from 1860 to 2006. The dotted black line, within an envelope of error shown in pale grey, indicates tidal gauge records that have been back-adjusted for land uplift; the mid-grey line shows actual tidal gauge measurements since 1950, and the solid black line is based on more recent satellite observations of sea level since the 1990s (drawing by T. Dixon; based on IPCC (2007) *Fourth Assessment Report: Climate Change* (AR4). Contribution of Working Group I to the Fourth Assessment Report of the Intergovernmental Panel on Climate Change. Solomon, S., Qin, D., Manning, M., Chen, Z., Marquis, M., Averyt, K.B., Tignor, M. and Miller, H.L. (eds) Cambridge University Press, Cambridge).

Belt of Scotland from Ayrshire to Fife and the Lothians, Northumberland, Durham, Yorkshire, Derbyshire, Nottinghamshire, South Wales and Kent. The burning of coal, however, releases carbon dioxide into the atmosphere that has been held in storage for millions of years, since the plant materials accumulated and became buried beneath younger strata. Carbon dioxide is the most important of the family of so-called greenhouse gases, which includes water vapour, methane and nitrous oxide, and its concentration in the atmosphere has increased by around 40 per cent since the onset of the Industrial Revolution. The natural process of heating the surface of the Earth by the sun's heat energy, visible as light, is called the 'greenhouse effect'. As surface temperature increases, the Earth radiates infrared energy, invisible heat rays, back into the atmosphere, some of which is absorbed by the greenhouse gases present. Above-normal concentrations of green-house gases, such as carbon dioxide, disturb the natural heat balance of the Earth, whereby greater amounts of heat are retained both on the Earth and in the atmosphere. Thus, the greenhouse effect is intensified; leading to global warming that has resulted in an average rise in global temperatures of about 0.74°C over the past 100 years.[7]

Such is the profound influence of human beings on global climate that the term 'Anthropocene' was coined by the Nobel Prize winning atmospheric chemist Paul Crutzen along with colleague Eugene Stoermer in the year 2000. By analogy with the word 'Holocene', this refers to the current period of geological time that began with the advent of the Industrial Revolution and which humans are currently experiencing.[8] The starting date has been arbitrarily assigned to the latter part of the eighteenth century, coinciding with James Watt's radical improvements to Thomas Savery's steam engine in 1784. Though not widely known, this term is progressively finding increased acceptance and usage. In 2007, the IPCC concluded that the 'enhanced greenhouse effect' resulting from fossil fuel burning, together with large scale deforestation, as in the Amazon Rainforest, has been the major cause of the observed temperature increase since the mid twentieth century and that warming of the Earth climate system is beyond doubt[9] and has been so since the mid 1990s; 'The balance of evidence, from changes in global mean surface air temperature and from changes in geographical, seasonal and vertical patterns of atmospheric temperature, suggests a discernible human influence on global climate.'[10] Similarly, the UK Climate Impacts Programme (UKCIP), a body that provides information and help to organisations to adapt to climate change, refers to such change as 'inevitable', pointing out that the effects of previous greenhouse gas emissions will continue to be felt for decades to come.[11] Even those who do not believe that there is a human-induced component to global warming cannot argue with the temperature data, which are unequivocal that the Earth's atmosphere is heating up. The ten warmest years on record have occurred since 1997 and global temperatures for the period 2000 to 2008 were almost 0.2°C warmer than the average for the decade 1990 to 1999.[12] In Britain, the longest available temperature record in the world, known as the Central England Temperature Series, extends back three and a half centuries to 1659. The data, representative of a triangular area of England that has London, Bristol and Lancashire at its corners, reveal that 2006 was the warmest calendar year since the records began. Moreover, ten of the twelve warmest years on record (1989, 1990, 1995, 1997, 1999, 2002, 2003, 2004, 2006 and 2007) have occurred in this area of England since 1989; with 1949 and 1959 being outliers from the recent cluster.[13] Thus global sea levels will continue to rise owing to a combination of ice melting and the thermal expansion of sea water, with each thought to be contributing around equal proportions of the observed trend,[14] as Earth surface temperatures continue to rise, as predicted, by between 1.1 and 6.4°C during the twenty-first century. This is computed to lead to global sea level rise in the range of 0.22 to 0.44 metres above present level, an average rise of some 4 millimetres per year projected towards the end of the twenty-first century.[15] Recent predictions to 2095, specifically for Britain, suggest increases in sea level within the range from 0.13 to 0.76 metres.[16] But by how much will *relative* sea levels change around the British Isles? This is a deceptively simple, yet a far from straightforward, question to answer.

Climate change and 'the roaring game'

Are winters in Scotland getting warmer? Ask this question to any curler of a certain age or devotee of the sport and he or she will answer unequivocally 'yes'. The basis for their response, unscientific though it may be and purely qualitative, comes from the playing of the 'Grand Match'. This bonspiel, held outdoors at one of several frozen freshwater lochs around the country, and for many the traditional highlight of the curling year, was first organised by the Royal Caledonian Curling Club, the sport's national governing body, in the 1840s. It first took place on 15 January 1847 at Penicuik to the south of Edinburgh.[17] Such was the general severity of the Scottish winters through the latter half of the nineteenth century that the event was to be held on a further twenty-one occasions until February 1900. The year 1886 was remarkable as it was the only one on record in which the tournament was played twice; in January and again in December.[18] Freezing weather conditions that generated the required thickness of ice, 7 inches for the purposes of safety, continued to characterise many winters in the first half of the twentieth century, permitting the Grand Match to take place on seven more occasions until 1935. However, milder winters since World War II have resulted in only three matches being possible; in 1959, 1963 and the last on the Lake of Menteith in Stirlingshire on 7 February 1979.[19] A resurgence of persistently cold temperatures in December 2009 and January 2010 led to eager anticipation for the first time in over three decades that the great bonspiel was not an extinct species. Despite the requisite thickness of ice being attained once again on the Lake of Menteith, health and safety concerns led to its cancellation, effectively dashing the hopes of so many who had waited so long. Was the 2009–10 winter just a blip? Only time will tell. However, notwithstanding the return to weather conditions that had not been experienced regularly in Scotland, or indeed within wider Britain, since the 1950s and 1960s, curlers with long, fond memories have no doubt whatsoever that global warming is a reality. Furthermore, they fear that the outdoor roar of stones, hewn from the Ailsa Craig granite[20] (Plate 13), on an ice-covered loch may be a sound never heard again.

**Ice floes in the nineteenth century contribute
to the eventual location of the Tay Railway Bridge**

*They were heading t'wards Americ's shore
In the middle of the night,
When the lookout spied an iceberg,
Which gave him quite a fright.*[21]

When the Tay Railway Bridge in eastern Scotland was opened on
31 May 1878, it was hailed as a triumph of Victorian construction
and ingenuity; the finest and longest bridge in the world. Spanning
the mighty Tay Estuary between Wormit and Dundee, along a
traverse over 3 kilometres in width, it was to have a working life of
less than twenty months. At about 7.15 p.m. on Sunday 28
December 1879, the central portion of the bridge, comprising
thirteen high girders, collapsed during a severe westerly gale – a
tempest even. A passenger train, en route from Burntisland in Fife,
was on the final leg of its journey to terminate in Dundee's Tay
Bridge Station. At the instant of collapse, the engine, five passenger
coaches and guard's van were passing within the high girders, so
they too were plunged into the waters below. Subsequently, forty-
six bodies were identified, but it was widely believed that there had
been over seventy passengers on the train. There were no survivors.
The eerie stumps of the old piers, exposed at low water alongside
the sturdy successor (Plate 15), are a poignant reminder of the so-
called Tay Bridge Disaster, still regarded today as the world's most
infamous railway accident. When the first bridge was constructed,
the route eventually chosen was actually the fourth that had been
considered.[22] The site of the first proposed crossing was some 20
kilometres upstream close to the small port of Newburgh where the
Tay is less than half the width off Dundee and subdivided by the
centrally located Mugdrum Island. So, a bridge at this location
would have been much shorter in length and, therefore, much
cheaper to build. Moreover, it could also have taken advantage of
the island as a stepping stone. Why was this route abandoned?
Recent research[23] has shown that one of the principal reasons why

the Newburgh crossing did not go ahead was that the structure would have caused an obstruction to ice floes on the Tay, thereby inhibiting navigation on what was then a very busy waterway. Furthermore, it was believed that such a constriction to the passage of ice masses could potentially cause flooding of homes and farmland in the Newburgh area and upstream. This provides another reminder of the severity of winter climatic conditions not only in this part of Scotland but elsewhere in Britain. During the nineteenth and early twentieth centuries[24] ice floes were an annual winter occurrence, and it was such an event in 1814 that effectively dammed the spans of John Smeaton's Bridge in Perth, at the head of the estuary, causing the highest flood level ever recorded in the city.[25] The last periods of winter weather sufficiently cold to promote substantial ice floe activity in the estuary were in January 1982 and, to a lesser extent, in January 1987.[26] With the exception of relatively minor events in December 2001 and 2009, the subsequent years have seen the Tay essentially ice-free, a local consequence of the general climatic amelioration that Britain is currently experiencing.

THE LAND–SEA BALANCING ACT

The term relative sea level refers to the balance between global or eustatic sea level rise or fall and the vertical movement of the land, either upward or downward, at any particular locality. If, for example, the sea level is rising at a rate of 4 millimetres per year and the land level in a district is rising at an identical rate as a consequence of isostatic uplift or positive isostasy, then the net effect will be zero, a situation that is known as sea level stillstand (Figure 2.3). There will be no observed relative sea level rise or fall. Similarly, if sea level is falling and the land level is subsiding (negative isostasy) at an equal rate, stillstand conditions will prevail and again there will be no observed relative sea level rise. Should the rate of isostatic uplift of the land exceed that of eustatic rise, coastal emergence will occur, as has been the situation at the Gruinard Bay location of the North West

Highlands of Scotland and at Collieston in Aberdeenshire. However, in the opposite scenario of eustatic rise taking place at a greater rate than vertical uplift of the land, or indeed in the event of vertical land subsidence, the consequence will be coastal submergence and transgression of the sea over formerly dry land. If the lands adjacent to the coastline are relatively low-lying plains characterised by very gentle, low angle gradients, then even a small rise in relative sea level can potentially inundate vast areas, as exemplified so spectacularly by the demise of Doggerland (see Chapter 1) and the isolation of Britain from the European mainland.

So, is there a problem in Britain? The short and unequivocal answer is 'yes'. However, the magnitude of the problem varies very considerably from locality to locality, according to the rate of relative sea level change. UKCIP data compiled in 2005 (Table 2.1) show how relative sea level is projected to rise as the twenty-first century unfolds within different regions of Britain according to two different scenarios of greenhouse gas emissions, 'low' and 'high', from the IPCC. The difference in relative sea level rise between the two emissions scenarios is 60 centimetres. Even the 'best estimate' figures of the low emissions situation potently illustrate the vulnerability of eastern and the southern parts of England, areas that are characterised by isostatic subsidence. In very broad terms, as the figures in Table 2.1 indicate, much of Scotland, where the thickness of Pleistocene

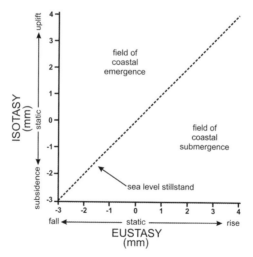

Figure 2.3 Graphical representation of how relative sea level at a particular locality around the coast depends on the balance between isostasy (vertical land subsidence or uplift) and eustasy (global sea level rise or fall). If isostasy and eustasy are of equal magnitude, either positive or negative, sea level stillstand conditions prevail (drawing by T. Dixon).

ice was at its greatest, is still subject to isostatic uplift which serves to moderate the effects of global sea level rise. By contrast, much of the south of England, where the ice cover was thin or absent, is sinking due to forebulge compression so the impacts of eustatic rise will be manifest more acutely. This is, however, rather a simplification in the UKCIP data as there are large regional variations, even at the scale of an individual water body such as an estuary in which there can be variations in the rate of relative sea level change from the landward reaches to the mouth. Even more recent predictions of relative sea level rise to 2095 have been made for the three capital cities of Britain (Figure 2.4).[27] These suggest very similar, virtually identical, rates of relative sea level rise for London and Cardiff according to high, medium and low emissions scenarios. For Edinburgh, owing to the greater amount of isostatic uplift, the rate of relative sea level rise according to the three scenarios through the twenty-first century is markedly lower. However, it is a popularly held rather broad-brush misconception that Scotland is 'bouncing back';[28] witness the Orkney Islands (see Chapter 1) which, along with Caithness, the Shetland Islands

| Region of Britain | Regional isostatic uplift (+ve) or subsidence (−ve) mm/year | Relative sea level rise projections (cm) compared with 1961–90 | | | | | |
| | | Low emissions: 'low' IPCC estimate | | | High emissions: 'high' IPCC estimate | | |
		2020s	2050s	2080s	2020s	2050s	2080s
East of England	−0.8	8	13	17	18	42	77
East Midlands	−0.8	8	13	17	18	42	77
London	−0.8	8	13	17	18	42	77
NE England	0.2	3	5	6	13	34	66
NW England	0.6	1	2	3	11	31	63
Scotland	0.8	0	1	0	10	30	60
SE England	−0.5	6	11	14	16	40	74
SW England	−1.0	9	15	20	19	44	80
Wales	−0.5	6	11	14	16	40	74
Yorkshire & Humberside	−0.7	8	13	17	18	42	77

Table 2.1 Regional isostatic uplift or subsidence rates in Britain and estimated projections to the 2020s, the 2050s and the 2080s of relative sea level rise according to 'low' and 'high' greenhouse gas emissions scenarios of the IPCC. Note that the estimates given here are averaged across the whole of Scotland and do not include Orkney, Shetland or the Western Isles, where isostatic subsidence is believed to be taking place (after UK Climate Impacts Programme (2005) www.ukcip.org.uk).

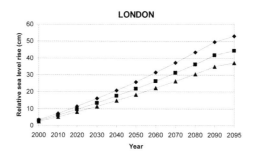

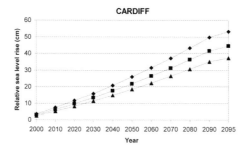

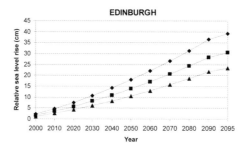

Figure 2.4 Graphs showing predictions of relative sea level rise to 2095 for the three British capital cities of London, Cardiff and Edinburgh according to high (diamonds), medium (squares) and low (triangles) emissions scenarios plotted from 2009 data presented in tabular format by the Department for Environment, Food and Rural Affairs (Defra) http://ukclimateprojections.defra.gov.uk /content/view/2145/499/.

and the Outer Hebrides, are actually subject to relative sea level rise. The tragic deaths of five members of the same family, spanning three generations, as they were swept away in two cars by waves during a severe storm in South Uist in January 2005, are a further poignant reminder.[29] In these north-western and northern areas, the rate of eustatic rise exceeds isostatic uplift as there the ice cover during the Pleistocene was generally thin compared with elsewhere in Scotland.

Monachs no more?

> Islands feed an appetite for the absolute.
>
> Adam Nicolson, *Sea Room*, 2001

Fringed with stunningly white beaches, now a National Nature Reserve, a haven for seals, sea bird and wild flowers, no human being has lived permanently on these tiny islands since 1948. Yet in the eighteenth century over 100 hardy souls eked out an existence from fishing and from farming the rich shell-rich soils of the blooming machair and dune lands.[30] In 1801, however, a great storm caused widespread devastation, stripping the islands bare of their machair carpet's pile. The people left, abandoning their homes but, by nine decades onward, they had made their way back and the population had risen again to 130 people.[31] These are the five tiny Monach Isles, or Heisgeir as they are also known, located some 6 kilometres to the west of North Uist in the Outer Hebrides. A famous 'tourist' was Lady Grange of Edinburgh, noted for her outrageous behaviour and her fondness for alcoholic drink, who, on 22 January 1732, was seized, bound and gagged by a party of Highlanders, dragged away on horseback and exiled to the island of 'Hesker' at the behest of her estranged Jacobite husband. There she remained for two years before being removed to the equally remote Island of St Kilda for a further seven years.[32] The most westerly of the Monach archipelago is called Shillay or seal island, a rocky speck which hosts a lighthouse. Constructed by David and Robert Stevenson, approval for the structure was granted in 1859 and the light was first exhibited from the 41 metres high tower in 1864. In 1862, it is said that the keepers of the lighthouse – then still under construction – were in fear for their lives when the structure was battered by a storm.[33] This light was in use until 1942, but in 1948 it was decommissioned after a brief period of re-use. A minor lighthouse was built on the island in 1997, but, a decade on, the decision was taken to discontinue this and to re-establish the light to prominence atop the Stevensons' red brick edifice.[34] Shillay gives some much needed shelter to the flat, machair and dune islands of

Ceann Iar, Shivinish and Ceann Ear from the might of westerly gales – which occur on around 160 days each year.[35] At low tide, these are all but one continuous mass, as exposed sandbanks provide fragile stepping stones between them. According to local tradition, the Monach Islands were at one time connected to North Uist and, at low tide, it was possible to make the crossing by horse and cart.[36] As relative sea level continues to rise, these tiny remnants of a once bigger mass are very vulnerable. Their dunes are the most exposed within Britain and, with their highest natural point at a mere 19 metres or so above sea level, the threat of overtopping in a storm surge like that of 1801 is all but inevitable. Moreover, gradual inundation of the Monach Islands is a longer-term prospect that is certainly not beyond the realms of possibility. It has even been predicted that this might take place by as soon as 2020,[37] though that is rather an extreme view. In that ultimate eventuality, the isolated eminence of Stevenson's lighthouse and a few, wave-battered rocky outcrops around its base will be all that will remain of Heisgeir at high tide.

The 'Little Ice Age'

Though there is debate about the precise dates, the late seventeenth and early eighteenth centuries in Britain and indeed in most parts of the world were characteristically a period of colder, wetter climate; this has become known as the 'Little Ice Age'. At this time average global temperatures were around 1.0 to 1.5°C cooler than they are today, glaciers advanced, winters were long and severe with strong biting winds and river flows were reduced. The Thames and other rivers froze over frequently. When the Little Ice Age came to an end, the climate became much wetter, more extreme and more variable and it has been suggested that these conditions were closely similar to those experienced in the present phase of global warming. It is noteworthy that the warming period from around 1700 until

1850, post-dating the Little Ice Age and with climatic conditions not dissimilar to those currently being experienced in Britain, has been associated with an increase in the reported occurrences of large coastal landslides, especially in eastern and southern England.[38] For instance, the Robin Hood's Bay landslide occurred in 1780 and the slippage of the village of Kettleness into the sea was in 1829 (see Preface). Indeed, many other major landslips took place around this time – some of the most spectacular will be explored in Chapter 5 along with their present day counterparts.

LOOKING TO THE FUTURE

Another complicating factor that also has to be taken into account is the form or structure of the coast. This is controlled fundamentally by the underlying geology (see Chapter 5), which can lead to variation between the two extremes of an essentially vertical, high, hard rocky cliff and a low-lying, low-gradient (almost horizontal) sand flat, dune field, salt marsh or muddy wetland. The former type of coast will, in general, be far less susceptible to relative sea level rise than the latter, which could be extremely vulnerable both to the risk of flooding and to relatively rapid erosion by wave attack. So, the most vulnerable parts of Britain, as in other countries of the world, are low-lying coasts, developed in 'soft', unconsolidated geological materials such as clay, sand and till (see Chapters 3 and 5) that are located in areas of relative sea level rise where the land might also, but not necessarily, be subject to isostatic subsidence due to forebulge compression. Thus, in England, the Holderness coast of east Yorkshire, the Humber Estuary, Lincolnshire, the Wash, the East Anglian coasts of Norfolk and Suffolk along with the coastal lowlands of Essex and the Thames Estuary are, as witnessed so forcibly in 1953, amongst the most in danger; areas that include numerous sites of not inconsiderable population density and valuable industrial infrastructure.

Three low-lying areas of England, two in East Anglia, the third at the opposite side of the country, are particularly vulnerable to future relative sea level rise – the Fens, the Broads and the Somerset Levels, regions that have been much modified by extensive human intervention over the centuries. At one time the Broads of Norfolk and Suffolk, a network of largely navigable, low gradient rivers and lakes, were believed to be natural features of the landscape, created at the meeting places of river and marine waters, with the former being ponded back against sediments pushed landwards by the encroaching sea.[39] However, subsequent research, involving inter-disciplinary collaboration between a botanist, a geomorphologist, a historical geographer, an archaeologist and a civil engineer, demonstrated that these features are unequivocally man-made.[40] The Broads are a legacy of the digging of turf, mainly peat, during the period from the eleventh to the fourteenth century. At that time peat was an important source of fuel, vital to sustain the rapidly growing population and it was extracted to depths of 3 metres and more. The digging techniques, known as turbary, mimic those of the Netherlands, and a highly organised and productive industry flourished in medieval times.[41] The East Anglian industry also prospered until rising sea levels began progressively to flood the excavations and, despite attempts to prevent this using wind pumps and embankments, eventually the extent of inundation was such that peat excavation was no longer possible. Human intervention had opened the door to the sea and by the sixteenth century the resulting flooded channels had become important commercial links. Thus, the Broads, today around 200 kilometres of waterways and a highly popular tourist and recreational destination, were created. It is hardly surprising that this area is extremely vulnerable to the threat of flooding as relative sea levels rise due to global warming.

To the west and north-west in Norfolk, Cambridgeshire and south Lincolnshire, the Fenlands, or Fens, occupy similarly low-lying terrain and are again the consequence of human endeavour. At the beginning of the Holocene, this was a forested area that merged with the estuarine marshes of the Wash. As relative sea levels rose, rivers draining the area were ponded back by the intruding sea waters. Swampy wetland conditions thus developed as the forests became inundated and the trees died, leading to the formation of thick sequences of rich, fertile peaty soils. To be of value to agriculture and food production, drainage of these soils was deemed essential, with early attempts to do so in the form of embankments to retain the sea being constructed by the Romans. Piecemeal drainage schemes continued to evolve over the centuries but it was from the mid seventeenth century onwards that drainage became both systematically engineered and large in scale. In consequence, the numerous shallow meres disappeared from the landscape. The naturally sinuous, meandering rivers and streams were widened, deepened and straightened over long distances and straight, artificial river channels were incised.[42] The conversion of marsh and fen to pasture and arable crops offered the prospects of profit and improved food security for the country.[43] Whilst the drainage schemes completely changed the natural character of this region, they resulted in the creation of some of the most fertile farmlands in England.

As the drainage of the Fens continued, the peat began to shrink in volume and thus the land level subsided at a remarkable rate, the southern parts being particularly susceptible. As a simple, but highly effective, means of monitoring this subsidence, a local landowner at Holme Fen, close to the village of Holme near Peterborough, had three oak piles driven through the peat into the underlying still clay. Their tops were cut level with the ground surface and used to measure the vertical extent of peat shrinkage. Three years later, in 1851, one of the wooden piles was replaced by a more substantial cast iron post salvaged from the old Crystal Palace buildings when they were dismantled after the Great Exhibition of that year. It was driven through about 7 metres of peat into the underlying clay until, like that of its predecessor, its top was level with the ground surface.[44] Today this iron pillar survives as what is known as the Holme Fen Post. In the first decade of drainage, it recorded almost 2 metres of ground subsidence. By 1932, it was projecting 10 feet 8 inches (around 3.75 metres) above the surface.[45] Further shrinkage caused the post to become unstable and in 1957 steel guys were attached to keep it upright. The post now protrudes to 4 metres above the present ground surface[46] and in so doing provides an impressive record of the still ongoing, but declining, rate of peat subsidence.[47] Holme Fen is today the lowest piece of land in Britain, about 2.5 metres below sea level.[48]

As the land surface sank through time, water could no longer drain into the rivers, which progressively became higher in elevation than the surrounding fields. Thus, wind pumps had to be installed to transfer the water from the land to the drainage network.[49] Today, most of the Fens lie close to or even below sea level and the networks of rivers and drains are supported by sluice gates, locks and electric pumps that replace former steam and diesel varieties. Some higher points once formed islands in the marshes, the largest of which was the Isle of Ely on which the cathedral city of Ely now stands. Were it not for flood embankments and pumping to prevent river and tidal flooding, the Fens would be all but completely inundated. As a result of numerous breaches over the centuries, these lands are certainly no stranger to flood damage; local people are acutely aware that flood hazards are part of life in the Fens.[50] Fortunately, the defences withstood the 1953 storm surge and the Fens remained relatively unscathed. However, if the surge had occurred under conditions of a high spring tide coincident with rivers in flood then the whole of the area would likely have been submerged by freshwater, held back by the force of the inrushing surge.[51] Since the 1950s, relative sea level has risen further and so too has the risk of tidal flooding should embankments fail or tidal doors at the lower reaches of the drainage systems fail to close in the event of a storm surge.[52]

The Somerset Levels, inundated so extensively by the 1607 tsunami (see Chapter 1), though smaller in area, have an origin and history in parallel with the Fens. These lands are only just above sea level so flooding by the sea has been a frequent occurrence over the centuries, until the defences were raised and strengthened in the early twentieth century. In the Greatest Storm of 1703 (see Chapter 1), waves overtopped the sea embankments.[53] Drainage inland to produce useable pasture, mainly for dairy farming, took place principally in the thirteenth and fourteenth centuries, from the late 1700s to the early 1830s and with a third phase of activity onwards from the Second World War.[54] Yet again, this area tells a story of embankments, ditches, peat extraction and stream diversions, the excavation of new channels and the incessant pumping of waters. Along with the Broads and the Fens, the Somerset Levels are thus a highly vulnerable part of shrinking Britain that will become increasingly difficult and costly to defend in the future.

To protect the capital from a tidal surge: the Thames Barrier

Although many storm surges have affected the Thames Estuary in the past, such as the one that occurred in January 1928 when fourteen people were drowned in Lambeth, the infamous 1953 floods, fortunately, caused no serious problems in the densely populated, urban area of central London. However, the stark realisation of the potentially appalling consequences had they done so could not be ignored by governmental authorities. This prospect and the associated devastation that could be caused by a major surge reaching the capital was to provide the stimulus to plan to protect it from this eventuality. This also marked a significant shift, a sea change in the mindset about the methods by which, for generations, estuarine flood events had previously been managed. As long ago as 1967 it was predicted that, 'a time may come when adjustments must be made to the level of dock sills, and a Thames barrage will be a necessity'.[55] Hitherto, the solution to prevent flooding in such areas had been the construction of static, containing structures in the form of retaining walls of masonry or concrete and embankments of earth. As flood levels increased through time, their upper surfaces were typically extended to higher and higher levels. By the late 1970s, however, it had become appreciated that the raising of walls and barriers progressively higher was not the solution, and that doing so would eventually block the Thames from ground level view, so other options had to be devised driven by necessity as the mother of invention. The result, a powerfully striking symbol, testimony to the vulnerability of south-east England to climate change and sea level rise, is the Thames Barrier, one of the largest *moveable* flood barriers in the world, designed to protect the central parts of London from tidal surges.[56] Spanning over 500 metres in length across the tidal reach of the Thames near Woolwich, the structure (Plate 14) took some eight years to build and was completed in 1982. All ten of its steel gates can be raised into position across the Thames within around one and a half hours, an operation ideally effected immediately after low tide, to hold back the incoming flood waters if a tidal surge is predicted. Some four months after it had been completed, in February 1983, the barrier was first put to the test, which it passed. By April 2010, it had been closed a total of 119 times for 'real' events, that is over and above routine monthly testing closures, with the numbers of closures per year generally increasing towards the end of this period with maxima of 24 and 20 in the years 2000/2001 and 2002/2003, respectively (Figure 2.5). This increase in usage through time in the past three decades or so is a reflection of the accelerating rise in

relative sea level in this part of England that has resulted in the high
tide in central London, at London Bridge, rising at a rate of around
75 centimetres per century since 1791. However, upstream flooding
along the Thames in London has been prevented successfully on
each occasion of its closure. The barrier was designed originally to
protect the city of London until about 2030 (it alone protects
property worth over £30 billion on the basis of 2007 prices)[57] but,
with suitable modifications in the future, it is now believed by the
Environment Agency for England and Wales that it is capable of
doing its job until at least the end of the twenty-first century.

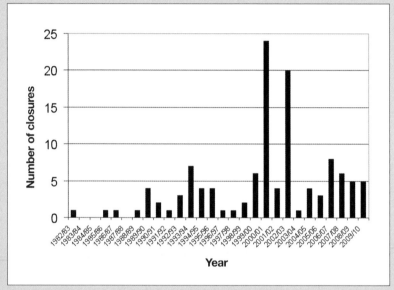

Figure 2.5 Bar chart showing the annual variation to April 2010 in the number of times
(totalling 119) that the Thames Barrier has been closed to protect London from floods
since it was completed in October 1982. Of these closures, 78 were to prevent tidal
surges and 41 to prevent flooding due to high rainfall. Note the general trend of
increasing closures per year through time and that the peak years with the highest
number of closures were in 2000/01 and 2002/03 (based on data presented on the
Environment Agency website http://www. environment-agency. gov. uk/homeand
leisure/floods/38359. aspx).

Along with increases in relative sea level rise around our coasts, the IPCC,
at the global scale, and both the UKCIP and the UK Department for
Environment, Food and Rural Affairs (Defra), at the more local scale,

present powerful evidence to support the suggestion that weather patterns will change through the next few decades with wetter winters and increases in storm strengths, which will increase offshore wave height and frequency.[58] Such increased storminess and more unpredictable weather will lead to more frequent extreme events, such as tidal surges. The latter is supported by the observations for the Thames shown in Figure 2.5 and by the historical record for south and south-west England, particularly during the twentieth century.[59] However, on the west coast, between Glasgow in Scotland southwards to Milford Haven in Wales, historical records point to a decline in flood frequencies due to storms in the same period.[60] Other more recent studies in Scotland, of tidal records from Aberdeen, Stornoway on the Isle of Lewis and Millport on Cumbrae Island, whilst recognising relative sea level rise in these areas, also suggest that there is no discernible evidence for changes in surges due to increased storminess.[61] Similar findings have been reported from monitoring stations in the Netherlands, which even indicate a slight decrease in storminess over the last four decades of the twentieth century.[62] So, to some extent the jury is still out with regard to this issue.

Even in the absence of storm surges and the aggravated problems they can bring, elsewhere from the south-east and east of Britain, many other estuarine settlements, as developed for example along the low-lying coastal fringes of Cornwall, Devon, the Severn Estuary, North Wales, the Wirral Peninsula, the Firth of Clyde, the Firth of Forth and the Moray Firth are also susceptible to the effects of rising relative sea levels. In addition, in such areas, as sea levels rise, saltwater intrusion into freshwater aquifers is likely to occur, thereby contaminating potable groundwater reserves. Such complex regional and even local variations in the susceptibility of Britain's coasts to sea level rise pose problems and complications for effective coastal zone management. It may come as a surprise to find that over a century ago in 1908, nearly half a century before the notorious 1953 storm surge, it was being asserted with considerable conviction in the foremost British textbook on coastal erosion of its day that, 'The problem of protecting our coasts from the attack of the sea has now acquired a national importance.'[63] This raises at least two key questions. Have attitudes to coastal protection changed in our island nation over the last hundred years or so? Furthermore, to keep the raging sea at bay, should we defend our coasts at all costs? These issues are explored in the following chapters.

3
ENEMY AND FRIEND:
DESTRUCTION, CONSTRUCTION AND SEDUCTION

But the deep and dark blue ocean – Oh, there is repose upon its vast expanse and enjoyment in its unmeasured sublimity which the pen cannot portray, and the tongue cannot enunciate. How complacently can the thoughts compose themselves into soothingly-grateful contemplations of that High and Holy One, who while He 'inhabits eternity, gives the sea His commandment' and commissions the tributary waves and waters – whether in calm or storm – to enrich, protect, and beautify the heaven-favoured circumference of Britain's sea-girt isle!

Robert Wake, *Southwold and its Vicinity, Ancient and Modern*, 1839

DESTRUCTIVE POWER

Erosion does not track across the ground at a constant and predictable rate like the sun across the sky. The land breaks off in lumps.

Richard Girling, *Sea Change: Britain's Coastal Catastrophe*, 2008

The previous two chapters have featured the shrinkage of Britain's landmass principally as a result of rising relative sea level since the last ice age. However, even if stillstand conditions prevail, that is there is no change in relative sea level, the sea's waves can erode and devour with great rapidity if the geological fabric of the land is soft and vulnerable to wave attack. Waves generated by the wind blowing over the surface of seas and oceans are the prime natural cause of coastal erosion. A key factor in determining the height, and, therefore, the energy, of wind-generated waves is the so-called fetch length. This is the horizontal distance of seawater surface over which the wind blows. Waves increase in height with increasing fetch up to a maximum of around 1,600 kilometres. Thus, for any given location, the direction that the wind is blowing from is of great importance in terms of the heights of waves breaking on a shore. A good way to visualise this is to look at a large puddle of water in a roughly surfaced road or car park on a windy day. The wind will generate small waves, known as ripples, on the water surface. The down-wind part of the puddle has the longest fetch and will have the largest ripples whereas the upwind end will have virtually no surface motion at all. Should the wind switch in direction, the down-wind location of the largest ripples will move accordingly and they will break onto another section of the 'shore'. Up-scale this from the puddle to a real coastal situation and the impact of wind direction on wave generation can be quite astonishing. For example, the 28 kilometres long Chesil Beach in Dorset is a remarkable formation of gravel ridges. A wind blowing onto it from the south, across the English Channel has a fetch length of around 120 kilometres from the Channel Islands. From the west, the fetch is much shorter, around 35 kilometres across Lyme Bay. However, a wind blowing onto Chesil Beach from the south-west has a fetch length that extends for around 8,000 kilometres, far exceeding the limiting distance (Figure 3.1). The nearest land in this direction is diagonally across the Atlantic Ocean, the north coast of South America. It is therefore not surprising that winds blowing from this

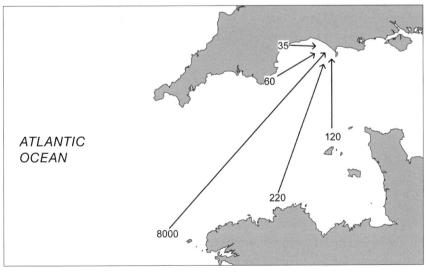

Figure 3.1 Fetch lengths in kilometres for waves approaching Chesil Beach on the English Channel coast of Dorset from different points of the compass (drawing by T. Dixon).

direction have the ability to generate very high and therefore powerful waves compared with those from other points of the compass. The energy of a wave is directly proportional to its height squared. The height of a wave is the difference in elevation between the crest of the wave and the trough. So this means that a wave with a height of, say, 2 metres, will have 4 times as much energy (that is, 2 multiplied by 2), and therefore 4 times as much potential to erode the coast, than a wave 1 metre in height. Similarly, a wave 3 metres in height will have 9 times as much energy (that is, 3 times 3) than a 1 metre high wave.

The energy of waves can thus be immense (see also Chapter 5). In December 1872, a violent storm battered the north-east coast of Scotland. At Wick in remote Caithness its effects were awesome; an emotive descriptor, yet the sea's power is just so. The storm destroyed the town's fishing harbour and in so doing tore from a breakwater, engineered by Thomas Stevenson, father of the acclaimed author Robert Louis Stevenson, a sandstone block 14 metres in length, 8 metres in width and 3.5 metres in thickness. This had remained fixed to its foundation by iron rods 9 centimetres in diameter for the previous four years and the mass removed by the force of the waves weighed around 1,350 tonnes. Following this devastating event, the harbour breakwater was rebuilt according to Thomas Stevenson's new design, replacing the stone block with another that, at 2,600 tonnes, was almost double the weight of its predecessor. Five years later, in 1877, it too was ripped away by the power of the waves in what has been referred to as an 'apocalyptic storm'.[1] For that gale, even awesome was an inadequate description.

Waves, however, have other, more subtle, ways of using their ammunition, yet still reminding us of their vast power. A few kilometres to the north-west of Wick is Dunnet Head, the most northerly point of the British mainland. Above the cliffs of this Devonian sandstone promontory projecting northwards into the Pentland Firth, stands a white painted stone lighthouse (Plate 16), 20 metres high, built in 1831 and engineered coincidentally by Thomas Stevenson's illustrious father, Robert. The windows of this tower, despite being at a height of 105 metres above the level of the sea, are from time to time damaged by pebbles thrown aloft by the force of the ferocious breaking waves that can develop frequently in the treacherous stretch of rocky strait below.

Writing over a century ago, in particular about the east and south coasts of England, Clement Reid, prior to *Submerged Forests* fame, propounded that, 'The Britain that Cæsar invaded was very different in its coastline from the Britain of to-day; the Britain of three thousand years ago was still more unlike.'[2] The rocky promontory of Flamborough Head that projects some 6 kilometres eastwards into the North Sea is one of the most spectacular coastal locations in Britain (Plate 17). Here the 120-metre-high cliffs are a paradise for sea birds such as guillemots, puffins, razorbills, fulmars, kittiwakes and herring gulls. To the south, however, the geological fabric of the Yorkshire coast changes and the Cretaceous chalk of Flamborough gives way to younger and very much softer, far less durable glacial till or boulder clay that was laid down during the last ice age. In fact, the boulders in these deposits are sparsely scattered, with the vast bulk of the materials being mud and sand. This is Holderness, a vulnerable region of Yorkshire's East Riding that extends south to Spurn Head that elongate, curious sand and shingle spit that extends, 'sickle-like',[3] in an arc southwards into the mouth of the Humber Estuary. Along this coastline, the dominant direction of longshore sediment transport, a topic that will be explored further in Chapter 4, is from north to south towards Spurn Head. With an elevation of no more than 9 metres above sea level and in places no more than this distance in width, there is no more fragile or indeed more striking strip of coastal land in Britain (Plate 18). A cluster of houses at the southern tip, along with the RNLI Lifeboat Station and jetty, are home to the only full-time resident lifeboat crew in Britain and their families. A National Nature Reserve owned by the Yorkshire Wildlife Trust, it is also a haven for birdlife who are oblivious to the almost constant flux that this narrow spit is in. A lonely road runs along its length, as from the First World War until the early 1950s did a light railway extending from Kilnsea. These wind- and wave-swept lifelines have been breached or overtopped many times by stormy seas over the years and the communities at the end of the spit continue to be cut off from the mainland periodically. For instance, during a north-westerly gale on 28 December 1849, a breach was made through the spit. In 1850 this breach was about 320 yards in width and 12 feet deep at ordinary high water and was used as a short cut by small vessels. By the following year, the cut had grown to 500 yards wide and 16 feet deep at high water.[4] Of the many lighthouses that have been built at Spurn over the centuries, two remain today, both in disuse; the close-on 40-metres-tall high light on land at the end of the spit, built in 1895, and the low light of 1852 on the beach to the west (Plate 19). Both were replacements for earlier structures.[5]

Using measurements collated by the then Borough Engineer of Bridlington, one E.R. Mathews, Clement Reid presented the first summary of the rates of erosion on a geographical basis from north to south along the Holderness coast (Figure 3.2).[6] The imperial unit of length in use at the time was the yard (1 imperial yard = 0.9144 metres) and the horizontal rate of erosion was expressed in yards per annum. Such values thus equate in a not unreasonable approximation, given the level of accuracy with which horizontal distance measurements are made, to metres per annum. This table shows that, unless protected by sea walls, the loss of land to the sea is, almost everywhere along this stretch of coast, in the range of 2–5 metres per year.

Similar rates of land loss to the sea have long been reported from south of the Humber, along parts of the Lincolnshire coast and in Norfolk and Suffolk.[7] For instance, observations at Sheringham in north Norfolk ascertained by Sir Charles Lyell showed that between the years 1824 and 1829 17 yards of land close to an inn were lost to the sea, equivalent to about 3 metres of erosion per annum[8] and similar to the values from Holderness. To put rates of land loss such as these into perspective, since the Roman invasion of Britain, roughly 2,000 years ago, the shoreline of these vulnerable parts of the east coast will have receded westwards by between 4 and 10 kilometres, according to locality.

Wilsthorpe, Auburn, Hartburn, Hyde, Withow and Cleton; these are just a further cluster of the towns, known collectively as 'The Lost Towns

Figure 3.2 Table of erosion rates from north to south along the Holderness coast (from Reid, C. (1906) Coast erosion. *The Geographical Journal*, 28, 487–495).

Part of coast.	Formation of cliffs.	Distance.	Rate of erosion in yards per annum.	Height of cliffs.
Flamborough Head to Bridlington	Chalk for 3 miles, then glacial drift	5	{ 0·5 yd. to 2 yds.	80 ft. to 130 ft.
Bridlington	Glacial drift	2	Protected	—
Bridlington to Barmston	,, ,,	5	3 yds.	10 ft. to 30 ft.
Barmstone to Ulrome	,, ,,	5	1½ yd. to 4 yds.	10 ft. to 20 ft.
Ulrome to Skipsea	,, ,,	1½	2 yds.	25 ft. to 35 ft.
Skipsea to Skirlington	,, ,,	2	2 yds.	—
Skirlington to Atwick	,, ,,	1	2½ to 3 yds.	30 ft.
Atwick to Hornsea	,, ,,	2	—	—
Hornsea	,, ,,	—	Protected	
Hornsea to Hornsea Burton	,, ,,	1	2½ to 4½ yds.	30 ft. to 40 ft.
Hornsea Burton to Mappleton	,, ,,	1½	2 to 3 yds.	50 ft.
Mappleton to Aldborough	,, ,,	3½	2 to 2½ yds.	70 ft.
Aldborough to Ringborough	,, ,,	2	3 yds.	50 ft.
Ringborough to Withernsea	,, ,,	7	3 to 4 yds.	25 ft.
Withernsea	,, ,,	—	Protected.	—
Withernsea to Dimlington	,, ,,	5½	3½ yds.	—
Dimlington to Easington	,, ,,	1	5 yds.	—
Easington to Kilnsea	,, ,,	2½	3 to 4 yds.	—
Kilnsea to Spurn point	Sandhills	—	—	—

SUMMARY re EROSION ON THE HOLDERNESS COAST.

of East Yorkshire' that have been eaten completely by the sea since the Roman occupation. In all, over thirty, once substantive, settlements are no more. It is thanks to the record of historical maps that their former existence can be documented[9] together with the rate at which erosion has taken place, the speed with which the sea has eaten away the land along this stretch of coast (Figure 3.3). Owthorne was another casualty. The foundations of its churchyard were being undermined in 1786, so the church itself (Plate 20) was largely pulled down, dismantled to prevent the sea from acting as its agent of demolition.[10] It was a common practice, in those days, not to permit the sea to destroy consecrated ground. What remained of the chancel finally succumbed to persistent wave attack in 1816, prior to which for several years:

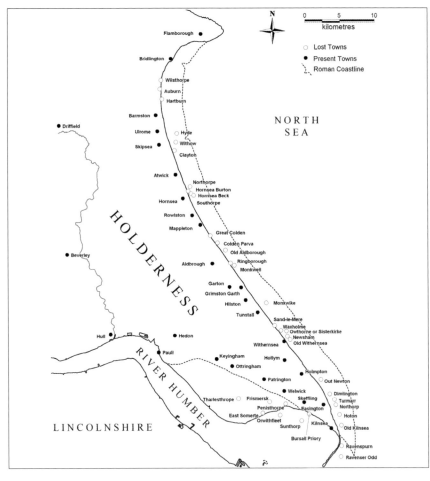

Figure 3.3 The 'Lost Towns of East Yorkshire'. The large area on the north bank of the Humber between Paull and Skeffling was claimed from the estuary since the mid eighteenth century (see Chapter 4; drawing by T. Dixon; from Sheppard, T. (1912) *The Lost Towns of the Yorkshire Coast.* A. Brown & Sons, London).

The churchyard and its slumbering inmates, removed from time to time down the cliff by the force of the tempest; whitened bones projecting from the cliff, and gradually drawn away by the successful lashing of the waves; and, after a fearful storm, old persons tottering on the verge of life, have been seen slowly moving forth, and recognizing on the shore the remains of those whom, in early life, they had known and revered.[11]

After the fall of the church, the vicar, the Reverend James Robson rescued those bodies from the foot of the cliff that had not been washed away and the corpses were re-interred at nearby Rimswell.[12] One coffin, smashed open by the force of the sea, contained the corpse believed to be that of a founder of the church, which had been richly embalmed with aromatic spices that had still not lost their aroma. A skull seen projecting from the cliff was observed to be occupied by a robin red-breast where she, undisturbed, built her nest and reared her brood. By 1838, there was scarcely a remnant of the churchyard left; the sea holds no respect for the dead and buried. Six years later, like so many other buildings in this area, the vicarage was to fall victim to erosion.

With reference to Hornsea, located towards the centre of the Holderness coastline, Sheppard has remarked wryly that: 'It occasionally happens that the erosion of a coast is not altogether a disadvantage. For example, in 1770, the corpse of a murderer and smuggler named Pennel, was bound round with iron-hoops and hung on a gibbet on the north cliff, until such time as the "ornament" was washed away.'[13] Hornsea is today right on the coast. An ancient local rhyme in *Folk Lore of East Yorkshire* provides an indication of just how much land has been lost to the sea hereabouts as, in 1861, it was noted that the church referred to in the verse was only half a mile from the shore:[14]

> *Hornsea steeple, when I built thee,*
> *Thou was 10 miles off Burlington,*
> *10 miles off Beverley, and 10 miles off the sea.*

Over the years, houses, cottages and hotels have had to be pulled down at Hornsea as a result of the persistent attack from the sea and many have been swept away.[15] In 1912, Sheppard noted with exclamation that at Withernsea, between Hornsea and Spurn Head, houses 'go over the cliff almost daily!'

Indeed, many of the towns lost to the sea were not insubstantial in size and significance. At the southern end of Holderness, Ravenser Odd was once a more important port than Hull. Here, as at Owthorne, in 1355, bodies were washed out of their graves in the chapel yard and a few years later, in 1361, the sea floods drove the merchants to Hull and across the Humber to Grimsby in Lincolnshire as the town was annihilated.[16] Nearby Ravenspurn, a gateway to the north, was featured several times by William Shakespeare under the name of Ravenspurgh including reference to its 'naked shore', an appropriate description of this exposed coast, in *Henry IV*, Part 1:

> *For all the world,*
> *As thou art to this hour, was Richard then*
> *When I from France set foot at Ravenspurgh;*
> *And even as I was then is Percy now.*
>
> *Henry IV*, Part 1, Act 3, Scene 2

> *Steps me a little higher than his vow*
> *Made to my father, while his blood was poor,*
> *Upon the naked shore at Ravenspurgh*
>
> *Henry IV*, Part 1, Act 4, Scene 3

> *Wipe off the dust that hides our sceptre's gilt*
> *And make high majesty look like itself,*
> *Away with me in post to Ravenspurgh;*
> *But if you faint, as fearing to do so,*
> *Stay and be secret, and myself will go*
>
> *Richard II*, Act 2, Scene 1

A fine stone cross was said to have been erected at Ravenspurn in memory of Henry IV landing there. The town was finally lost to the sea in the fourteenth century.[17]

New settlements – towns and villages – subsequently developed and evolved inland, as the land and buildings on it were consumed by the sea. The people relocated and rebuilt landward, often time and again, as if accepting, with reluctance no doubt, the realism, the eventuality of what is a natural process – coastal erosion. In the words of Thomas Sheppard, a century ago:

There can be no question that the changes on the south-east coast
of Yorkshire have been as great as those in any part of Britain, and
in various ways geologists and antiquaries have placed on record a
mass of information relative to these changes. The result is that,
probably more than is the case with any other district, we are able
to get reliable information in reference to one of the most interesting chapters in the geography of our islands.[18]

Is land still being lost at these rates along our eastern shores? The Hull
Geological Society, with reference to a fixed point so dear to the hearts of
most geologists, has recounted that, when the Blue Bell Inn at the village
of Kilnsea, at the northern end of Spurn Head, was rebuilt in 1847, a wall
plaque states that it was 534 yards from the sea. The very placing of such a
notice is a clear measure of the rapidity of erosion to be anticipated in the
area. No longer an ale-house but a visitor centre, by 1989, the former inn
was 217 yards from the sea; in 1994, the building was 190 yards; and on 17
May 2004, it was 160 yards from the sea.[19] Thus, 374 yards of land had been
lost in 157 years at Kilnsea, a long term average erosion rate of a little over
2 metres per year (Plate 21). This is comparable with, but towards the lower
end of, the range of values reported from this length of coastline, a
reflection of the much longer time frame over which the observations of
land loss were made. The average loss of land is still around 2 metres per
year but the rate does fluctuate greatly both over time and from location
to location.[20] For instance, a recession of 6 metres in just two days was
reported at Barmston south of Bridlington in October 1967 following a
big storm.[21] The actual process of recession occurs as a series of land slips;
the soft cliffs collapse and slump towards the unsupported face leaving
often large bites at the cliff top, which may be 10 or even 20 metres across
(see Chapter 5). Wave action gradually removes the slumped material from
the back of the beach, at the toe of each landslide, transporting it offshore
and alongshore in suspension. There may be long periods of relative
stability before the next landslides take place, and, by these means,
Holderness shrinks (Plate 22). A look to seaward from any high vantage
point along this coast, on all but the calmest days of the year, will reveal
brown, turbid water extending almost to the horizon, an indication of the
high concentrations of fine particles, silts and clays, being held and transported in suspension.

Observation of the older cottages and churches in many of the Holder-

ness villages reveals that they are not built of cut blocks of so-called
dimension stone; rather they are constructed from water-worn cobbles
(Plate 23). Indeed, buildings in Holderness have used cobbles in their
construction for many generations, and certainly into the early twentieth
century. Therein, however, is another intriguing story. What was the source
of these building materials? Erosion and slumping of the soft till cliffs
provided a continuous source of gravel and cobbles to the beach below;
they have been transported here from afar by ice, and are known as glacial
erratics. These were then moved by the prevailing wave-generated
longshore currents towards Kilnsea and onwards to Spurn Head, where
they accumulated. Cobble and gravel extraction in the Spurn area, not
only for building houses but also for road construction in Yorkshire and
across the Humber in Lincolnshire, was once big business, peaking in the
mid nineteenth century with sloops being the main mode of transport.
These raw materials were continually collected onto carts along the
seaward side of the spit, taken over to the Humber Estuary shore and piled
into heaps, awaiting loading onto the sloops as they came alongside the spit
at low tide.[22] The 'Spurn gravel trade' almost inevitably led to a conflict
between commerce and coastal erosion along this fragile finger of land.
There is abundant evidence to indicate that the excessive extraction of
gravel and especially cobbles was a major contributor to the 1849 breach
of the spit, which took place in an area where extraction was concentrated.
A few years prior to this event there were signs of incipient breaches along
the spit and, in 1842, one of the main gravel extractors was directed by
Trinity House not to remove materials from the shore near the low lighthouse due to the effects of the 'German Ocean'; a direction that appears
to have gone unheeded.[23] Additional damage was caused by the continual
use of horse-drawn carts to shift thousands of tons of cobbles and gravel
per year, flattening and trampling the fragile dunes forming the higher
ground in the centre of the spit. In the 1840s, extraction was quite simply
being carried out at a faster rate than natural process could supply the raw
materials. Moreover, the wave energy absorbing capacity afforded by the
protective veneer of gravel and cobbles had been taken away. Even today,
this fragile environment has not fully recovered from the effects of the
Spurn gravel trade; the cobbles and gravel had likely taken centuries to
build up in commercial quantities and, still depleted in these materials, it
presents relatively easy prey to wave attack.

Was it an act of stupidity to construct a North Sea gas processing plant close to the edge of one of the most rapidly eroding parts of Britain, indeed of Europe? Between the small town of Withernsea and Spurn Head is the village of Easington. Located here on the cliff top (Plate 24) is a nationally important gas terminal, a processing plant that today receives and separates around a quarter of the total demand for natural gas in Britain. This is now piped 1,200 kilometres diagonally across the North Sea from Norway by way of the world's longest undersea gas pipeline. Constructed in the late 1960s, Easington was the first place in England to have a gas terminal, which begs the obvious question; *why* locate such an important facility on one of the most rapidly eroding coasts in the country? Surely, this was absolute folly? Even the public house in the village's main street is prophetically called 'The Neptune Inn'. When the terminal was constructed, however, it was done so at a position far enough back from the cliff edge to permit its safety on the basis of the best available knowledge at the time, that the life expectancy of North Sea gas reserves would be around twenty-five years. It would thus have been very much a fixed-life structure; by the time erosion threatened it seriously, gas production would have ceased. No-one could have predicted, when it was built, that North Sea gas would still be produced. Although it no longer receives gas from the offshore UK fields that originally supplied it, the terminal has substantially exceeded its assumed lifespan and so there has been a necessity to protect it subsequently from coastal erosion. This has been done by the installation of a large rock armour revetment, accompanied by lowering the angle of the cliff and improving drainage within it to lessen the possibility of slumping and gully formation. Attempts to protect this coast have, more often than not, however, made the situation worse, exacerbating the rate of erosion elsewhere (Plate 25), a topic that will be explored in Chapter 4.

The above are still not the highest rates of coastal erosion in Britain though. That dubious honour belongs to Suffolk in East Anglia, which has some of the fastest retreating coastlines in Europe. In Waveney District, in the north-east corner of the county, the long-term average erosion rates of soft, undefended cliffs are 1 to 2 metres per year; however, losses of farmland of up to 10 metres can occur over one winter season as, for example, close to the town of Southwold.

A unique piece or artwork in the Suffolk Coastal District, close to the town of Bawdsey, provides a highly unusual but nonetheless important insight into the contemporary rate at which land can be lost to the sea in this fragile part of Britain. The art project, 'If Ever You're in the Area', took place in 2005 and 2006 and relates to the memory of war and the fear of enemy invasion. 'Lines of Defence' was part of this project and involved the placement of thirty-eight flags, in five lines each 1 metre apart, each flag bearing a letter which together spelled out in capital letters the phrase: 'SUBMISSION IS ADVANCING AT A FRIGHTFUL SPEED'. These were located on the top of rapidly eroding cliffs, where, of course, the sea was cast to perfection in the role of the enemy invader. The site chosen was that of First and Second World War military installations, adjacent to Bawdsey Manor. This country estate was selected in 1935 as a site for a new research station for the development of radio direction finding, subsequently to become known as radar. Nearby, the hamlet of Shingle Street, requisitioned in 1940 for invasion defences, is the mysterious site of the rumoured German invasion attempt of 1940, Operation Sea Lion; a myth or, perhaps, black propaganda that hit and fired up the British national press into frenzy in 1992, on the early declassification of government papers.[24] As the sea eroded the soft cliffs away, the progressive destruction of the flags in their lines was captured by time lapse webcam, positioned on a nearby Martello Tower from the Napoleonic Wars, and webcast every fifteen minutes from 15 January 2005 to 15 January 2006. Today the time lapse movie can still be viewed on the Internet on 'You Tube' (Lines of Defence).[25] It provides a compelling visual reminder of the power of the sea, but especially a unique quantification of the rapidity and ease with which land can be eaten away from soft cliffs. During the twelve months of time-lapse image recording, a remarkable 17 metres of this part of Suffolk was lost to an enemy that was at one time, after all, known as the German Ocean. This is most likely the highest rate of erosion recorded in Britain, albeit monitored over a comparatively short period.

The Suffolk-born historical writer and poet Agnes Strickland, most famous for her 'Lives of the Queens of England', whose sketch map of the lost land of Lyonesse between Cornwall and the Isles of Scilly featured in Chapter 1, also told the story of the demise of once proud Dunwich:

Oft gazing on thy craggy brow,
We muse on glories o'er;
Fair Dunwich! Thou are lowly now,
Renowned and sought no more.

How proudly rose thy crested seat
Above the ocean wave;
Yet doomed beneath that sea to meet
One wide and sweeping grave!

The stately city greets no more
The home-returning bark;
Sad relics of her splendours o'er
One crumbling spire we mark.

Unlike when ruled by Saxon powers,
She sat in ancient pride,
With all her stately halls and towers
Reflected on the tide.

Those who through forgotten age,
With patient care will look,
Will find her fate in many a page
Of Time's extended book.

Nor will they coldly turn away,
Because my verse shall tell
A story of that fearful day,
When mighty Dunwich fell.[26]

Located a little distance to the south of Southwold, this Suffolk village of Dunwich is today a small settlement that belies the fact that it was once an important and very prosperous North Sea trading port.[27] Legends and folklore abound around our shores of the eerie sound of church bells tolling from 'neath storm waves where towns and villages once clustered before the sea devoured them. None, however, is richer or more vivid than that of the sound of the bells of Dunwich; Britain's Atlantis. Some say that their peal can be heard on a quiet day; others hold that fishermen will not put to sea as their ghostly ringing is a sure sign of a gathering storm. There is little wonder that the sound of bells is so inextricably linked with this spot, since so many churches have been lost to the sea here over the centuries.

Of 'tis said
Below the waves; and oft the mariner,
Driven by the whirlwind, feels his vessel strike
Upon the mingled mass.[28]

When Daniel Defoe made his tour through the eastern counties of England in 1722 as part of his mammoth 'Tour Thro' the Whole Island of Great Britain' he found:

Yet Dunwich, however ruined, retains some share of trade, as particularly for the shipping of butter, cheese, and corn, which is so great a business in this county, that it employs a great many people and ships also; and this port lies right against the particular part of the county for butter, as Framlingham, Halstead, etc. Also a very great quantity of corn is bought up hereabout for the London market; for I shall still touch that point how all the counties in England contribute something towards the subsistence of the great city of London, of which the butter here is a very considerable article; as also coarse cheese, which I mentioned before, used chiefly for the king's ships.[29]

Today, Dunwich is little more than a hamlet, but it was once the seaport capital of East Anglia, and one of England's ten largest cities. Grain and wool were exported with return trade of wine, furs, fish and cloth from, among others, France, the countries of the Baltic and the Netherlands. In the words of Cuming Walters, 'Truly it was no mean city.'[30] So familiar, however, is the loss of land to the sea in this part of England that eminent British Geographer, the late Sir Laurence Dudley Stamp, wrote rather dismissively that: 'There are stretches where normal sea erosion is eating into low cliffs of boulder clay and the rapid regression of the coastline in the neighbourhood of Dunwich is too well known to need description.'[31]

As more powerful testimony to the rapid coastal erosion that characterises this part of Suffolk, the churches once dedicated to St Peter, St John the Baptist, St Nicholas, St Leonard, St Martin, St Bartholomew, St Michael, St Patrick and St Felix are all no more, along with the Church of the Knights Templars, St Francis' Chapel, St Katherine's Chapel, St Anthony's Chapel and the Black Friars' Monastery.[32] Hereabouts, as along the Holderness coast, owing to the optimum geological circumstances of extremely soft cliff materials (see Chapter 5), the power of the sea to devour all in its path is exemplified. There was still one final church to fall, however. All Saints, dating back to the sixteenth century, survived into the early twentieth century. The last part of its stone tower fell on 12 November 1919; no longer serving as a prominent landmark for ships as it had done for many years and finally beyond the care of Trinity House who had maintained it in that role.[33] As at Owthorne, human bones could still be seen protruding from the soil at the top of the cliff many decades after the church itself had fallen. The fate of Dunwich was, however, sealed as long ago as the thirteenth and fourteenth centuries when violent storms in 1286 and 1328 rendered much extensive damage. A further storm in 1347 is said to have alone claimed 400 buildings; houses, shops, churches and windmills, comprising around one quarter of the then city, were destroyed.[34] Three of the city's churches, St Bartholomew, St Leonard and St Martin, were lost together in another severe storm in the fourteenth century. Horrific devastation was brought about by a storm with an associated surge that lasted for several days in 1740 – this was the storm of storms.[35] Coffins and skeletons from the churchyards of St Nicholas and St Francis were strewn onto the beach; Dunwich was, 'in cradle of the rude imperious surge'.[36] By 1829, Dunwich was so much eroded in size that it comprised just forty-two houses, half a church (All Saints), 200 inhabitants and a mere eighteen voters.[37] By the dawn of the twentieth century, once proud Dunwich merited the description: 'Half-sunk in the sea, half-vanished from the eye of man, a great name in ancient history, and a fading name in the present, the former capital of East Anglia is to-day an impressive and pathetic spectacle as its cluster of small cottages is viewed dipping down towards the ravenous ocean.'[38] And so the sorry story of its still further reduction to hamlet status has continued largely unabated to this day. As if destruction by the sheer force of waves was not enough, Dunwich has also had to contend over the centuries with the continual choking of the creek that formed its natural haven on the north side, by sand pushed ashore, thrust landward in storms.[39]

The English romantic artist William Turner, in one of his lesser known works, painted 'Dunwich, Suffolk' in around 1827. Held by the Manchester Art Gallery and one of a series of east coast watercolour paintings, this small image depicts a violently stormy scene with the ghostly pale ruins of a church on the cliff top, a distant shipwreck and a group of men pushing a small boat out into the breaking waves. Using full

Did William Shakespeare have an appreciation of coastal erosion?

Whether or not Shakespeare ever visited the vulnerable British coasts of Holderness or Norfolk or Suffolk we will never know. There is indeed, however, some potent evidence to suggest that Shakespeare was well aware of the process of wearing away of the land by incessant wave attack, as illustrated by his Sonnet 64, revealed especially by the couplet of the fifth and sixth lines:

> *When I have seen by Time's fell hand defaced*
> *The rich proud cost of outworn buried age;*
> *When sometime lofty towers I see down-razed,*
> *And brass eternal slave to mortal rage;*
> *When I have seen the hungry ocean gain*
> *Advantage on the kingdom of the shore,*
> *And the firm soil win of the watery main,*
> *Increasing store with loss, and loss with store;*
> *When I have seen such interchange of state,*
> *Or state itself confounded to decay;*
> *Ruin hath taught me thus to ruminate*
> *That Time will come and take my love away.*
> *This thought is as a death which cannot choose*
> *But weep to have that which it fears to lose.*

Within this 'little song' the overall theme or message conveyed is that of the swift passage of time and the eventual destruction of *all* things. The rate at which the hungry ocean is capable of eating away the land is but part of this 'whole' and we should realise that it could potentially involve the destruction of an entire kingdom. Perhaps Shakespeare once visited Dunwich?

artistic licence, Turner has rotated the ruins of All Saints through 180 degrees,[40] but nonetheless this is a moody, fantasy image of land against the sea at the site of one of Britain's most famous and very real lost cities, now all but effaced from the map of Britain.

The Goodwin Sands: could lost Lomea become an airport?

> In what census of living creatures, the dead of mankind are
> included; why it is that a universal proverb says of them, that
> they tell no tales, though containing more secrets than the
> Goodwin Sands.
>
> > Herman Melville, *Moby Dick* or *The Whale*, 1851

In addition to Dunwich, coincidentally, romantic artist William
Turner also painted 'Cricket on the Goodwin Sands' sometime
between 1828 and 1830. That notoriously treacherous sandbank in
the English Channel, emergent at low tide, around 10 kilometres to
the east of Deal in Kent, has claimed hundreds if not thousands of
shipwrecks over the centuries. In 1830, Sir Charles Lyell reported
that: 'When the erection of a lighthouse was in contemplation by
the Trinity Board, twelve years since it was found, by borings, that
the bank consisted of 15 feet of sand, resting on blue clay.' These
observations led Lyell to conclude that the over 15 kilometres long
Goodwin Sands are the eroded remains of an island of clay, much
like the low-lying Isle of Sheppey off the northern coast of Kent in
the Thames Estuary,[41] an island much damaged in the 1953 floods.
This was reinforced by the suggestion that the Goodwin Sands are
the remnants of the fruitful rich pastures of the 'Isle of Lomea'; the
'Insula Infera' or Low Island of the Romans.[42] Though the evidence
might be open to debate and based largely on myth, Gattie asserts
that Lomea, 'occupying the exact position of the present Goodwin
Sands, must have been, as stated by the old writers, none other than
the sea-girt island said to have formed part of the vast possessions, if
not the actual home of the great English statesman and warrior, the
famous Earl Godwine, the councillor and friend of Edward the
Confessor, sometimes called the Earl of Kent'.[43] Once many
thousands of acres 'of goodlie pasture',[44] it had been suggested since
the 1970s that an additional airport serving London might be built
on the Goodwin Sands, and serious proposals to that end were put
forward as recently as 2003.[45] This would have involved raising a
new island to the east of Deal on which two runways would have

been built. The scheme was, however, rejected on the grounds of poor economic benefits;[46] at least for the foreseeable future Lomea and its mysteries remain another casualty of rising sea levels.

South of Dunwich, Aldeburgh has also waged a continual battle with the sea but perhaps on a less dramatic scale. In the guise of 'Seaburgh', this town was the setting for 'A Warning to the Curious', penned in 1925 by that master of the antiquarian ghost story, M.R. James. In the eighteenth century, wave attack progressively washed away Aldeburgh's market place and an entire street.[47] Writing in 1861, Mackenzie Walcott recounted that the inhabitants had been obliged to build progressively further and further inland. The former town stood a quarter of a mile to the east of the then existing shore, but there was now 24 feet of water over the site where it had once existed. This pattern of inland relocation continued as, in 1898, the town was severely damaged again in a storm.[48] As storms have periodically broken through the dunes that build up during times of strong onshore winds and afford some temporary protection to the town from the sea, Aldeburgh has thus gradually had to migrate inland to avoid the fate of its more infamous neighbour.

The wearing away of rocky cliffs is not always as obvious as the recession of those made of soft materials as for instance along the coast of Holderness. In some places in Britain, the rates of erosion of our rocky shores are all but imperceptible, but in others they can be almost as dramatic as those of their softer counterparts. The chalk cliffs of the English Channel coast of Sussex are a prime example. The spectacular cliff line that extends from Seaford Head to Beachy Head near Eastbourne is known as the 'Seven Sisters', so called because of the seven distinct peaks apparent in the form of the white chalk cliffs. Between each of the 'peaks', which rise to heights of around 150 metres above sea level, lie dry valleys that are perpendicular to the coast where the cliff heights are at their lowest. The deepest dry valley, that is the lowest point of all, along the Seven Sisters, is Birling Gap, the location of a small hamlet where rates of erosion have been monitored for many decades.[49] Long-term average rates of cliff retreat of 71 centimetres per year have been measured, with a report of this value being higher, 91 centimetres per year, between 1950 and 1961. As a result, almost 90 metres of this part of Sussex were lost in the period from 1873–74 to 1997.[50] Not surprisingly, there are considerable seasonal variations, with the majority of recession taking place during the stormy winter months. Although this is an unusually undeveloped part of the south coast of England, the rate of recession of the cliffs has necessitated the demolition of cottages at Birling Gap, most recently in early 2001 (Plate 26).

'Seahenge'

This circular structure of Holme Timber Circle comprising some fifty-five wooden timbers discovered in the late 1990s off the Norfolk coast near Holme-next-the-Sea was more popularly named by analogy with its famous onshore stone counterpart. The early Bronze Age oak timbers of Seahenge have been dated back to around 2050 BC and were exposed as winter storms lowered the level of the beach. At the centre of the 6 to 7 metre diameter oval ring of posts, each around 2 metres in height, stood a large upturned oak stump.[51] By counting the tree rings, it was determined that this massive central tree was around 160 years old when it was felled. Controversially, the structure was excavated and it is now preserved for display in the local Lynn Museum.[52] Many people objected to the removal of what they saw as part of their local heritage and others objected on religious grounds, even staging sit-in protests, despite the fact that archaeologists are by no means certain for what purpose Seahenge was built. It has been postulated that the circle may have been used during the burial of an important person such as a priest or local chief; with a body perhaps placed over the central altar of the inverted stump to decompose prior to committal to the earth. Pieces of rope made from honeysuckle vines were found beneath the stump and it is thought that these were used to move it into its final position.[53] Had the structure been left *in situ*, however, there is little doubt that the erosive forces of the waves that exhumed it, along with the numerous visitors that it would have attracted, would eventually have undermined it and ultimately destroyed its integrity. Originally built some distance inland from the sea, the discovery and subsequent removal of enigmatic Seahenge provides a thought-provoking epitome of 'this shrinking land'.

Hugh Miller on the coastlands of his birthplace

The self-taught Scottish geologist and writer, stonemason to trade, Hugh Miller, became most famous for his work *The Old Red Sandstone or New Walks in an Old Field* published in 1841. His earlier and less well-known *Scenes and Legends of the North of Scotland* (1834) is subtitled *The Traditional History of Cromarty*, in homage to the town of his birth on the southern shore of the Cromarty Firth, at the northern tip of the Black Isle of Easter Ross. Chapter 3 of this book, Miller's first major narrative, not only contains numerous inspiring accounts of the loss of land and homes to the sea in the local area but also descriptions of sites where relative sea level has apparently fallen, as exemplified by:

> In the valley of Munlochy, the remains of oyster-beds, which could not have been formed in less than two fathoms of water, have been discovered a full half mile from the sea; beds of cockles still more extensive, and the bones of a porpoise, have been dug up among the fields which border on the bay of Nigg; similar appearances occur in the vicinity of Tain; and in digging a well about thirty years ago, in the western part of tile town of Cromarty, there was found in the gravel a large fir-tree, which, from the rounded appearance of the trunk and branches, seems to have been at one time exposed to the action of the waves. In a burying-ground of the town, which lies embosomed in an angle of the bank, the sexton sometimes finds the dilapidated spoils of our commoner shell-fish mingling with the ruins of a nobler animal . . .

Concerning loss of land in the Cromarty area to the sea, Miller continues:

> It is a well-established fact, too, that for at least the last three hundred years the sea, instead of receding, has been gradually encroaching on the shores of the Bay of Cromarty; and that the place formerly occupied by the old burgh, is now covered every tide by nearly two fathoms of water.

The last vestige of this ancient town disappeared about eighteen years ago, when a row of large stones, which had evidently formed the foundation line of a fence, was carried away by some workmen employed in erecting a bulwark. But the few traditions connected with it are not yet entirely effaced. A fisherman of the last century is said to have found among the title-deeds of his cottage a very old piece of parchment, with a profusion of tufts of wool bristling on one of its sides, and bearing in rude antique characters on the other a detail of the measurement and boundaries of a garden which had occupied the identical spot on which he usually anchored his skiff. I am old enough to have conversed with men who remembered to have seen a piece of corn land, and a belt of planting below two properties in the eastern part of the town, that are now bounded by the sea. I reckon among my acquaintance an elderly person, who, when sailing along the shore about half a century ago in the company of a very old man, heard the latter remark, that he was now guiding the helm where, sixty years before, he had guided the plough.[54]

CONSTRUCTIVE POWER

Strong winds blowing onshore over wide sandy beaches can also have immense constructive power. At low tide, when the sands are exposed, the particles can be blown inland building often very extensive and sometimes highly elevated dune fields (Plate 27). Through time, if the onshore winds are persistent, fields, houses and even whole towns can be covered over, obscured, depopulated and lost to the sands of time. Thus, a moderate degree of subsequent erosion can often be friend to the coastal archaeologist in such areas, since it can expose to view artefacts and sites, sometimes of huge cultural heritage value, that might have been obscured beneath beach and dune sands for centuries. In enemy attacking role, however, severe erosion acts as their very agent of destruction. Some portable artefacts, like the oak timbers of Seahenge, can be conveniently, but sometimes controversially, removed from coastal areas to museums and laboratories for study but other assemblages of remains require not only examination but also preservation *in situ*.

Europe's most complete Neolithic village had lain completely hidden under sand dunes for millennia, preserved by the constructive help of wind. It was a violent storm that hit the coast of the Northern Isles in 1850 that exhumed the remains of eight houses at Skara Brae, occupied from around 3200 to 2200 BC, on the exposed Bay of Skaill on the western fringe of the mainland of Orkney. A subsequent storm in 1925 caused damage to the remains and so a sea wall was built to provide some protection. It is a twist of cruel irony that this remarkable and archaeologically important monument, one that has been accorded UNESCO World Heritage Site status, should today be under renewed threat of damage (Plate 28), even complete obliteration, from storm wave attack coupled with rising relative sea level.

This is no isolated example of destruction taking place following previous preservation beneath a constructive, protective veneer of wind-blown sand. Writing in 1913, Clement Reid observed:

> If we resume our journey northward along the Norfolk coast we come to the well-known locality of Eccles, where the old church tower described and figured by Lyell in his *Principles of Geology* long stood on the foreshore, washed by every spring tide. The position of this church formed a striking illustration of the protection afforded by a chain of sand dunes. The church was originally built on the marshes inside these dunes, at a level just below that of high-water spring tides. But as the dunes were driven inland they gradually overwhelmed the church, till only the top of its tower appeared above the sand. In this state it was pictured by Lyell in the year 1839. Later on (in 1862) it was again sketched by the Rev. S. W. King, and stood on the seaward side of the dune and almost free from sand. For a series of years, from 1877 onward, I watched the advance of the sea, and as the church tower was more and more often reached by the tides, its foundations were laid bare and attacked by the waves, till at last the tower fell.[55]

A large mound of sand is all that remains of the old Crosskirk at Quendale, the former parish church of Dunrossness in the south of Shetland. This sometime place of worship had to be abandoned in the late seventeenth century owing to continually drifting sand; it remains today as an entombed relic within a sand-blown knoll of 2 to 3 metres in height. But this and the foregoing examples of the constructive force of the wind at the coast prompt a reminder that the sand has had to be blown from somewhere else; thus construction and destruction are often juxtaposed closely. At Quendale, whilst the church itself was buried, in the nearby graveyard the corpses were entirely bare, relics of interments exhumed by violent wind erosion ripping coffins asunder, and in many instances were described as being bleached white.[56]

Kenfig: a town engulfed by sand

> But oft there swirls a woeful wind
> That shrieks with dread portent,
> And ever drives its golden charge
> In flurries from the shore;
> Until at last with frenzied blast
> The demon hour-glass breaks,
> And street and moat lie choked in sand,
> A broken keep remains.
> There time stands still and plovers sob
> A bittersweet lament.
>
> A. Leslie Evans (*c.* 1960)

Just as the inhabitants of Skara Brae in Orkney must surely have had to relocate as the wind-blown sands buried their homes, the people of Kenfig between Porthcawl and Port Talbot in South Wales were obliged to re-settle elsewhere for the same reason. Famed in folklore, Kenfig was situated on what is a highly dynamic stretch of coast, directly exposed to the force of the Atlantic Ocean and large dune fields, like the Kenfig Burrows, have formed at many places along it. Here in the Severn Estuary the tidal range, the difference in sea level between high and low water, is exceptional, the second highest in the world at up to 14 metres in the vertical. In consequence, large near-horizontal expanses of beach sand deposits are exposed between successive high tides, which have time to dry out and become blown inland by onshore winds. Beneath what today forms the Kenfig Dunes National Nature Reserve, renowned for the diversity of its flowering plants and birdlife, is the buried town of that name, a town that was accorded borough status in the Middle Ages. From at least the fifteenth century and probably much earlier, homes and pastures became gradually engulfed by wind-blown sand until by the seventeenth century all that remained visible, and so to this day, was part of the ruined keep of its Norman castle amongst the dunes to the north of Kenfig Pool, Glamorganshire's largest freshwater lake (Plate 29). Many residents relocated to a nearby inland site called Pyle where the parish church was built in 1471 using stone transferred from that of Kenfig.[57] A wall of the 'new' structure reveals smaller stones at its base and larger blocks at higher levels, reflecting the order in which they would have been moved from Kenfig. The nearby Pyle and Kenfig Golf Course, moulded amid the spectacular dune lands, links by nature and by name the past with the present.

A postscript to this story is that, in the 1960s, two jetties were constructed at the mouth of Port Talbot Harbour to permit larger vessels to enter to serve the steelworks. These jetties starved longshore sediment transport from the north-west and as a result caused substantial beach lowering at Kenfig. However, since 25,000 or more jobs depended on the steelworks at the time, it was considered politically expedient to construct the jetties.[58]

Hidden from view, on a secluded sandy eminence within the mature pines of Tentsmuir Forest in north-east Fife stands an almost forgotten, engraved sandstone monolith. Erected in 1794, as its inscription explains, this is a March Stone delimiting the former boundary of salmon fishing rights. When it was positioned atop the dune edge, long before afforestation of the moor, the waves broke just a few metres beneath its base. Today, however, the high water mark is some 1 kilometre distant to the east. If not the most rapid, this is certainly one of the most swiftly accreting parts of the British coast. This stone's present location indicates that sand has built up at an average rate approaching 5 metres per year in the more than two centuries since it was set up. But where has all this sand come from? A prominent legacy from the Second World War helps to illuminate the answer. They may not be pretty, but the line of concrete anti-tank blocks along the northern and eastern lengths of the Tentsmuir coastline, placed at high water mark in 1940, in an attempt to prevent an enemy invasion from the sea along this low-lying shore, are an invaluable time-line in the sands against which coastal change, either construction or destruction, accretion (Plate 30) or erosion (Plate 31), can be measured with considerable accuracy. Maps and aerial photographs of the area that succeed the installation of the line of blocks show that the northern extremity of the area, Tentsmuir Point, has advanced with an average increment, varying with position, of from 7 to as much as 14 metres per annum.[59] Since accurate mapping in 1812, shortly after the erection of the March Stone, the area has been accreting in a north-eastward direction at a long-term average rate of a little less than 5 metres per year; an impressive and sustained rate of growth.[60]

Further south, however, a very different picture is revealed by these means. Hereabouts, the coast is eroding and the concrete blocks lie detach-ed, some displaced by wave erosion, now located several tens of metres seaward from the high water mark. Overall from 1812 to 1990, the land at Tentsmuir Point advanced around 870 metres in a north-eastward direction and eroded approximately the same distance inland in the south.[61] In this area, the dominant direction of longshore sediment transport is from south to north towards the mouth of the Tay Estuary. The Tentsmuir coast is thus encapsulating the intimate relationship between destruction and con-struction as the southern part of the area *naturally* supplies sediment by erosion and the northern part *naturally* accretes by a combination of wave-generated longshore sediment transport and the activity of the wind. In this undeveloped terrain, natural processes continue unabated; there is a powerful message here for those who seek to 'manage' the coastal zone in developed areas elsewhere.

SEDUCTIVE POWER

Man has an inherent fascination with the sea, yet he fears it. It charms, it thrills, it inspires; it has immense seductive power. *Sleeping with the Enemy*, the title of the 1991 psychological thriller film directed by Joseph Ruben, is eminently applicable to coasts; the sea is simultaneously our close friend and our worst enemy. It is a sobering thought that, were it not for coastal erosion, there would be no beaches and, therefore, no opportunities for beach recreational pursuits.

Worldwide, people in their millions like to live by the sea; around 50 per cent of the population of the industrialised world is estimated to live within 1 kilometre of the coast, and tiny island Britain is no exception. People have clearly been doing so for thousands of years, at least since Neolithic times in Orkney. Aside from the practicalities of transport, trading, communication and seafood supplies, people are lured to the coast and seduced by the very sounds, the smells, the clean air, the views and the perceived quality of life. Breaking waves, salty spray and constantly changing vistas are but part of the romance, the exhilaration of owning a home at the coastal fringe, of living on the edge (sometimes in Britain far too near the edge). Railway mania in the mid to late nineteenth century saw routes constructed radiating from the industrial heartlands of Britain to numerous coastal resorts, leading to increasing numbers of both permanent residences and holiday properties. There were even branch lines from Hull to Hornsea and Withernsea, but these arteries fell victim to Dr Richard Beeching's axe in the 1960s. Doctors and medical consultants, at this time, played their part in promoting an exodus of both holidaymakers and local residents from the hinterland to our coastal towns as in their surgeries all over the country they prescribed little more than a dose of clean, bracing sea air for a whole host of physical and mental ailments. This is epitomised by the rhyme used on the Great Northern Railway's (GNR) early posters (1908) advertising day trips to Skegness from London King's Cross on non-stop corridor trains for the return fare of 3 shillings (£0.15):

> *For all the ills we have to bear*
> *There's nothing cures like East Coast air*
> *It's so bracing.*[62]

In 1851 the population of this Lincolnshire coastal settlement was 366.[63] Immediately prior to the arrival of the railway in 1873, Skegness was still a rather insignificant village of around 500 citizens. Within a few years of railway mania, it grew into a substantial town, a fashionable seaside destination for those wanting to escape the industrial heartlands of the country, and by 1907 the resort was attracting some 300,000 visitors per year by train.[64] Similarly, the Great Western Railway's posters enticed visitors to Weston-super-Mare in Somerset with its promise of 'air like wine'.

Southwold: attractions of no ordinary character

Before the coming of railways, railway mania and the lure of their colourful advertising posters, putative seaside 'resorts' had to use the printed word to attract visitors who would have been obliged to travel by far less speedy means of transport. Before travel guide books, replete with maps and pictures, texts on the history of a town were all that was available to attract those that could make the journey to their charms. A short distance north of Dunwich in Suffolk is the town of Southwold, itself no stranger to attack by the sea:

> Up rose old Ocean from his bed,
> And landward drove his billowy car;
> And headlands, spires, and villas fled
> Before the elemental war.[65]

In 1839, Robert Wake by means of breathless sentence structure, used the printed word to hypnotic effect, painting a picture to perhaps inland, grim city dwellers of not only a scenic but also an intellectual paradise by the sea that they might one day aspire to visit should their means permit:

> If a summer visit to any sea-coast town usually frequented with this single object in view, be not without its charms; and if recreation and health may not necessarily be required, at such seasons, to supersede entirely the more refined acqui- sition of intellectual improvement, in the case of sea-bathers and fine-weather excursionists, in whatever point of the island they may pursue their pleasant researches – we are sincere in our impression that Southwold will present them with attractions of no ordinary character. The distinctive features of the favourably-situated and handsomely-furnished town – its neat and commodious lodging-houses – its

comfortable, capacious, and well-served inns – its tastefully-built and respectably-tenanted dwelling houses – its sea-side and landscape scenery, graceful, complete, and picturesque – these and other features of our locality are not slightly enhanced by their contiguity to, and connection with, the deeply-furrowed face of long-lived antiquity presents its solemnizing recollections to the explorer of elder time, and to the student of remoter history.[66]

It is no surprise that, once the railway network evolved, so many people were mesmerised and flocked to our shores, some never to return, and that coastal populations multiplied. A sea view was the imperative along with the bracing air, the spray and the sound of crashing waves; little wonder that so many homes were built in extremely vulnerable, inappropriate locations, storing up problems for future generations. Intellectual paradises perhaps, but intelligence it would seem was largely overruled by the heart. The sea has immense power.

Island murder, mystery and eccentricity

There was something magical about an island – the mere word suggested fantasy.

Agatha Christie, *Ten Little Niggers*, 1939

Small islands hold a special allure and none more so than Burgh Island. Reached by sea tractor at high water, the tiny tidal island is a mere 250 metres off the south coast of Devon near Bigbury-on-Sea, and it was once, like St Michael's Mount and Lyonesse, a permanent part of mainland Britain. The eccentric access vehicle is driven along the causeway with its wheels underwater while its driver and passengers sit on a platform above the water (Plate 32). For decades, the island's 1920s Art Deco style hotel has been a draw for discerning tourists, the rooms being named after its famous guests such as Noël Coward, Winston Churchill, Edward and Mrs Simpson. It was also a favourite writing place of Agatha Christie who based her famously politically incorrectly entitled *Ten Little Niggers* in a fabulous mansion on 'Nigger Island, Sticklehaven, Devon'. With this enchanting magnet, the murderer lured the various fickle characters to their death by the romantic thrill of a trip to isolation by the sea. Subsequently, Christie was obliged to rename the work to *Ten Little Indians* and the island became known as 'Indian Island'. She used the site again as a place of writing and as setting for a second novel, this time transforming it into Smugglers' Island, Leathercombe Bay in *Evil under the Sun*. As sea levels rise, it is likely that the novel sea tractor's journeys to and from the mainland will become more frequent throughout the tidal cycle as Burgh Island looks towards complete isolation.

The awesome power of waves was captured in Victorian and Edwardian postcard scenes as a means of inspiring and seducing day trippers and holidaymakers alike. Clearly, such images of the sea in the guise of the enemy did nothing to deter the influx of visitors to fashionable resorts like Scarborough (Plate 33); people were seduced in their tens of thousands, drawn as if by a powerful magnet. Even the erratic British weather could not prevent the allure.

The wind blew with a fury from the sea; it was hard to walk against it. The people in hundreds waited in their dull apartments for a lull, and when it came they poured out like hungry sheep from the fold, or like children from a school, swarming over the green slope down to the beach, to scatter far and wide over the sands. Then, in a little while; a new menacing blackness would come up out of the sea, and by and by a fresh storm of wind would send the people scuttling back into shelter. So it went on day after day . . . [67]

The Victorians referred to the cure of 'taking ozone' at the seaside. Similarly, regular bathing in seawater at resorts like Scarborough, Blackpool, Bournemouth, Cromer, Margate, Skegness, and so many more, was purported to be a treatment and possibly a cure for many conditions. Even very recently, the *Daily Telegraph* broadsheet (Monday 11 August 2008)[68] carried a story that doctors *now* advise that just being beside the sea can boost your health in a range of natural ways. But well over four centuries ago, in 1581, Richard Mulcaster, the pedagogical writer and first Headmaster of Merchant Taylors' School in London, was teaching that:

> The swimming in salt water is very good to remoue the headache, to open the stuffed nosethrilles, and therby to helpe the smelling. It is a good remedie for dropsies, scabbes, and scurfes, small pockes, leprosies, falling awaye of either legge, or any other parte: for such as prosper not so, as they would, though they eate as they wishe, for ill stomackes, liuers, miltes, and corrupt constitution.[69]

Swimming, coupled with the sea air, clearly assured a healthy constitution.

A ship is sunk by a church

> You should have gone to Cromer, my dear, if you went anywhere. Perry was a week at Cromer once, and he holds it to be the best of all the sea-bathing places. A fine open sea, he says, and very pure air.
>
> Jane Austen, Emma, 1815, Vol. 1, Chapter 12

> *Wonder is excited in the bosom of a visitor to Cromer, when some old salt, stretching a rough and tanned forefinger to the northward, indicates in the far distance a solitary upstanding rock, lashed by the waves, and says,* 'Yonder is old Cromer Church, which used to be in the middle of the town. When there is a storm you can hear the bells chiming in the belfry.'
>
> Beckles Willson,
The Story of Lost England, 1902

At the time of the *Domesday Book*, completed at the behest of William the Conqueror in 1086, there is no record of the north Norfolk coastal 'gem' of Cromer. The only mention is of its seaward predecessor, Shipden, a town that has, like so many in this part of eastern England, been lost to the sea by erosion.[70] It survived as a trading and fishing port until the late fourteenth century to be replaced by the fishing settlement of Cromer constructed further inland. In the nineteenth century, especially with the coming of the railway, Cromer became a fashionable tourist resort where doctors like Perry in Jane Austen's *Emma*, even before the railway had arrived, were advising their often hypochondriac patients to go to take the waters and inhale the bracing sea air. On 9 August 1888, a curious accident took place offshore from the town, indeed, one that could have been a great human disaster, but fortunately this outcome was averted.[71] The pleasure steamer *Victoria* had, early that day, left Great Yarmouth to the south-east, laden with passengers on a day trip to Cromer. The passengers were landed safely at Cromer by transhipping them into a smaller vessel, since Cromer had no pier at the time. On the return voyage, the vessel struck something hard and began to take in water. Fortunately, local fishermen had observed the collision and acted quickly to evacuate the passengers who made their return journey to Great Yarmouth from Cromer by train. The *Victoria*, it transpired, had struck what fishermen knew as the 'Church Rock', the submerged ruins of St Peter's church of the lost town of Shipden. Local custom has it that this was subsequently blown up to avoid the occurrence of a similar incident.[72] Whilst shipwrecks are sadly part and parcel of life around an island nation, this is, if not a unique, certainly a highly unusual cause.

It comes as no surprise that in the twenty-first century it is still far from uncommon for people to own second homes by the sea or to retire to our coastal resorts, towns and villages. This dream of owning a cottage by the sea is illustrated cleverly, to great amusement, in Dick Millington's *Daily Mail* cartoon strip (Figure 3.4), but behind the fun there lies a serious message; coasts can be dangerous places to live and many who choose to live there either do not appreciate or are in ostrich-like denial about the vulnerability of their homes and properties. It is said that, 'Cliff Drive is still the most aspirational address for anyone with a decent pension' in Britain.[73] If so, 'Salubrious Terrace' in the Cornish resort of St Ives must surely have comparable allure?

There is even a British glossy monthly magazine entitled simply *Coast* and published by The National Magazine Company Ltd, that is devoted specifically to all aspects of 'living by the sea'. With sections focusing on features of coast living, coast property, coast travel and even coast people, the brand aspires: 'To feed the dreams of people who want to live by the sea or who have a particular fondness for the many and varying aspects of the British coastline, *both natural and man-made*' (italics added for emphasis). Moreover, 'It offers its readers escapism – the chance to dream about living by the sea by showing them the homes of those who already do so. It caters for those with nostalgia for the seaside. It appeals to the British love of the sea and gives readers a renewed appreciation of what it means to be an island nation'. A sister publication devoted to the *Interior* or the *Hinterland* seems inconceivable.

The intensity of our love affair with the coast is, however, equalled or even exceeded by the deep passion of the centuries-held perception that the sea is 'the enemy' that 'steals' land and, as a result, has to be controlled at all costs. Indeed, it is completely understandable for land and property owners to react in defensive mode and seek to protect their assets if they become subject to wave attack that leads to erosion. However, such actions, typically involving the building of hard engineering structures such as various designs of sea walls, can more often than not lead to major problems, as will be explored in Chapter 4.

Figure 3.4 Cartoon strip originally published in the *Daily Mail* (Dick Millington).

St Ouen's Bay, Jersey:
the essence of destruction, construction and seduction

> On the coast of Jersey, while wandering among the rocks on
> its northern coast, a curious example of the power of the
> waves was encountered. It was a basin of considerable size
> scooped out of the rock, at the sea level, and filled with large
> water-worn and rounded blocks of stone. These blocks did
> not seem to have fallen from the rocks above, but appeared to
> have been lifted up and deposited in the cavity by the force
> of the waves which incessantly strike upon this rugged and
> precipitous coast.
>
> 'A Naturalist', *Rambles among the Channel Islands*, 1855

Accounts of the British coast often forget about the Channel
Islands, perhaps because they lie closer to France than Britain. Jersey,
for instance, has long been victim of powerful wave erosion and
rising sea levels. St Ouen's Bay that forms most of the west coast of
the island is exposed to Atlantic waves providing some of the best
surfing conditions in Europe. The 'old and pious'[74] Jersey historian,
the Reverend Mr Falle, noted in his eighteenth century writings:
'those high westerly winds that blow here, at almost all seasons of
the year, and that, on this side of the island, are daily seen to drive
the sands to the tops of the highest cliffs'.[75] The extensive dunes
with a rich diversity of habitats, dunes that have been constructed
inland by onshore winds, are one of the most important systems in
northern Europe and incorporate the Les Mielles conservation
area.[76] But destructive forces characterise this area also, as Falle
continued: 'In the parish of St. Ouen, the sea has, within these 250
years, swallowed up a very rich vale, where, to this hour, at low
water, the marks of buildings appear among the rocks, and great
stumps of oaks are seen in the sand after a storm.'[77] Erosion problems
at this site, now a honey pot for the island's coastal tourist industry,
continue to this day but now, as is so often the case, exacerbated by
human intervention.[78] Construction of a sea wall, which began in
the nineteenth century, was an initiator of problems. In the period

1940–45, however, the Second World War necessitated that previously isolated sections of sea wall be incorporated into a continuous structure (Plate 34) during the German occupation of Jersey to provide an anti-tank defence. The exigencies of war were such that sand was sourced locally, indeed adjacently, being mined from the beach and nearby dunes for the concrete mix.[79] These activities have, not surprisingly, contributed to reduced sediment supply to St Ouen's Bay and to beach lowering, thus promoting enhanced erosion; a story which is sadly all too familiar that will be explored further in the following chapter.

4

WAS KING CANUTE RIGHT?
CAN WE HOLD BACK THE SEA?

Sex began 380 million years ago, a fossil of a pregnant fish suggests

Philip Larkin was nearly 380 million years out when he wrote that sexual intercourse began in 1963, it appears, after scientists found an ancient fossil of a pregnant fish.

The Daily Telegraph, 13 April 2011

INTRODUCTION

Despite the abundant evidence presented to the contrary in the previous chapters, there is a popular misconception that coastal erosion is something of a new phenomenon fuelled by climate change. However, long before climate change and global warming hit the headlines, newspapers were reporting on the damage caused by the power of the sea. For instance, over a century ago, on 10 January 1900, the *Dundee Courier and Argus* carried the story that:

> The need to protect Carnoustie golf course around the second hole from the ravages of easterly gales has been intimated by Dalhousie Golf Club. During the past year a large slice of country was washed away while deviation of the Barry Burn has removed a trap for drifting sand.

Such reports of wave erosion have been commonplace in Britain ever since the golden age of newspaper publication in the nineteenth century. Moreover, in this example the pun concerning the amount of land lost to erosion at this famous championship venue will not escape golfers. In general, at the turn of the twentieth century, such was the concern about the wearing away of Britain's fringes that the government of the day established a Royal Commission to assess the magnitude of the 'problem'. This body made its evaluation in 1911 with the publication of the catchily titled, 'Report of the Royal Commission Appointed to Inquire into and to Report on Certain Questions Affecting Coastal Erosion, the Reclamation of Tidal Lands, and Afforestation in the United Kingdom'.[1]

Coasts are complex. They are naturally dynamic, often highly dynamic, sometimes dangerous, ever changing, ever evolving, and erosion is part and parcel of that dynamism. Just as sexual intercourse was not invented in 1963, as Philip Larkin so famously miscalculated in his poem 'Annus Mirabilis' (1967), coastal erosion has been going on throughout the millennia of geological time, for as long as land and sea have been in intimate contact. Erosion is, first and foremost, a natural earth surface process; it can, in many cases, also be a problem, often a severe problem, but not necessarily so. More often than not if it does become a problem, it is of our own making or exacerbated greatly by our actions. Similarly, the accretion of sediment in coastal zones is also a natural process. It too can be a problem, as, for instance, for the inhabitants of Kenfig (see Chapter 3), but today it is generally of far lesser concern around the British coastline than is erosion.

How do coasts 'work' – can we hold back the sea? Despite Canute's widely misperceived failure to stem the tide (Chapter 1), even reiterated recently in the Editorial of the *Independent* newspaper,[2] humankind has waged an endless and relentless battle against the encroachment of the sea upon its land. Coastal zones may best be thought of as a 'complex mosaic' of interactions among natural processes, like waves and tides, and human activities. They are like a giant, three-dimensional, mobile, jigsaw puzzle and an appreciation of this is paramount to the understanding of how coasts work. The inter-linkages between the differing coastal components, pieces in the jigsaw, have been likened by eminent coastal specialist Professor Peter Burbridge[3] to a Roman arch bridge. The individual wedge-shaped blocks of stone that make up such semi-circular arches, which can span wide spaces whilst supporting great weight above, owe their stability to the forces of compression between them and to their resistance to shear, holding them in position over the centuries. Remove just one block, one piece from the jigsaw, and the arch will fail, often suddenly and catastrophically. Similarly, if one component of a coastal zone is damaged or disturbed or changed from its natural state by human intervention, the whole of that zone will be weakened and this may lead potentially to 'collapse' of the system. Extending Burbridge's analogy, a whole series of arches may be thought of as representing discrete sections of a coastline (Plate 35) or, to use the modern term, coastal cells. Each is independent of the other. If a stone from one arch is displaced, the others will remain intact, in just the same way that cells are sections of coastline in which the sand and gravel sediment transport processes are more or less independent of one another.

According to eminent coastal engineer Cyril Galvin,[4] on a worldwide scale, 'all examples of shore erosion on non-subsiding sandy coasts are traceable to man-made or natural interruptions of longshore sediment transport'. This bold assertion underlines the imperative for those who are responsible for the management of our coasts, especially their defence, to have a more than robust understanding of this process, not only within their jurisdiction but beyond. Unfortunately, this was seldom the case in the historical past, but, even now, in the twenty-first century, mistakes are continually being made in Britain and elsewhere in the form of inappropriate interventions at the coast, that simply shift a problem 'downdrift' in the direction of longshore sediment transport from one site to another. A subsequent attempt, for example, extending a sea wall, to address a problem induced by a previous intervention, i.e. the original wall, shifts the problem downdrift yet again and so it goes on and on, like a chain reaction, as the wall continues to be lengthened. So, what is longshore sediment transport, more commonly abbreviated to longshore drift? Before answering this question, it is important to appreciate that some coasts are natural suppliers of sediment; that is they erode easily and they act as sediment sources for beaches and other nearshore coastal environments. Put bluntly – were it not for natural erosion, there would be no beautiful sandy beaches. The sediment supplied can, of course, range in size from boulders through cobbles, gravels and sand down to fine silt and clay, depending on the local geology of the 'supplier'. The Holderness coast of East Yorkshire is a prime example of a supplier of largely fine particles.

When waves move into shallow water close to the shore, they become distorted and break, spilling water forward in what is called the surf zone. If they approach the shore at an angle the breaking so called swash will surge up the beach, moving sediment with it at the same angle towards the back of the beach. The return flow down the beach, or backwash, acting under gravity, then draws sediment back down the face of the beach perpendicular to the shore following the steepest gradient. Thus sediment

Bramblewick and the sound of erosion

Bramblewick is a 'real spot'. This is Leo Walmsley's reincarnation of Robin Hood's Bay (see Preface) on the coast of North Yorkshire. The name first appeared in one of his novels, but it stuck and he used it subsequently in works of non-fiction. Walmsley's description of the sound of waves breaking onto the soft, vulnerable rocks (Plate 36), ripping into nature's suppliers of sediment particles and the removal of the crumbling and crushed debris out to sea is not only haunting; it cannot be bettered:

> From the Cove we were obliged to climb to the top of the clay cliff, and follow a rough path along its edge towards the village. Dusk was falling. Westwards the land was obscure. The gale-torn surf, however, gave a peculiar light, and the sweeping cliffs of the bay were sharply defined against a continuous ribbon of churned-up water by collision of the incoming breakers with the backwash of the broken waves that preceded them. A deep, steady thunder filled the air. Yet above this we heard the direct impact of seas launching themselves against the foot of the crumbling cliff below us, the thud of tumbling earth and clay, the awful rasping of the backwash, carrying away its spoil, crunching it with the shingle like an animal crunching bones.[5]

particles move along the face of the beach in a zigzag fashion. This so-called longshore drift will vary in direction according to the direction the wind is blowing from and, therefore, the angle of breaking-wave approach. However, for all coasts, one direction of longshore sediment transport will be dominant and an understanding of which direction is very important. Should an obstruction be placed in the path of the dominant direction of longshore drift, the transported sediment will be prevented from moving as nature intended and will become deposited against the barrier. 'Downdrift' beaches will thus become starved of their natural sediment supply. Where estuaries, such as the Humber, meet the sea, deposition from longshore transport typically occurs in the form of projections of sand and gravel known as spits; Spurn Head is a spectacular example, and it demonstrates that the dominant long-term direction of longshore sediment transport is from north to south along the Holderness coast.

Human intervention at the coast in Britain, including the construction of sea walls, harbours, jetties and other structures, rose gradually through the centuries until the Industrial Revolution. It has been noted that from around the beginning of the nineteenth century, coastal modifications began to move from, 'incidental or accidental actions to direct modification in response to changes in population pressures, perception of resources, income, leisure time and technological advances'.[6] So many people had migrated to the coast and so much industry had been developed there that there was a need to protect the asset. The period from around 1800 until as recently as the 1980s can thus most appropriately be thought of as one of 'man against nature' and during that time hard engineering, in the form of sea walls, rock armour revetments and groynes, was seen by engineers as the predominant panacea to coastal erosion and the protection of our land. Even a surgeon offered solutions to coastal erosion in 1844 in, 'An Essay on the Encroachments of the German Ocean along the Norfolk Coast, with a Design to Arrest its Further Depredations; Dedicated to the Right Honourable the Lords Commissioners of the Admiralty'.[7]

Lawyer, James Ferguson, writing over a century ago, specifically with respect to Scotland and Scots law, stated, 'A landowner is entitled to erect works for his own protection against the inroads of the sea, and he is not debarred from this, or rendered liable for protected works for his neighbours, or in compensation to them, by the fact that his defences cause the sea to flow with greater violence against adjoining land. The sea is a *common enemy*, against which each proprietor must protect himself' (italics added for emphasis).[8] These unequivocal assertions epitomise the protectionist, 'beggar thy neighbour' approach of that time.

DEFENDING THE INDEFENSIBLE

Essentially, we can build two varieties of coastal defence structures: those that trend along the shoreline that are known as shore parallel and those that project out from the shore into the sea that are usually shore perpendicular. The former comprise a wide range of sea walls and rock armour whilst the latter are walls that project seawards from the shore and are known as groynes. Sea walls are designed to reflect wave energy, just like light is reflected by a mirror, and must be designed to withstand immense shock pressures, as at Wick in Caithness. They were traditionally built of wood or masonry, but through time concrete forms with buttresses or piles to provide extra stability have become predominant. The earliest such structures were constructed vertically but, as long ago as the late 1800s, it was appreciated that when waves collide with a relatively smooth, solid vertical wall the reflected backwash removes sediment from the base of the wall. This scour at the toe of the structure causes a lowering of the beach level known as beach draw-down. By this means, a beach may reduce substantially in width or in the extreme disappear completely. To reduce this impact, which can ultimately undermine the foundations and, therefore, the integrity of a wall, inclined, curved and stepped forms have been developed. Such sloping or concave sea-wall profiles reflect incoming waves far more efficiently, especially during storm events, helping to lessen scour at the base and also to prevent wave overtopping onto adjacent roads and promenades.

Even a century ago the Royal Commission asserted that sea walls, unless properly constructed are, 'agents of their own destruction',[9] a reference in particular to the potential for undercutting at the base of such structures. The report also expressed concern that the age-old practice of the removal of sand and gravel from beaches, that fed the building construction industry until as recently as the 1960s, was increasing the rate of coastal erosion in many places. For ease and sheer convenience, to minimise transport costs, it was not unusual in Britain for sea walls to be built using concrete mixed on site using sand and gravel aggregate extracted from the very beaches adjacent to them. In this way, such a beach had already been lowered in level, even before the wall behind it had begun to induce any scour or undercutting at its toe. Even stone blocks were, in some cases, sourced locally. Sandgate Castle, on the shore near Folkestone in Kent, was built in the 1530s by Henry VIII. Today much of this fortification has been destroyed by waves. Had it been constructed from stone quarried from an inland site, it might have survived intact. However, the materials were obtained from adjacent intertidal reefs, thereby increasing its likelihood of storm wave attack. Its partial destruction must have been exacerbated by this ill-advised activity.[10]

Erosion is not just a horizontal thing:
the importance of fixed-point photography

Fixed structures like sea walls that are designed to prevent what might be called horizontal erosion often afford the opportunity to demonstrate the extent of beach lowering that can take place in front of them – that is, vertical erosion. Two photographs of a sea wall, constructed in 1954, at Montrose on the Angus coast were taken from approximately the same location, the first in 1986, the second twenty-four years later in 2010 (Plates 37 and 38). In the intervening period, the beach has drawn down by as much as 2.5 metres as measured against the sheet steel pile section at the base of the wall. This has necessitated the placement of rock armour boulders against the piled foundation of the wall to prevent its being undermined and, as a result, the change in character of the area is dramatic. The access steps at this spot, in use in 1986, have subsequently had to be decommissioned. The photographic record shows that the level of the beach in 1986 was only a few centimetres lower than at the time the wall was built over thirty years previously. So, in this case, the wall could not in itself have been responsible for the dramatic beach draw-down that was to take place thereafter. Conditions must have changed subsequently; either an increase in storminess leading to more vigorous vertical erosion at the toe of the wall or a starvation of the natural longshore sediment supply to the area – or perhaps both.

Though they might not be pleasing aesthetically, people actually like sea walls. This is because such solid structures make them feel safe and secure; out of harm, the raging sea will be kept at bay, houses will be safe and land will not be eroded away. However, the tell tale signs of patchwork repair of old sea walls confirms that they are not invulnerable to attack and cannot last for ever (Plate 39). Furthermore, a wall or a section of rock armour is of finite length. Typically, it will have been installed to protect an individual's property or that of a local authority that might be subject to erosion. Such intervention has therefore been historically on a piecemeal or ad-hoc basis, with no consideration whatsoever of the potential impact of the structure on natural processes operating within the coastal zone or on the unprotected coast beyond either end of the structure. Coastal processes, in particular longshore sediment transport systems, do not, however, map conveniently onto land ownership boundaries or onto local authority administrative, county or even national boundaries. Nevertheless, such boundaries have for decades constrained the limits of strategic thinking in terms of coastal management and in many cases still continue to do so.

Canvey Island: a tale of two pubs

At length we descried a light and a roof, and presently afterwards ran alongside a little causeway made of stones that had been picked up hard by. Leaving the rest in the boat, I stepped ashore, and found the light to be in a window of a public-house. It was a dirty place enough, and I dare say not unknown to smuggling adventurers; but there was a good fire in the kitchen, and there were eggs and bacon to eat, and various liquors to drink. Also, there were two double-bedded rooms – 'such as they were,' the landlord said. No other company was in the house than the landlord, his wife, and a grizzled male creature, the 'Jack' of the little causeway, who was as slimy and smeary as if he had been low-water mark too.

Charles Dickens, *Great Expectations*, 1860

The sense of security and safety afforded by sea walls can surely be felt no better nor illustrated more dramatically than on Canvey Island in Essex. Devastated in the 1953 storm surge (see Chapter 1), the population of this claimed land at the time was less than a third of that today. Six decades on, it has become developed into an urbanised and industrialised island, home to large numbers of oil storage tanks, flare towers, jetties and other associated infrastructure. An encircling girdle of over 20 kilometres of considerably heightened concrete sea walls now protects around 40,000 inhabitants from the risk of flooding. Their homes, many with upper floor sitting rooms, are located on ground that is wholly below the level of normal high tides. The lowest part of the island is in the centre; it is thus like a bowl and all surface water drainage from rainfall has to be evacuated over the seawall into the Thames by pumping. From street level, it is easy to forget that this is an island; the enclosing sea is invisible, out of sight and largely out of mind, obscured by the high perimeter defences. However, a reminder of the island's long and bloody conflict with its enemy, a tempestuous relationship with the Thames Estuary, is the name of a public house on busy Canvey Road (Plate 40). Another inn, the Lobster Smack, dating back to the seventeenth century and reputed to have been the loneliest on the Thames marshes, the 'dirty' pub where Pip and fugitive Magwitch spent the night, nestles defiantly in the shadow of the island's front line of defence, the apex of its roof reaching only just above the top of the wall (Plate 41).

Structures that are built parallel with the shore, whether designed to reflect or to absorb the energy of incoming waves, have one thing in common; they cause wave energy to be transferred laterally along the shore. This leads to erosion being both focused and accelerated beyond the ends of a seawall or extent of rock armour, a process that is known as flanking erosion, which typically leads to the formation of a receding embayment, so-called an 'erosional bight' (Plate 42). Think of the largest bight of all, the Great Australian Bight that eats into the southern coast of that island continent.

In this way, the location of the erosion that a structure was built to defend becomes transferred along the coast; the sea is thus compensating for the decrease in sediment input from the length of coast that has been defended. In addition, the length of naturally eroding coast that a wall or rock armour is defending from the force of the waves is no longer able to contribute sediment particles to the coastal transport system – its natural contribution as a sediment source has effectively been cut off by the structure. This leads to both a reduction in sediment supply to any adjacent beach and, importantly, to the longshore sediment transport regime that characterises the particular coast. A consequence of the latter is the acceleration of erosion downdrift of the wall. Hence a sea wall or a length of rock armour is potentially both inducing adjacent flanking erosion and contributing to enhanced downdrift erosion some distance away from it. These effects may impact on land owned by the same proprietor as that of the defended land or on that of one, or indeed several, other landowners.

In the nineteenth century the civil engineer was not only a man but was also king

Man against the sea. In fact, in nineteenth-century Britain, there would appear to have been no bounds whatsoever to man's abilities to tame nature and harness the resources of the planet. This is captured quintessentially by the powerful words of Sir John Rennie. In his inaugural address to the Institution of Civil Engineers in 1845, the third President of that august professional body concluded:

> When we look around us and see the vast strides which our profession is making on every side, and the deservedly high place it holds in public estimation, we cannot but feel justly proud; for without the slightest disparagement of the pursuits or studies of other professions, I may confidently ask, where can we find nobler or more elevated pursuits than our own; whether it be to interpose a barrier against the raging ocean, and provide an asylum for our fleets; or to form a railway, and by means of that wonderful machine – the locomotive engine – to bring nations together, annihilating, as it were, both space and time; or to construct the mighty steam vessel, which alike regardless of winds or waves, urges onwards its resistless course; or to curb and bring within proper bounds the impetuous torrent, converting its otherwise destructive waters to our use and benefit, whether for navigation, trade, or domestic comfort; or the drainage of the unwholesome marsh, and converting it into fields of waving corn; or illuminating our cities with gas, changing, as it were, night into day; or the fabrication of machinery of endless form and ingenuity, by means of which every article, which can tend to man's comfort and luxury, can be produced in the greatest

perfection, at the smallest cost; or to recover from the bowels of the earth nature's exhaustless treasures, and forming and preparing them to our use. In fact we may almost say, that there is nothing in the whole range of the material world, which does not come under our observations, or where the skill, and science of the engineer is not required, in a greater or less degree, to render the bounties of Providence subservient to the good of mankind.[11]

This lengthy but evocative quotation resonates the prevailing spirit of that time for not only the construction of hard engineered sea defences around our shores to protect the realm but also the 'reclamation' of land from the sea – by its self-styled rightful owner, of course.

Rock armour revetments, also known as riprap, are constructed of large blocks of durable rock that are arranged in elongated sloping mounds along the shoreline (Plate 43). The blocks are angular ideally so that they fit together like an imperfect three-dimensional jigsaw puzzle in a stable structure that presents a rough, sloping and permeable surface to incoming waves. Such structures therefore absorb or dissipate wave energy rather than reflect it and they offer a lower cost option than solid concrete sea walls. Rock armour is often emplaced as an apron along the toe of an existing sea wall in an attempt to prevent ongoing scour (Plate 44). The use of natural materials predominates, but reinforced concrete blocks of various forms, such as enormous pre-cast cubes and interlocking, four-legged, so-called tetrapods, are also employed as 'rock' armour. Old oil drums filled with sand, building rubble, lumps of asphalt, concrete and brickwork, indeed all manner of waste objects are also dumped illegally at the coast to serve as 'rock' armour. This often, but not always (Plate 45) takes place at remote sites and is without any consideration for aesthetics, nature conservation or natural processes. In addition, this practice can pose a health hazard. In terms of beach draw-down, wave absorbing armour structures are, in general, preferable to wave reflecting walls since their capacity to induce scour is far less. However, the associated problems of flanking erosion and enhanced erosion due to downdrift sediment starvation are still just as prevalent.

Erosion is prevented, but a harbour has to be abandoned: coastal legacies of Old King Coal

For nearly 800 years coal mining thrived in Fife in eastern Scotland. The decline of this industry in south Fife provides an interesting perspective on the long-term dumping of colliery waste along the shore. Along the north-east to south-west trending stretch of coast between Buckhaven and Dysart, the custom, long before environmental awareness had taken hold, had been to tip large amounts of colliery waste directly onto the beaches and rocky foreshore, locally building headlands of loose fragments of coal, shale and sandstone that were then reworked along the coastline by prevailing longshore currents. Such was the extent of dumping that, along this stretch, the coastline moved seaward by 100 to 170 metres. Colliery waste migrated north-eastwards and gradually infilled the harbour at Buckhaven; thus, by 1946, the once proud fishing harbour had to be abandoned, silted up by human action. This age-old practice of dumping continued until the closure of the last of the three deep mines in the area; the Wellesley in 1967, the Michael in 1968 and the Frances in 1984 (Plate 46). As a result, this progressive reduction of mine waste discharge to the coast led to a greatly improved beach amenity in terms of aesthetics and ecology. No longer was the beach black. The dumping of waste had, however, been having another and more positive effect, neither realised nor appreciated until the practice ceased. A very important consequence was the reduction in material available for transport by the longshore current system of the area, a source that had been depleted when the dumping stopped. This, in turn, led to greatly increased erosion of the underlying natural beach and rock materials, which was exacerbated by coastal subsidence due to the long history of coal mining in the area. The response to the enhanced erosion was, ironically, the installation of substantial sections of rock armour to provide coastal protection.[12] An environmentally unfriendly practice in the extreme had been imperceptibly protecting this coast from erosion for centuries.

Over the decades, the understandable, knee-jerk reaction to flanking erosion and other enhanced erosion downdrift has been quite simply to extend along the coast the very defence that is the root cause. So begins a chain reaction of the progressive extension of defence structures such that the flanking erosion is shifted laterally along the coast potentially threatening coastal settlements. As the structure becomes extended, the supply of sediment to the beach and longshore transport system becomes correspondingly further depleted so that downdrift erosion continues to accelerate and, furthermore, to affect areas progressively further downdrift of the wall. As a consequence of this progressive extension of defences, over 50 per cent of the coastline of south-east England is today protected by some type of artificial structure. In North Wales, a staggering 45 kilometres of Conwy Borough Council's 73 kilometres of coastline is artificially defended.[13] Had natural processes of erosion in this area been allowed to continue unabated, one can but speculate that the lost land of Tyno Helig would have been of far greater extent and the drowned palace of Llys Helig even further from the coastline (see Chapter 1).

Sea walls and rock armour also cause other, often less obvious impacts. The reduction in sediment supply to an adjacent beach has already been mentioned. However, where a soft coast that is characterised naturally by sand dunes is defended, such structures reduce or cut off entirely the two-way onshore–offshore sediment interchange between dunes and beaches

When will it end? Elie: the epitome of transferring erosion along the coast

The Fife coast provides yet another classic example of a coastal issue, this time encapsulating the chain reaction that can be set in by building sea defences. At the small resort of Elie, a length of inclined concrete sea wall was built originally to defend a number of properties and a minor road from wave attack. The remedy to the erosional bight that this induced was to extend the defence with a section of vertical wall constructed of sheet steel piling. Following further flanking erosion, stage three of this defence saga was to install a length of rock armour revetment, beyond the end of which the inevitable is now taking place (Plate 47).

causing once active, mobile landforms to become stabilised and sterile or even destroyed completely. Thus, not only the landforms but also their associated habitats become modified, damaged or destroyed. This loss of habitat is not restricted to sand dune systems; eroding rocky cliffs are host to numerous plant and animal species whose environments for life are lost when stabilising structures are built over them. The work of the sea on naturally eroding rocky coasts progressively reveals new exposures, especially after severe winter storms. These are vital to the geologist who uses the structures within rocks like the pages from nature's diary, as clues to understand Earth history and evolution. Once protected by a hard defence, such geological evidence is obscured and there is a consequent reduction in so-called geodiversity.[14] Eroding cliffs in sedimentary rocks can yield fossils such as those of reptiles and amphibians, the study of which is the key to understanding the evolution of animal and plant life through geological time. Again, when such sites are built over, their geological value by virtue of their exposure and natural erosion potential, yielding specimens continually, is obliterated.

Strong points are uncommon coastal protection measures in Britain. They are relatively small mounds of rock armour that are positioned at strategic points along an eroding shore in much the same way as those strongly fortified and heavily armed points in a military defence system. They are usually placed in groups with the aim that erosion will continue in the unprotected stretch between each adjacent pair but at a controlled rate, leading eventually, at least in theory, to a stable embayed coastline with the mounds of rock acting as artificial promontories. In practice, however, such bays seldom evolve into a truly stable configuration. A series of strong points was installed in the late 1980s to protect strategic parts, tees and greens, of the threatened golf links, which sit on top of an eroding dune system at Montrose on the Angus coast of eastern Scotland (Plate 48). These have worked with some degree of success, slowing down the inevitable, the need to realign the course. However, the boulder mounds are continually subject to becoming isolated from the steep dune cliffs they abut by flanking erosion as the sands become scoured away from behind them by wave activity, thereby necessitating their relocation landward. Strong points are far less extensive than rock armour revetments, so correspondingly cut off less supply of sediment from eroding coasts to the longshore transport system. Nevertheless, their impact in this regard is not negligible.

A lower cost option to sea walls and rock armour is the installation of what are known as gabions (derived from the Italian word gabbione, meaning 'big cage'), which have been in use since the late nineteenth century. These consist of wire mesh cages; usually in the form of rectangular boxes that contain typically cobble sized fragments of rock. Rounded cobbles are preferable to angular ones since they are less likely to cut the wire mesh should the baskets be rocked by storm waves. Clearly, gabions offer less resistance to waves than walls and as such they are unsuited to use on exposed coasts that experience extreme wave activity. They often become damaged after storms; the wires can become severed if the cobbles within are not tightly packed and jostle around, thus they usually require very frequent maintenance. Gabions may be stacked in large numbers vertically or in stepped and inclined forms mimicking sea-wall types, a flexibility that rock armour does not have. However, they create the same set of problems, flanking erosion and downdrift sediment starvation, as their more solid counterparts. Gabions often trap masses of dead seaweed which become entangled with the wire meshes. Whilst this affords extra protection against wave attack, the seaweed mats acting as energy absorbers, the effect can be displeasing aesthetically at low tide. Entanglement with the wires results in the seaweed being difficult to remove and, furthermore, the rotting of dead seaweed in hot weather leads to unpleasant smells and attracts flies. As a result, gabions are not liked by many beach users.

Groynes are visually intrusive, solid barriers usually built at right angles to a shoreline that are intended to prevent sediment, such as sand and

Once more to Fife

It seems patently obvious that the size of the rock fragments within gabion baskets must be larger than the mesh aperture of the wire framework. However, this simple tenet was overlooked by those who installed them along the southern shore of the outer part of the Eden Estuary of Fife to protect the famous St Andrews links in the 1970s. Needless to say, the defences soon had to be replaced and the exotic cobbles strewn in an area of naturally sandy beach (Plate 49) are a lasting legacy of needless human error.

Plate 31 (above) Compared with Plate 30, the picture is very different at the southern end of the Tentsmuir National Nature Reserve where the line of concrete blocks reveals the extent of erosion by the sea (photo R.W. Duck).

Plate 32 (left) Photograph of the Burgh Island tractor ferry from *Everyday Science and Mechanics* (August 1935). This US magazine alluded to the English eccentricity of the mode of crossing: 'Not a boat, but a caterpillar-tractor car, is this public utility, located at an English seaside resort.'

Plate 33 Record wave at Scarborough's North Bay (from postcard dated 1909).

Plate 34 The lengthy sea wall of St Ouen's Bay, Jersey (photo courtesy of L. Booth).

Plate 35 A series of Roman Arches – a useful analogy for the coastal system; remove just one wedge-shaped stone block and an entire arch can fail, but each arch acts independently from the others (photo R.W. Duck).

Plate 36 The soft Jurassic sedimentary rock cliffs on the north side of Robin Hood's Bay, Leo Walmsley's Bramblewick, seen at low tide when no wave attack is taking place. The broad rocky platform reveals just how much land has been lost by erosion over time (photo R.W. Duck).

Plate 37 Sea wall at The Faulds, Montrose, Angus, in 1986 (photo R.W. Duck).

Plate 38 Sea wall at The Faulds, Montrose, Angus, in 2010 – compare with Plate 37 (photo R.W. Duck).

Plate 39 Nineteenth-century masonry sea wall at Elie in Fife, Scotland, showing signs of repeated repairs and strengthening (photo R.W. Duck).

Plate 40 'The King Canute' on Canvey Island's Canvey Road – a reminder of the vulnerable island's long battle with the sea (photo R.W. Duck).

Plate 41 'The Lobster Smack' at Hole Haven Point on the southern edge of Canvey Island adjacent to the sea wall that has been heightened many times in its history (photo R.W. Duck).

Plate 42 Flanking erosion producing an erosional bight at Monifieth, Angus, on the north shore of the outer reaches of the Tay Estuary, Scotland, caused by an expanse of rock armour that ends in the middle distance at the boundary between different landowners. Wave attack has strewn rubble and debris used in former land claim onto the beach. The concrete blocks becoming exposed in the foreground were placed in the former dunes in 1941 to prevent an enemy landing during the Second World War. The site has now been landscaped, a coastal pathway reinstated and the rock armour extended (photo R.W. Duck).

Plate 43 Part of the largest extent of rock armour revetment in Scotland, protecting the eastern side of the promontory of Buddon Ness, looking towards the town of Carnoustie, Angus. Interchange of sand between the dunes and the beach is now inhibited by this form of hard engineering, and the dunes in the middle distance are beginning to degrade (photo R.W. Duck).

Plate 44 Part of the lengthy extent of rock armour installed in 2008 to prevent scour at the base of the pre-existing Victorian sea wall, which protects the unstable cliffs of soft Jurassic rocks along Scarborough's 100-year-old Marine Drive. The grassed-over hummocky topography forming the lower slopes of the cliff is the result of former landslides. It is roughly at this spot that the record wave shown in Plate 33 was breaking (photo R.W. Duck).

Plate 45 Inexpensive, but both aesthetically displeasing and hazardous, the practice of dumping is one of the worst forms of coastal protection measures and is sadly all too common in Britain even in the twenty-first century (photo R.W. Duck).

Plate 46 The pit head winding gear of the former Frances Colliery at Dysart on the Fife coast stands proud on the cliff top as a protected monument as the now spoil-free coast below is today protected against erosion by rock armour (photo R.W. Duck).

Plate 47 Three generations of coastal protection at Elie in Fife, Scotland. The concrete section in the foreground was built first, followed by the central, sheet steel piled section and finally the rock armour revetment in the distance was installed (photo R.W. Duck).

Plate 48 Strong points adjacent to the golf links at Montrose, Angus. These have protected strategic parts of the course with some success, slowing down the need to realign it. They are continually becoming isolated from the dune cliffs by flanking erosion thereby necessitating their periodic relocation landward (photo R.W. Duck).

Plate 49 An inclined mattress of gabions installed to protect a section of dunes along the southern shore of the Eden Estuary in Fife, as seen in 1995. Cobbles of black basalt, washed out from a previous set of failed baskets, despoil the naturally sandy beach (photo R.W. Duck).

Plate 50 Although it was not built with the intention of impeding longshore sediment transport, the old harbour wall at Auchmithie, dating back to the 1890s, on the Angus coast of eastern Scotland is acting like a large groyne. It has trapped gravel on the updrift side (to the right of picture), thereby starving the natural sediment supply downdrift. As a result, an erosional bight has been formed on the opposite side of the wall and this has now scoured around the landward end of the structure (photo R.W. Duck).

Plate 51 Flanking erosion immediately to the south of the southern rock groyne and shore-parallel rock armour defences at Mappleton in Holderness. Vehicle tracks draw a line through the middle of the beach beneath where the land has been eroded away (photo R.W. Duck).

Plate 52 What is thought to be the world's first tarmac beach at Porthcawl, on the Glamorganshire coast of South Wales, located in front of a concrete sea wall constructed with a curving cross section to help to reflect wave energy (photo R.W. Duck).

Plate 53 Stone-faced embankment on the southern side of the Forth Estuary in eastern Scotland built in the nineteenth century to claim intertidal land for agriculture. Salt marsh plants have subsequently colonised the area on the seaward side of the wall (right), the new marsh being displaced from its natural location. Heavy rainfall has caused flooding of the field to the landward of the wall (left) in the distance. The line of trees in the distance behind the flooded field marks the natural shoreline of the estuary. Owing to such embankments, the capacity of this estuary and many others in Britain to respond to natural coastal changes and relative sea level rise has been limited (photo R.W. Duck).

Plate 54 Bow Fiddle Rock, Portknockie, Banffshire (photo R.W. Duck).

Plate 55 Wave-cut platform over 200 metres in width at Cowie in Kincardineshire, Scotland. This is cut into near vertically bedded sandstones of Devonian age, thus it has an irregular, serrated upper surface (photo R.W. Duck).

Plate 56 Incipient cave formation on the coast near Sunderland, Tyne and Wear, in thinly and near-horizontally bedded limestone of Permian age cut by vertical joints. The voids are the result of the plucking out of blocks by wave action, and their shapes mimic those defined by the discontinuities (photo R.W. Duck).

Plate 57 Relict caves, associated with a raised shoreline, eroded into Permian age sandstones at An Cumhann, Isle of Arran – the largest, on the left of the view, is the so-called King's Cave. A higher, vegetated terrace cut into the cliff marks the position of a still older sea level (photo R.W. Duck).

Plate 58 The collapse of part of the roof of a cave at Arbroath in Angus has led to the formation of a blow hole (photo R.W. Duck).

Plate 59 The archetypal geo – the long narrow inlet, with near-to-vertical side walls, known as Trollochy near the hamlet of Crawton on the Kincardineshire coast, is eroded into Devonian lava and conglomerate sequences along a series of parallel joints and faults (photo R.W. Duck).

Plate 60 The natural arch of the Needle's Eye at Arbroath has been drilled by the sea through interbedded sandstone and conglomerate of the Devonian. Note the joints cutting through the rocks of the beam at its narrowest part (photo R.W. Duck).

Plate 61 Lot's Wife in the book of Genesis was turned into a pillar of salt as a punishment. The stack of that name at Marsden Bay near South Shields, Tyne and Wear, is probably so-called because the magnesian limestone out of which it is eroded was laid down in a warm, shallow, evaporating marine environment in which different mineral salts were precipitated. Subsequent dissolution of these salts has led to deformation of the overlying layers as seen in the cliffs (photo R.W. Duck).

gravel, from migrating in the natural longshore transport direction. They interrupt and slow down the sediment movement along a beach face causing particles to be deposited on their updrift sides. They may be constructed of rock armour, gabions, steel or concrete sections but timber varieties are by far the most common. Normally, groynes are built in groups known as groyne fields, thus they are designed to increase the storage of sediment along a particular stretch of beach. They are often placed in an attempt to stem beach draw-down adjacent to sea walls. However, whilst unnaturally plentiful amounts of beach sediment might prove beneficial to the economy of a specific tourist resort, its downdrift neighbours will be starved of their natural sediment supply. This will lead inevitably to the deterioration of downdrift beaches and enhanced erosion rates in such locations. Other structures projecting seawards from the coast, such as harbour walls and jetties, though not intended to trap sediment, act in the same way as groynes (Plate 50). Indeed jetties, which are usually longer than groynes, can cause major interruptions to natural longshore sediment transport systems. The 1911 Royal Commission noted that, 'The evidence laid before us goes to show that in many cases on the coast of the United Kingdom groynes have been constructed to a greater height than was necessary to fulfil the required conditions, with the result that they have so unduly interfered with the travel of the shingle as to lead to impoverishment of the beach to leeward, causing in many districts serious injury to the coast.'[15] Indeed, contemporary studies worldwide reveal that groyne fields, almost without exception, cause more problems at the coast in the long term than they purport to solve. Moreover, they are potentially dangerous for beach users.

Another less well known, less obvious and, therefore, less visually intrusive form of hard engineering coastal defence structure is the offshore breakwater. Such a structure may well eventually prove to be the best solution in Orkney's Bay of Skaill to arrest the erosion of Skara Brae. These are offshore, shore-parallel ridges or reefs, typically of rock armour, concrete blocks, tetrapods and even old rubber tyres, that are intended to prevent large waves from breaking on the coast. Some are designed to emerge at low water; other varieties remain submerged throughout the tidal cycle. They act as barriers that intercept incoming waves before they reach the shore, thereby dissipating the wave energy further offshore than would be the case under natural conditions. This, in turn, allows sediment to accumulate in the calmed waters in the landward shadow of the

Holderness revisited: human intervention causes fivefold increase in rate of erosion

A highly controversial scheme to protect the village of Mappleton, located 3 kilometres to the south of the resort of Hornsea on the Holderness coast, from rapid erosion took place in 1991. Along this coastline, as described elsewhere, the dominant direction of longshore sediment transport is from north to south towards the elongate, curving spit of Spurn Head. This scheme involved the installation of a rock armour revetment at the base of the soft cliffs along with two large rock groynes. The £2 million project made use of highly durable, large blocks of granite imported by barges from Norway and was a welcome success for the Mappleton community inasmuch as it brought about the accumulation of a wide sandy beach on the updrift, north side, of the rock groynes. Furthermore, the beach build up has slowed down greatly the natural cliff recession rate of around 2 metres per year. Enthusiasm for the protection scheme was not, however, shared by the residents of coastal communities to the south of Mappleton as the shore parallel rip-rap together with the two projecting groynes not surprisingly cut off the natural downdrift sediment supply (Plate 51). As an inevitable consequence, the rate of erosion has increased substantially, some estimate fivefold to around 10 metres per year, at locations like the nearby village of Aldbrough (see Chapter 3); epitomising to perfection the maxim of 'one beach's gain is another beach's loss'.

structure. Whilst this might be advantageous to beach users, the deposited sediment has been 'stolen' from its natural longshore transport pathway. Thus, downdrift sediment starvation and accelerated erosion are almost inevitable consequences. In addition, the focusing of wave attack on the coast to either end of a breakwater usually results in localised flanking erosion.

The 'man against nature' hard engineering, traditional ad-hoc approach to coastal protection prevailed in Britain and, indeed, elsewhere until as recently as the 1980s. Since that time, however, there has been an increasing, though not entire, realisation that alternative methods, the so-called soft engineering techniques, are in many situations far more appropriate. The underlying principle of such methods is that they work in sympathy *with* nature, rather than in a combative way *against* it.

SOFT SOLUTIONS

The most widely used and simplest soft engineering method is known as beach feeding or beach nourishment, where a beach is recharged with sediment sourced from elsewhere to counterbalance sediment loss due to erosion caused typically by updrift structures. Beach recharge schemes can make good use of unwanted sediment dredged to maintain navigation channels and harbours; for instance, the materials removed from the major port of Harwich Harbour in Essex are regularly used to recharge nearby beaches. However, it is essential that the range of particle sizes in the recharge sediment matches closely that of the natural beach materials. Ideally, sediment is used that is very slightly coarser grained than the natural materials, so as to inhibit beach erosion. Should the recharge sediment be too coarse, then aeolian processes, wind activity, on the beach are likely to be less effective, leading to the potential starvation and degradation of any dunes that might be present. If the recharge materials are finer than the natural beach sediment, they will be removed rapidly from the system by wave activity, thereby necessitating further nourishment. In addition, some grains will become washed into the pore spaces between the existing particles causing the beach to become unnaturally waterlogged. Although offshore sources for recharge sediment are the most common, such materials are sometimes derived from onshore sites potentially leading to many environmental problems associated with sand and gravel extraction. Since this technique only replaces sediment that has been eroded, recharge is a process that has to be repeated continually depending on the rate of sediment loss by natural longshore process and any accelerated erosion. For example, the renowned seven miles of golden sands at Bournemouth on the English Channel coast have to be replenished every eight to ten years or so, the natural supply to the area being cut off due to a sea wall.[16] Bournemouth beach and that at Portobello on the eastern side of Edinburgh were the first major recharge schemes in Britain, dating back to the early 1970s, both utilising sand dredged from offshore which was pumped ashore from barges. Like Bournemouth, Portobello beach needs to have its sand replenished, roughly every ten years.[17] However, its original deterioration was due to direct extraction of sand from the beach to feed the local glass bottle industry in the nineteenth and early twentieth centuries. Even larger schemes have since taken place at Mablethorpe in Yorkshire and Skegness in Lincolnshire and along the Norfolk coast, notably between the villages of Winterton-on-Sea and Happisburgh.

Dredging offshore sands and gravels, whether for beach recharge purposes or, as is more commonly the case, for the building industry, might appear innocuous and a harmless means of acquiring much needed aggregates. However, this practice has many associated problems. Aside from the obvious damage caused to seabed habitats, to spawning grounds and the increased turbidity of the water column, which can cause damage to fish and decrease light penetration, offshore dredging can, in fact, have significant onshore influences if the rate of extraction of sediment from a site exceeds that of natural replenishment. In this situation, the seabed will become artificially lowered and thus the water depth over the site will increase. If the water becomes deeper then the potential for the wind to generate larger waves is increased. This, in turn, can lead to higher energy waves impinging on coastal areas that would not naturally receive such large breakers and thus erosion rates can locally be exacerbated. Furthermore, sands and gravels, often in very large quantities, have been removed from the natural sediment transport system. There are conflicts of opinion, sometimes passionate, as to the onshore impacts of offshore dredging and it is often difficult to prove a causal link. This is certainly an emotive issue in many coastal communities of East Anglia. For instance, the 'Marine Environmental Information Network (MARINET)' has reported on a survey of a 10 kilometre length of the Norfolk coast near Winterton-on-Sea, Great Yarmouth, between 1972 and 1997. During this period, offshore sand extraction increased from virtually zero to a cumulative total of around 260 million tons. An advance in the mean high water mark by around 115 metres and in places a lowering of beach levels by up to 6 metres has been attributed directly to this increase in dredging activity.[18] Similar links have been suggested at sites elsewhere in Norfolk, in Suffolk, in the Bristol Channel and on beaches of the Glamorgan Heritage Coast, Pembrokeshire and the Gower Peninsula in South Wales.

In unsheltered coastal dune fields, sand fences are sometimes erected with the aim of trapping and accumulating wind-blown sand by creating a zone of calm air to encourage deposition. A wide range of materials is used for this purpose including timber planks, paling, netting, brushwood, wattle and textiles; all of these are visually unattractive and despoil the natural landscape. Yet, where successful in stimulating sand deposition, such fences will eventually become buried and hidden from view. They can help to create new embryo dunes and prevent the erosion of existing dunes. In addition, if located appropriately, they can stop or reduce the problem of sand blowing onto roads and into nearby homes and gardens. The stabilisation of bare, desolate expanses of blown sand can be effected in several ways with the overall aim of preventing or slowing down erosion and establishing vegetation cover. Planting dune grasses such as marram, sea lyme or couch is the most natural and unobtrusive technique. These species have long rhizomes that help to bind sand grains at depth below dune surfaces (see Chapter 6). In addition, their leaves trap blowing sand and they have the ability to continue growing upwards as the sand accumulates. Planted grasses or re-seeded areas can be protected by means of mulching, thatching or binding.

Mulching involves the use of a layer of seaweed, peat, reeds, straw or manure to retain moisture and prevent erosion, thus pungent odours are an almost inevitable side-effect. Thatching is the process of spreading brushwood over the surface, especially in exposed locations. It is a traditional method of stabilising sand that was in operation at Culbin Sands, Morayshire (see Chapter 6), as far back as the late nineteenth century. It has even been used as an effective, sustainable method of disposing of old, shredded Christmas trees. In recent years, Castle Morpeth Borough Council has worked with coastal conservation volunteers to create fences of Christmas trees at Druridge Bay in Northumberland, to stabilise sections of the extensive sand dune system.[19] Through time, the trees, which are highly effective in slowing down the wind as it blows over the dunes, become buried completely by trapped sand. Binding involves the use of chemical sprays, which act as glues, binding the surface grains of sand together to form an outer 'skin'. It is often used along with mulching, and is particularly effective on the unstable slope faces of dunes.

A little known, virtually unnoticeable, simple, yet highly innovative soft engineering method of preventing sand loss from beaches due to wave action is known as beach face dewatering or beach drainage. This is a technique that was first developed in Denmark in the early 1980s and has subsequently been applied with success at sites around the world, including Newquay, the surfing capital of Britain, in Cornwall.[20] It involves the lowering of the groundwater table beneath a length of beach by pumping; hence 'dewatering'. Field and laboratory observations have shown that a relatively low groundwater table encourages the build up of sand on beaches, thereby preventing erosion. As is often the case, the viability of this method was discovered originally quite by accident. A public marine aquarium at a site in north Jutland was acquiring its seawater by pumping from beneath a beach. Such groundwater was used as a clean source for the tanks owing to the natural filtering effect of the beach sand. As pumping progressed, however, the sand on the beach built up to such a great extent that it became a nuisance, blowing into nearby houses, gardens and onto a road. Thus the potential for beach face dewatering to be developed into an erosion control method was realised. If the water table is low, the water from a breaking wave, as it advances up the beach face as swash, can soak quickly downwards, percolating into the empty pore spaces between the sand grains. By contrast, if the water table is naturally at or near the surface, this enhanced infiltration is not possible and the receding backwash has greater flow volume and therefore capacity to remove sediment particles seawards down the beach face. Drain systems, comprising permeable pipes that are buried below the beach face parallel with the coastline, intercept the collected seawater to a sump and pumping station, from where it can be pumped back to sea or to other nearby sites, such as marinas and coastal lagoons. The accumulation of sand that this method stimulates causes beaches to maintain or even increase in width. In turn, the increased availability of sand to aeolian processes acting on a beach can help to maintain and build fringing sand dunes and their associated habitats. Thus, the method has an added benefit. On the negative side, however, it can reduce the natural rate of downdrift sediment transport, potentially contributing to sediment starvation and enhanced erosion elsewhere.

ONLY IN BRITAIN

Britain can lay claim to some seemingly oddball methods of coastal protection. At Porthcawl, on the Glamorganshire coast of South Wales, is what is believed to be the world's first tarmac beach (Plate 52). The cobbly

Town Beach in front of the promenade of the town was partly covered over with tarmac in the 1980s to stabilise the sediment and to help dissipate wave energy at the base of the sea wall. This part of the beach now acts like an inclined revetment; the sediment has been immobilised and, moreover, the aesthetics of this approach to coastal management are questionable.

Another unusual method of protecting a shoreline involves the sinking of vessels and the placement of the hulls so that they act in much the same way as offshore breakwaters. This was the approach in response to erosion of the very vulnerable Essex marshes. In the mid to late 1980s, following substantial erosion by a large storm in January 1978, the sunken hulls of many Thames barges and lighters, filled with sand, were grounded offshore from Sales Point and Marsh House on the extensive Dengie Marsh. They were arranged a few hundred metres offshore parallel with the marsh edge with the aim of lessening wave attack along the fragile Dengie Peninsula to the north of the Thames Estuary.[21] First World War blockships, deliberately wrecked to prevent access by the enemy to the natural deep, sheltered harbour of Scapa Flow by way of five narrow straits between the Orkney Islands, act in much the same way. Attack by natural forces was, however, far from the minds of those whose job it was to scuttle the vessels at the time.

Several unusual approaches to curb erosion rates of hard rock cliffs have been made, often without success, along the Glamorgan Heritage Coast of South Wales, an area of high wave energy.[22] The cliffs, up to 90 metres in height, comprise inter-bedded limestone and mudstone of Lower Jurassic age. The presence of extensive networks of near vertical fault and joint systems, which intersect the sedimentary bedding planes, contributes to cliff instability; erosion rates in the area are generally around 10 centimetres per year. At Colhuw, near Llantwit Major, blasting with explosives was carried out in 1969 to remove dangerous upper cliff overhangs. This procedure caused debris to collapse to the base of the cliffs in the form of a cone with the aim that this should provide protection at the toe like a rock armour apron.[23] Unfortunately, the engineers greatly underestimated the size of the debris cone that they created, the wave energy and the power of longshore sediment transport in the area. Thus, the displaced materials were removed completely within five years from the foot of the cliff that they were intended to protect. Moreover, the hazard of rock fall still remains, but also the scenic quality of the cliffs has been impaired by the blasting operation. A plan to remove loose blocks of rock at Southerndown involved the use of high-pressure water jets. The power of the jets was unfortunately sufficient to dislodge only the weaker mudstone blocks and had no effect on those of limestone. The scheme thus had the reverse effect and induced enhanced erosion at the site. A low cost method used at Nash Point met with rather more success. Here natural limestone blocks were cut, inserted and cemented into the wave-cut notch at the base of the cliff to prevent wave undercutting. A similar method has been employed to stabilise the Carboniferous sandstone cliffs at St Andrews, Fife. Such cliff strengthening techniques can also include the infilling of open joints and other gaping fractures in a cliff with concrete, a practice known as dentition, together with the use of meshwork and bolts to hold large blocks of rock together.

Blasting of cliffs to prevent erosion is not, however, as novel as it might seem. On 21 September 1850, the *Illustrated London News* carried an article entitled 'Grand Explosion at Seaford Cliff'. This provided a description of events two days earlier in the East Sussex town, where blasting of the chalk cliff had been carried out amid great spectacle; a special train even brought onlookers from the capital. The aspiration was that this would, at minimal cost, create a rock groyne that would prevent sediment from being carried out of Seaford Bay and thus prevent erosion.[24] Naturally, however, the rock debris was soon removed by waves and currents and the enterprise was a complete failure.[25]

A method of coastal erosion and flood protection first developed in the United States that involves the recycling of old rubber tyres has now reached our shores. In Britain alone, we manufacture a staggering 25 million tyres per year. Tyres must be durable and non-biodegradable, which means that they are very difficult to dispose of, so their recycling as a means of coastal protection is becoming an increasingly attractive idea. In an experimental defence scheme at Pevensey, on the coast of East Sussex, a large excavation was made into the gravel beach in 2002. This was filled with 350 tyre bales in an arrangement of five by five by fourteen bales.[26] Each bale comprised somewhere in the range of 100 to 120 tyres that had been compressed mechanically into blocks of roughly 1.33 cubic metres in volume and held together with either stainless steel wire or nylon cord. The bales were subsequently covered over with a substantial veneer of beach gravel. By this means, the large volume of material removed from the excavation was available for use to recharge

Paying the price: what do sea defences cost?

What are the actual monetary costs of the various types of coastal engineering methods that have been discussed? Since specific costs rapidly become out-dated, it is more appropriate to look at the differing techniques in *relative* cost terms, as high, medium and low, and as multiples of a given notional unit. A further consideration is that of ongoing maintenance costs, which vary according to the technique in use; a gabion basket will possibly require yearly repair, whilst a reinforced concrete sea wall might need little or no attention for thirty years or so. Costs also depend on the individual location, ease of access, distance from sources of materials, types of materials used and so on. In general, however, sea walls are the most expensive form of coastal defence, whilst soft engineering forms like sand fencing and planting are the least. The costs of groynes, gabions and beach nourishment schemes occupy the middle ground, somewhere between these two extremes. If 2010 prices are used as a guide, concrete sea walls can cost anything from £800 to around £9,000 per linear metre, the range being a function of the height and thickness of the structure. Sand fencing, at the other extreme, is likely to cost as little as 0.0025 of the lower end of this range (especially if recycled Christmas trees are installed in the dunes by a volunteer labour force).

other parts of the beach at Pevensey that were eroding. There are, however, environmental concerns regarding the use of tyres in this way and in other forms of coastal defence as some research indicates that they can release zinc which is toxic to crustaceans, such as burrowing crabs.[27]

CLAIMING WHAT IS RIGHTLY OURS?

The 'man against nature' period from around 1800 until the 1980s was also one when 'reclamation' was seen as a solution to a perceived lack of space at the coast, although this activity has been carried out since, at least, Roman times in Britain. Intertidal areas of salt marsh and mudflat, particularly within estuaries, were then regarded as 'waste' lands; their ecological importance was either unknown or disregarded offhandedly as insignificant.

So-called reclamation, the very word implying quite incorrectly that humans were taking back land that had previously been 'stolen' by the sea, became widespread in lowland coastal and estuarine areas where industrial and urban development was rampant. Just as sea defence structures were built on an ad-hoc basis, so land 'claim' (a far more appropriate term) progressed, especially from the mid eighteenth century until well into the nineteenth century. Within the Forth Estuary of eastern Scotland, for example, around half of the intertidal mudflat and salt marsh areas had been claimed from the sea for agriculture by 1840,[28] typically by the construction of earth embankments (dykes) with cores of impermeable clay (Plate 53). These were faced on the water side with cut stone blocks to prevent wave erosion. Another method of land claim in the area and elsewhere, such as in the Humber Estuary and the Wash, involved raising the level of mud flats by warping. This involved the use of stakes set into the mud, interlaced with brushwood to create quiet backwaters that promoted the sedimentation of fine particles and, therefore, vertical build-up of deposits. Subsequent land claim schemes in the Forth Estuary that continued into the 1920s were principally for industrial rather than agricultural purposes, often using nearby colliery and oil shale mine waste to raise the land level behind the retaining embankments.[29] In the last 150 years or so, at least one third of the intertidal land in the Forth Estuary has been lost. Land claimed for industry includes large areas of the foreshores of Bo'ness and Grangemouth on the southern bank. The latter area now hosts not only the largest container port in Scotland but the adjacent oil refinery that is Scotland's main fuel supplier. Clearly this is an area of claimed land that is the foundation of infrastructure of enormous economic importance to the country and thus it must, at all costs, be maintained from encroachment by the sea for the foreseeable future. So too, the port of Felixstowe in Suffolk must be protected; the largest deep water container port in Britain and one of the largest in Europe, it is also mainly located on expanses of land claimed from the sea at Bathside Bay in the 1980s.

Extensive land claim around the wide estuarine embayment of the Wash on the north-west margin of East Anglia took place from the seven-teenth century onwards resulting in a loss of 47,000 hectares of formerly intertidal lands, the greatest area excluded from the sea in any British

Whitby's Penny Hedge

On the side of a jetty at the mouth of Whitby Harbour in North Yorkshire, where the River Esk meets the North Sea, there is a plaque erected by the former North Riding of Yorkshire County Council. Its inscription reads:

> From time immemorial at or near this place in Whitby Harbour the ceremony of the Horngarth popularly known as the planting of the Penny Hedge has been performed each year on the morning of the eve of Ascension Day.

This is a reference to a tradition that goes back eight and a half centuries to the year 1159,[30] a ceremony that takes place on the morning of Ascension Eve at approximately 9.00 a.m. Legend has it that a band of three Norman noblemen, William de Bruce, Ralph de Piercie and Allatson, murdered a hermit monk from Whitby Abbey, who had provided sanctuary in a local chapel to a wounded wild boar that they were hunting with hounds. On his deathbed, the hermit is said to have forgiven his killers, but the Abbot of Whitby, Sedman, gave orders that the three nobles should serve an annual penance. Every Ascension Eve, thirty-eight days after Easter Sunday, the men were to gather at the Wood of the Strayhead where the Abbot's officer would deliver to William de Bruce 'ten Stakes, ten Stout-Stowers and ten Yedders' to be cut 'with the knife of a Penny Price'. Ralph de Piercie was to take 'one and twenty of each sort, to be cut in the same manner', whilst Allatson 'shall take nine of each sort to be cut as aforesaid'.[31] The killers were then to carry these materials on their backs to the harbour and erect them in the form of an inter-woven brushwood fence – the hedge – within the intertidal zone. The structure had to be sufficiently robust that it would withstand the forces of the rise and fall of water over three tides. If the so-called Penny Hedge failed, the men would forfeit ownership of their lands to the Abbot or his successors. Today the pliable hazel fence is still constructed faithfully in accordance with the legend, as captured on film by Pathé News in 1938,[32] keeping

alive the lengthy tradition that has become part of Whitby's heritage.
Once the task is completed, a horn is blown three times by the
Abbot's officer, followed by the cry 'Out on ye' three times, once for
each nobleman. It has been suggested that the penitential hedge
with its Canute-like nuance might 'represent a garbled memory of
former boundaries now lost to the sea'.[33] Equally striking, however,
the erection of such a brushwood structure across the foreshore
bears more than a little resemblance to the centuries-old means by
which sedimentation has been stimulated and land has been claimed
by warping in muddy estuaries like the Humber and the Forth.

estuary.[34] The practice was so widespread, that of 155 British estuaries, 136
(88 per cent) have experienced some land claim for agricultural,
commercial, industrial or recreational uses. Along with the Wash, very large
areas of land have been claimed around the Severn, Dee, Humber, Thames
and Tees estuaries, with the British grand total of formerly intertidal land
area excluded from the sea being estimated at nearly 89,000 hectares.[35]
This may best be visualised in terms of a single square of land measuring
30 kilometres by 30 kilometres that has been 'won' from the 'enemy' over
time. Whilst this is a significant area of Britain, it is small in comparison
with the Netherlands where about 18 per cent of the country's landmass
has been claimed from the North Sea. Not only do such actions result in
modifications to natural tidal and sediment flow pathways and speeds, the
areas of claimed land represent once natural habitats that have been
destroyed, that are no longer able to provide, among others, bird breeding
or feeding sites, fish spawning or juvenile feeding grounds. So too, the
natural capacity for estuaries to respond to natural coastal changes and
relative sea level rise has become constrained.

A resurgent phase of land claim schemes seemed poised to begin in
Britain following the Second World War, as the post-war, victorious and
euphoric 'anything is possible' spirit prevailed in the country. Authors such
as Ogilvie[36] did little more than draw lines on maps across estuarine
embayments, inlets and the mouths of coastal bays to demarcate areas that
they believed could potentially be won from the sea. No consideration was
given whatsoever to the impacts of isolating these areas from the sea, such
as loss of habitat or the consequences for natural sedimentary processes. In

Scotland alone, nearly fifty sites were identified totalling approximately 170,000 hectares in surface area, equivalent to a square of land measuring 13 by 13 kilometres being cut off from the sea (Figure 4.1). The largest single site proposed was within the Tay Estuary on the east coast of the country, where over 1,000 hectares of intertidal flats would have been lost from what today is a Special Protection Area (SPA), as designated in accordance with the European Community Birds Directive (1979). This area is noted for hosting the largest continuous reed bed in Britain, which supports nationally important populations of reed bed birds. Furthermore,

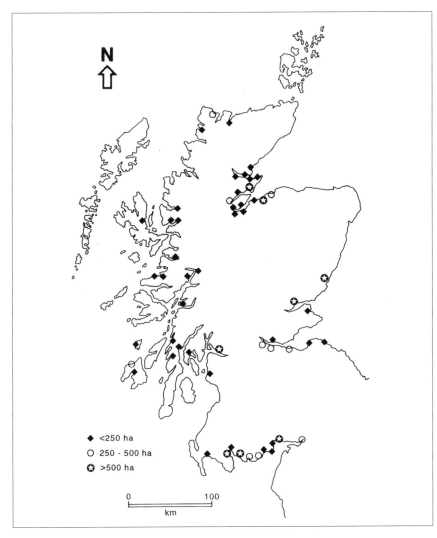

Figure 4.1 Sites of proposed land claim in Scotland according to their area (adapted from Ogilvie, A.G. (1945) Land reclamation in Scotland. *Scottish Geographical Magazine*, 61, 77–84).

internationally important populations of wading birds, sea-ducks and geese, are dependent on the extensive intertidal flats. Mercifully, the lines that Ogilvie and others drew on maps in such an ad-hoc cavalier fashion in 1945, without any regard for or appreciation of natural process, ecology or nature conservation, were soon erased from memory and in most locations, including the inner Tay Estuary, common sense won the day.

It is somewhat ironic that the now very extensive Tay reed beds that provide such an important habitat within the SPA are of a species (*Phragmites communis*) that is not native, but was introduced to the area by local riparian landowners. Planting took place in the late eighteenth and especially the early nineteenth centuries as a novel, soft engineering (though the term was not known at the time) means of reducing bank erosion by waves. The slowing down of current speeds around the closely spaced stems further stimulated fine sediment particles to be deposited among the reeds, thereby augmenting the early land claim schemes of this area. Newly built earthen embankment walls were protected from wave action by the baffling effect of the reed stems within which sediment accretion raised the surface level of the intertidal flats in readiness for additional land claim.[37]

Warping in the Leame Estuary creates Cold Harbour Colony

Cold Harbour Colony owed its existence to a nineteenth century philanthropist, Sir Rupert Calderdyke, who believed in making two acres grow where one had been before. He had set thorn fences in the mud of the Leame Estuary, against which receding tides piled clay and drift-wood that slowly from week to week grew from piles to banks, from banks to shallow islands, from islands to outworks of the coast itself, then, mile by mile into level arable land, lightish towards the river where the tides drained off the clay, and heavy as pudding farther in. Sir Rupert raised dykes, dug drains, built heavy double cottages in pseudo-gothic style marked with their varying dates, 1845 to 1889, then died full of plans and debts, leaving to his heirs his many problems.

Winifred Holtby, *South Riding*, 1936

The little village and parish of Sunk Island, its very name evokes mystery, is neither sunk nor is it today an island. It is, however, in an area vulnerable to sea level rise. Situated on the north side of the Humber Estuary to the east of Hull, this spot was the inspiration for Winifred Holtby's 'Cold Harbour Colony' in her most famous novel, 'South Riding'; a forlorn settlement 10 miles from Withernsea where fictitious victims of war struggled against despair and poverty among the drains and dykes of land claimed from the mud of the 'Leame Estuary'.[38] The eerie sight of big ships in the Humber apparently making passage in a neighbouring field, an illusion resulting from the high retaining embankment in the line of view, is the reality of today as recounted in Holtby's myth. Along with other areas along both banks of the Humber, such as Broomfleet Island to the west of Hull and Read's Island on the south side, Sunk Island was gradually claimed from the estuary since the mid eighteenth century, largely by a process known as warping.[39] It started off life as little more than an intertidal bank of estuarine deposits; although isolated from the north shore by the Patrington Channel, island would have been too grand a name to begin with. Warping is the technique, used extensively in the Wash, by which sedimentation is encouraged by the flooding of areas, retained from the estuary with artificial embankments, by sediment-laden waters fed along a network of drains at high tide. As the water drains away, it leaves behind a thin deposit of sediment, typically mud. If, however, this process is carried out repeatedly, so the level of the land is raised gradually then section by section it can be claimed from the estuary. As much as 1 metre of sediment, known as warp, can accumulate in this way in a year.[40] Warping can typically be aided by the use of brushwood 'dams' that promote sedimentation in the drains by slowing down the flow and it can also incorporate the dumping of excavated sediments brought to a site by cart from elsewhere.[41] It is remarkable to note that, in the nineteenth century, in this part of England, the mole was referred to colloquially as a moundwarp.[42] By a combination of warping, leading to as much as 3 metres of mud deposition,[43] and the construction of embankments, Sunk Island eventually became an integral part of the East Yorkshire mainland by 1808 as the Patrington Channel became infilled.[44] Land claim by these means continued for decades and by the close of the nineteenth century[45] the basis for 'Cold Harbour Colony' was realised. Sir Rupert may have died leaving many problems, but that of sea level rise was never to exercise his mind.

In estuaries that are characterised by substantial areas of land claim, the natural volume of the water body has been reduced and so too the natural capacity to accommodate the tidal influx of water which, excluding any fresh water discharges from rivers, is known as the tidal prism. Such areas are, therefore, particularly vulnerable to relative sea level rise as there is simply far less space available than nature intended to accommodate the progressively increasing volumes of water. As an example, to put this into quite dramatic perspective, it has been shown by means of a computer simulation model that, were the Patrington Channel to be reinstated in the Humber Estuary to the north of Sunk Island, tidal levels at Hull would fall by a maximum of 0.5 metre.[46] The blockage of this channel as part of the successive Sunk Island land claim schemes has thus had a profound impact on tidal levels in this estuary.

The Tees: industrialisation and the destruction of an estuary

Although more land has been claimed from the Wash than any other estuary in Britain, the much smaller Tees Estuary has lost the greatest percentage of its intertidal area to the extent that it has been almost completely destroyed (Figure 4.2). Plentiful supplies of coal from the Durham coalfield coupled with iron ore from the nearby Cleveland Hills fuelled the development of the iron and steel industry in the upper parts of this estuary in the eighteenth century. As the local iron ore supplies became depleted, the need to import raw materials became acute and so the steel works migrated to the lower reaches of the estuary and in the early nineteenth century new docks and urban areas were developed apace at Middlesbrough,

Cargo Fleet, South Bank, Redcar and elsewhere. The rapidity of industrial growth in the region was so voracious that the estuary's intertidal areas became devoured on all flanks by successive and rather piecemeal episodes of land claim that continued until as recently as the 1970s. In 1850, the Tees was characterised by very large areas of intertidal sand and mudflats fringed by salt marshes; only minor amounts of land had been claimed for agriculture. By the mid 1970s, however, these intertidal areas had been all but obliterated with only small parts of the former Seal Sands on the north side and Bran Sands on the south side remaining. In little over a century, a staggering 83 per cent[47] of the intertidal area of the Tees Estuary had been claimed for the needs of industry and port-related activities. Today, it is sad, but nonetheless ironic, that the Teesside area is ravaged by industrial decline and much of the land claimed from the estuary is no longer required and lies derelict.

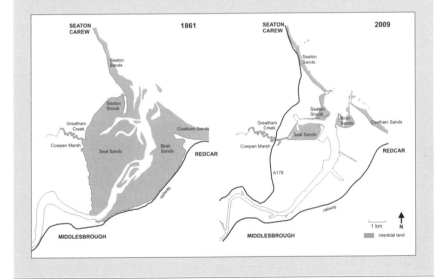

Figure 4.2 Shrinking estuary – comparison of the Tees Estuary in 1861 with 2009 showing the spectacular loss of intertidal land due to extensive land claim (drawing by T. Dixon).

A modern response to alleviate the impact of relative sea level rise in estuaries and other coastal areas that are characterised by such historic, extensive land claim schemes is that of so-called managed retreat or managed realignment, a form of soft engineering. This process can also mitigate for loss of intertidal habitats, for example by initiating the redevelopment of salt marshes from what has been used as arable land for centuries.

It involves the removal or breaching of old land claim defences, thereby permitting tidal waters to re-flood land that they previously inundated.[48] In England, the first such managed realignment site was at Northey Island in the Blackwater Estuary, Essex, in 1991 where about 0.8 hectare of land was allowed to re-flood. Similar, larger managed retreat projects have been carried out at other locations on the Essex coast at Abbott's Hall in 2002, Orplands and Tollesbury in 1995, together with other schemes elsewhere in low-lying coastal areas of England, such as that at Freiston Shore on the Wash in Lincolnshire in 2002. It is ironic that the latter is the very estuary from which the greatest area of land in Britain was claimed from the sea in the past. In 2003, as part of the Humber flood defence upgrade works, a site at Paull Holme Strays was breached thereby recreating 80 hectares of inter-tidal habitat.[49] Also in 2003, a small, 25 hectare, managed realignment scheme in Scotland at Nigg Bay on the Cromarty Firth in Easter Ross, in which an embankment was breached to recreate intertidal habitats,[50] paved the way for similar schemes elsewhere in the country, notably in the upper reaches of the Forth Estuary. In 2010, in what is known as the Skinflats Tidal Exchange Project (STEP Forth) a pipe was driven through the embankment at the Royal Society for the Protection of Birds Skinflats Reserve, thus permitting the Forth to flood over what was previously a 10 hectare grass field.[51] On the falling tide, the water can be held back by a sluice at the outflow which should lead to the re-establishment of salt marsh and the creation of saline pools, simultaneously of benefit to many different types of birds and a novel, controlled means of estuarine flood alleviation.

In many places the sea has already undertaken the work of bulldozers where the retaining embankments of centuries-old land claim schemes have not been maintained and have become breached naturally through disrepair. Such abandoned reclamations are common around the low-lying, muddy estuaries of the south-east of England, in Suffolk, Essex and North Kent. These sites are showing the re-establishment of salt marshes and intertidal mudflats without the human intervention of managed realignment, but with identical consequences. The sea has been biding its time and is merely claiming back what was once, perhaps centuries previously, taken away from it, stolen by man.

Where relative sea level is rising (see Chapter 2), areas that are charac-terised by land claim embankments or sea walls and developments close to the shoreline are now experiencing what is called 'coastal squeeze'. What would, under natural conditions, have been intertidal land has been enclosed from the influence of the sea. Such areas are becoming progressively unable to accommodate erosion; intertidal sand or mudflats, wetlands and salt marshes that would naturally migrate landwards as sea level rises are unable to do so as they encounter man-made barriers, hence the term 'squeeze'. If sediment availability to such areas has been depleted, as is so often the case, for example, by the construction of walls in the updrift direction, then the squeeze is exacerbated with the result that beaches become narrower and steeper in profile or indeed vanish completely due to erosion.

A recent large-scale survey of England and Wales[52] has shown startlingly that the majority, 61 per cent of the length of the coastline, is showing steepening whereas 33 per cent is showing flattening. This indicates a progressive exposure of large numbers of beaches to damage from erosion, which has clear implications for coastal management. The greatest steep-ening has taken place along both defended and undefended coasts of north-west England, South Wales, the Solent, the Thames Estuary, large parts of East Anglia and the whole length of Holderness. Many of these areas are well known to be subject to long-term coastal erosion as described elsewhere in the book.

EPILOGUE

King Canute was right – he knew that the sea cannot be held back indefinitely and, as noted in Chapter 1, was merely trying to demonstrate to his people that his kingly powers were not limitless. As Robert Burns wrote in 1791 in his most famous narrative poem, *Tam o' Shanter – a Tale!*, 'Nae man can tether time or tide'. Yes, the sea can be held back temporarily, perhaps for decades, by walls and other structures, but, as this chapter has shown; such defence schemes invariably create more problems that they solve. The simple message that eroding coasts are natural suppliers of sediment and those that are accreting are natural depositional 'sinks' is still so often overlooked. Locate centres of habitation along the former and it will just be a question of time before there are demands for defences. Between such sources and sinks are natural longshore transport pathways, and it is the intentional or unintentional interruption of these by human intervention, such as installation of hard defences or land claim, that is the root cause of almost all coastal problems not only in Britain but worldwide.

5

WHY ARE THE COASTS IN NORTH-WEST SCOTLAND NOT LIKE THOSE IN SOUTH-EAST ENGLAND?

The coast is exposed to the destructive force not only of weather but of the sea. The waves pound it with countless tons not merely of water but of rock fragments and pebbles, and rasp at its surface with thousands of tons of gritty sand. They rush into its crevices, compressing the air within them, and then retreat, allowing it to expand violently. Thus, like the weather, they destroy the rocks not only on the surface but a little below; and, like the weather, they have hardly destroyed one surface before they begin on another.

I.O. Evans, *The Observer's Book of Geology*, 1968

A WHISTLE STOP JOURNEY AROUND THE FRINGES OF BRITAIN: PAINTING WITH A BROAD BRUSH

The simple answer to the question posed in the title of this chapter is twofold; 'rock type and age'. At one geographical extreme of Britain, the rocks are relatively old, hard and enduring; at the other, they are relatively young, soft and fragile. For a small island, from outer space rather an inconspicuous speck on the surface of the Earth, Britain is made up of an enormous variety of rock types and ages; arguably more so than any landmass of comparable size on our rocky planet. These span virtually the entire gamut of the geological column from some of the very oldest rocks in the world, over 2,600 million years of age, to the newborn at the other extreme (Table 5.1).

Cape Wrath, that far north-western extremity of mainland Britain, is a convenient location to begin a clockwise geological circumnavigation of the island. Here the ancient Precambrian metamorphic rocks, Lewisian gneisses, amongst the oldest in the country, give way eastwards to younger gneisses and schists along Scotland's north coast. Caithness, in the north-eastern corner, is strikingly different, however. Here, sedimentary rocks of Devonian age, sandstones and siltstones, form spectacular vertical cliffs like those found in Orkney. South of Caithness, the coast of east Sutherland is formed of younger Jurassic formations followed by sandstones, primarily of Devonian age, around the shores of the inner Moray Firth from Dornoch south to Inverness, and thence east to Lossiemouth. The southern shore of the outer part of this great firth, through Nairnshire, Morayshire and Banffshire, is fringed with a variety of Precambrian metamorphic formations – schists and quartzites – that continue to crop out along the Aberdeenshire fringe as far south on the open North Sea coast as Stonehaven in Kincardineshire. Here the Highland Boundary Fault, a major fracture in the Earth's crust that slices through Scotland, meets the coast. To the south, the rocks are very much younger; in Angus, sandstones and contemporaneous lavas of the Devonian; south of the Tay Estuary in Fife, principally sandstones, limestones, shales and coals of Carboniferous age. These continue to skirt the Firth of Forth and the East Lothian coast south to Dunbar.

The Berwickshire coast is dominated by sedimentary rocks of Silurian age, grey mudstones and associated sequences that have been contorted by folding. At Berwick-upon-Tweed itself, limestones of the Carboniferous form the coastal rocks continuing south into Northumberland. The southern fringe of this county is dominated by the Carboniferous Coal Measures that continue south to the mouth of the Tyne. Southwards, along the Tyne and Wear coast to Hartlepool, limestones of Permian age dominate. Jurassic sedimentary sequences of shales, sandstones and limestones crop out along the Cleveland and North Yorkshire coastline as far south as Filey. These give way to the Cretaceous chalk forming the prominent white cliffs of the promontory of Flamborough Head. Though the chalk forms the bedrock continuously through Holderness, Lincolnshire and onwards to north Norfolk, it is draped with thick veneers of soft glacial till that form the friable coastal edge. Apart from a few isolated occurrences of 'hard' cliffs, as at Hunstanton, unconsolidated sediments of Tertiary and Quaternary age form the Suffolk and Essex shorelines southwards to the Thames Estuary. Indeed the first real cliffs seen south of Flamborough Head are those at Margate in Kent's projecting Isle of Thanet, formed similarly from chalk. If a rock is considered as an Earth material that 'rings' when it is hit with a hammer, the almost complete absence of such materials at the coastal edge from Flamborough Head southwards to Margate is remarkable. As the crow flies, this is around 350 kilometres, but very much longer if the shape of the coastline is followed and equivalent to over 70 per cent of England's east coast – little wonder these parts are so susceptible to erosion.

The chalk cliffs of east Kent continue to become the famous White Cliffs of Dover on the English Channel coast. Jurassic and Cretaceous sedimentary sequences dominate along the south coast of England extending westwards from Sussex into Dorset and east Devon. However, younger Tertiary deposits overlie these to the north of the Isle of Wight in Hampshire between Portsmouth and Bournemouth. Permian sandstones occupy the Exmouth and Torbay area, with Devonian age sandstone forming much of the west Devon and Cornwall coast from Brixham to Padstow and Tintagel. The exception is the Land's End area, eroded out of a large granite intrusion. Thereafter, Carboniferous rocks, dominantly sandstones, form the north Devon coastal fringe. Fine-grained mudstones of the Triassic encircle the Severn Estuary passing into Jurassic limestones of the Glamorgan Heritage Coast, after which mixed Carboniferous sedimentary formations crop out along much of the South Wales coastline westwards into Pembrokeshire.

Slates, mudstones, limestones, lavas and ashes of Ordovician and Silurian age dominate the Cardigan Bay coastline of west Wales continuing to crop out along the northern fringes of the country east to Llandudno. The coastal stretch from the Wirral Peninsula to Barrow-in Furness is underlain principally by soft Triassic-age mudstones and sandstones that continue to St Bees Head near Whitehaven in Cumbria. Hereabouts, the Carboniferous Coal Measures recur in the section north to Maryport. Permian and Triassic sandstones and mudstones underlie the inner Solway Firth, with the Ordovician and Silurian rocks, like those of the Berwickshire and west Wales coasts forming much of the fringes of the Southern Uplands of Scotland to Girvan in Ayrshire. Carboniferous and Devonian sedimentary rocks – limestones, sandstones and coals – dominate the Ayrshire coast with local lavas and igneous intrusions. The Highland Boundary Fault reaches the west coast of Scotland near Helensburgh north of which Precambrian metamorphic rocks, principally various types of schists underlie the deeply indented and embayed coasts of Argyllshire and Wester Ross. From Loch Alsh northwards along the west Sutherland coast, the Torridonian Sandstones of Precambrian age dominate as far north as Enard Bay. Thereafter, to the point where this

Period	Years before present
Quaternary (Holocene and Pleistocene)	0–2 Ma
Tertiary	2–65
Cretaceous	65–114
Jurassic	144–213
Triassic	213–250
Permian	250–286
Carboniferous	286–360
Devonian	360–408
Silurian	408–438
Ordovician	438–505
Cambrian	505–590
Precambrian	>590★

Table 5.1 Simplified geological timescale (Ma = million years)

★ The oldest Precambrian rocks are in the Outer Hebrides and Sutherland in Scotland and date back as far as around 2,600 Ma.

journey began, the oldest rocks of Britain, the Lewisian gneisses are rejoined. Offshore, these rocks form the greater part of the islands of the Outer Hebrides, whilst the Inner Hebrides are formed largely from very much younger igneous rock varieties, volcanic and intrusive, of Tertiary age – in sharp contrast to the unconsolidated sedimentary rocks of the same age in south-east England.

Although robustness, durability, resilience, sturdiness and the age of rocks, as with so many things, go by and large hand-in-hand, this can sometimes be rather too simplistic a picture in terms of resistance to coastal erosion. However, it is hardly surprising that approximately 44 per cent of the English and Welsh coastlines are defended compared with only 6 per cent of those of Scotland.[1]

ROCKY CLIFFS: SYMBOLS OF PERMANENCE?

The Butt of Lewis is a desolate, wild and windswept place. This, the northernmost tip of the Isle of Lewis in the Outer Hebrides of Scotland, is one of the windiest in Britain. The continually wave-battered and wave-pounded rocks that make up this promontory and, indeed, comprise most of the island itself are the very oldest in the country. The Lewisian gneisses are crystalline rocks that have been transformed over millennia deep within the Earth's crust by processes involving elevated temperatures and pressures that are collectively termed metamorphism. From a coastal perspective, the most important property that these metamorphic rocks possess is their inherent durability. They are very tough and are able to withstand and resist the incessant force of waves breaking upon them. They therefore offer resistance to breaking waves and wear away or erode at imperceptibly slow rates forming cliffs that are typically characterised by smoothed and rounded outcrop surfaces. However, it is essential to note that, just as a chain is only as strong as its weakest link, 'a cliffed coast is only as strong as its weakest part'.[2]

Bow Fiddle Rock: the arch in the stack

Off the Banffshire coast at the village of Portknockie stands a remarkable piece of sculpture, carved not by the hand of man but by the power of the sea (Plate 54). Here the rocks are arranged in layers, not horizontal but inclined. The so-called Bow Fiddle Rock stands isolated from the cliffs – a stack, cut off from the mainland, of which it was once part, by incessant wave erosion. Through it there is a spectacular aperture, a natural arch. The eccentric shape of this is controlled by the angle of inclination of the ancient Precambrian quartzite rocks, metamorphosed sandstones laid down originally in a shallow sea themselves, which comprise this stretch of the southern Moray Firth coast. In essence, here is a rocky remnant that has been punctured, almost but not quite severed into two, by wave attack. When the slender, inclined beam gives way, which it will do surely one day, two stacks will be formed, one very much larger than the other.

Surely high rocky cliffs are fine, upstanding symbols of permanence, of solidity and often of striking, never changing aesthetic appeal? But look to the foot of such a cliff at low tide, when the waves are breaking elsewhere and that unchanging nature of such a coastline is often brought into question. Here lie pieces of broken rock detached by the erosive forces of waves that break against the base of the cliffs at high water. Indeed, these blocks themselves can be hurled and battered repeatedly at the base of the cliffs by storm waves, thereby empowering the waves even more. By this process of undercutting and collapse of material above, a cliff will recede sometimes gradually and imperceptibly but sometimes spectacularly, and the signs of its former seaward positions often remain sawn almost horizontally in the form of a wave-cut platform − a flat-lying rocky surface, with perhaps a thin veneer of sediment on top, that is left as the sea has undermined the rocks above (Plate 55). In previous chapters, this book has featured coastlines developed out of what might be called 'soft' cliffs, such as at Holderness and East Anglia. But Britain is also shrinking around its 'hard' coastal fringes, albeit at very much slower rates.[3] As a result, there have been far fewer studies of the typically less spectacular rates of recession in such areas; that at Birling Gap on the Sussex coast is one such exception (see Chapter 3). As Alfred Steers noted four decades ago, 'It is easier to study the problem where the coastal rocks are relatively weak.'[4]

In broad terms, ancient crystalline rocks are the most durable. Such rocks may be 'fire-derived' igneous varieties that have crystallised from the molten state; either as lavas spewed from a volcano or as intrusive bodies that have cooled at depth in the Earth's crust to be exposed after millions of years of wearing away of the land above. So-called metamorphic rocks have been transformed from older rocks of any type, by the agencies of elevated temperatures and pressures, and they too can be intrinsically tough and hard wearing. Sedimentary rocks, which began life as sediments, such as sand and gravel, laid down in various environments at the surface of the Earth, present a range of durability that is largely a function of the natural bonding agent or cement than binds their component grains together. Thus sandstone can be quite tough or it can be friable depending on the nature of the bond between the mineral grains. The weakest of all rocks and, therefore, those most vulnerable to attack from the sea's power, are those that are geologically young, are in essence unconsolidated and have little or no bond between the component grains. In a coast of mixed rock varieties of differing resistance to erosion, the igneous and metamorphic varieties will typically form headlands, whereas softer sedimentary types are likely to be embayed. Within purely sedimentary sequences, finer grained varieties like shale and siltstone will often be far less durable to attack by the sea than sandstone or conglomerate.

But this is rather an over-simplification. Although it might appear contrary, rock hardness in itself is not necessarily an indication of resistance to marine erosion. This is because rock is seldom, if ever, a continuous, homogeneous, uniform body. Rock masses are sliced through by fractures, known as joints, which can be very close together or wide apart. Unlike joints along which no offset movement has taken place, faults are also present in many rock masses. To add to the complication, naturally layered rocks of sedimentary varieties, like sandstone and limestone, have another set of discontinuities subdividing them – the bedding planes themselves. Bedding planes are the manifestation of natural breaks in the deposition of a sedimentary sequence; a reflection of the episodic, as opposed to continuous, nature of the accumulation of sediment particles. So rock masses are typically cut in several different orientations by planes of weakness that are the primary control on how they will resist wave attack and the impact of the weather.

Waves do not only attack the bases of cliffs

At exposed sites on the deep water coasts of Scotland – around Shetland, Orkney, Caithness and the Outer Hebrides – extreme storm waves are capable of dislodging huge blocks of rock from cliff tops, shifting and depositing these at high altitudes and at significant distances inland. Such cliff-top storm deposits are found at varying elevations that can reach up to 50 metres above sea level. Eye-witness accounts, field studies and modelling have shown that boulders between 1 and 40 cubic metres in volume can become quarried by waves from cliff tops in these harsh environments. Occasionally, much larger blocks can become dislodged by the slam forces generated. Waves are capable of overtopping cliffs of 10 to 30 metres in height and, as they do, bores of water develop that surge across the flat cliff top platforms, quite literally bulldozing the dislodged boulders inland.[5]

Open discontinuities in rocks can permit the ingress of rainwater. If the temperature falls such that this freezes, it will swell in volume by around 10 per cent and, just as ice can exert bursting pressures within household plumbing systems, blocks of rock may become dislodged by this expansion. Repeated cycles of freezing and thawing are very powerful

breakers of rocks. Thus, the weathering of cliffs by this process of disintegration due to freeze–thaw action can be an important contributor to and
promoter of coastal rock falls, especially following the winter months.
Rock strength is no indicator of resistance to freeze–thaw action. Soft
rocks that are permeable with inter-connected pore spaces offer room for
expansion as water freezes within them. By contrast, crystalline rocks, that
are tough with little or no permeability, can be far more susceptible to frost
shattering. The sea, breaking waves in particular, will exploit these
weaknesses mercilessly (Plate 56), eroding caves along the zones of crushed

Isostatic uplift preserves a legendary place of refuge

On the west coast of the Isle of Arran in the Firth of Clyde, several
caves have been eroded by the waves into sandstones of Permian age
at An Cumhann near Blackwaterfoot. The largest of these is the
King's Cave, its name derived from the legend that it sheltered
Robert the Bruce while he was hiding on the island.[6] It has,
however, been noted that this cave was at one time known as
Fingal's Cave and the popular story of Bruce's occupation is without
foundation.[7] Thus, it has been reputed as a residence of the
legendary Fionn mac Cumhaill and the Fianna when hunting in
Arran.[8] But whoever they have given shelter to from wind, rain and
enemy over the centuries, the eccentric shapes of the mouths of the
caves can be seen to be controlled by the orientations of inclined
faults that slice through the sedimentary rocks (Plate 57). With
grassy welcome mats, these caves are now, however, high and dry.
Beyond the reach of waves for some 5,000 years or so, and thus no
longer being actively eroded by the sea, they have been elevated
above present day high water mark by isostatic uplift (see Chapter
2). They are thus relict features. Above the roofs of the caves, a higher
uplifted terrace cut into the cliff, now covered with vegetation,
marks the position of a still older sea level. Should the time come
when eustatic sea level rise exceeds isostatic uplift in this part of
Scotland, then these caves and others like them will become reacti-
vated, and the cliffs into which they are eroded may find themselves
subject to marine-driven retreat once again.

or broken rock that are often found along the planes of faults, along joints and along weak bedding planes.

As caves become progressively widened and deepened landward, parts of their roofs can collapse to form blow holes (Plate 58). Such features are also known by the term 'gloup', a quintessentially onomatopoeic descriptor of the sound made by the lapping waves below as heard funnelling through the rocky hornpipe to the cliff top above. With further collapse, as the sea cuts back into a cliff, long narrow slotlike features, given the name geo from the old Viking word, are chiselled out (Plate 59). Sometimes arches are formed if the rocks that comprise the beam are sufficiently strong to support themselves (Plate 60), but collapse is inevitable at some point in the future. Isolated remnants of cliffs stand proud and removed as pinnacles known as stacks, sometimes in lines or clusters, but often spectacularly alone. The Needles, Old Harry Rocks, Lost World, Tower of Babel, Chocolate Finger, Fist and Finger, The Old Man of Stoer, the Herdsman, the Old Man of Hoy, the Knee, Gibb's Craig, Tom Thumb, Little Stack, Muckle Stack, the Deil's (Devil's) Head, Rock and Spindle, Lot's Wife (Plate 61) – magical names, all of which refer to dramatic, erect, but isolated rocky remnants around the shores Britain – sea stacks – each one a stark reminder of the power of the sea eroding our islands. Nearby, low stumps of reefs with waves engulfing and spraying over them at high water afford a reminder of the eventual fate that awaits such currently proud eminences like Orkney's Old Man of Hoy. Stacks like these, moreover, are subject to a double whammy; at the perpetual mercy of marine erosion at their bases whilst disintegration due to freeze–thaw action in the winter is weathering away their upper reaches (Plate 62).

The coast is dynamic, ever changing – today's cave is tomorrow's natural arch or tomorrow's geo; today's natural arch is tomorrow's stack; today's stack is tomorrow's reef (Plates 64, 65 and 66). To paraphrase the late Professor Derek Ager, who described the history of any one part of the Earth in such terms; change at the coast, 'like the life of a soldier, consists of long periods of boredom and short periods of terror'.[9] On rocky coasts, 'tomorrow' may seem a long way away, as though true to its word it never comes, and then a sudden and violent storm event may alter its form almost beyond recognition within the span of just a few hours. Along our soft coasts of Holderness and East Anglia, the periods of natural terror are rather more frequent, the periods of relative tranquillity rather shorter and the cumulative consequences more severe.

Marsden Rock: sometimes man has to help erosion

A refuge for cormorants, fulmars, and kittiwakes, Marsden rock off the coast of South Shields (Plate 63) is isolated at high tide; a striking stack eroded out of the Magnesian Limestone, a Permian age sedimentary formation. Actively eroding, itself, punctured by caves and incipient arches, the beam of a particularly large and high arch, cut through it by the sea, eventually gave way in 1996, collapsing to create two separate stacks. The smaller was held to be unstable and in the interests of public safety, Marsden Rock's owner, the National Trust, demolished it the following year using explosives. Man had simply been obliged to carry out, for safety's sake, what the power of breaking waves would have done anyway in the fullness of time.

At Nash Point, exposed to violent south-westerly waves, on the Glamorgan Heritage Coast of South Wales, the cliffs are composed of thinly and quite uniformly bedded, pale grey limestone of Jurassic age (Plate 67). Here, the almost horizontal bedding planes that separate the individual sedimentary layers are typically the same dimensions apart as the near to vertical joints that slice through the rock mass. As a result, the rocks are cut into almost perfect cubes by the discontinuities that dissect them. As the waves batter against these rocks in stormy weather, blocks become plucked away and tumble to the beach and broad rocky platform beneath. There, they become jostled, abraded and worn away by the action of swash and backwash, rubbing against each other, against the base of the cliff and against the rocky platform below. The protruding corners of the cubes are the most vulnerable and as they wear away the small cubes progressively become more and more rounded and reduced in size; eventually taking on the form of some of the most near-perfect spherical pebbles that can be found on any beach around Britain's shores (Plate 68). In most places, the pebbles eroded from cliffs will be far less uniform, a reflection of the differences in the spacing between and ordinations of the various planes of weakness that pre-determined their primary block shapes and sizes; the pebbles of Nash Point are all but unique.

The now one-legged Old Man of Hoy: how old is 'old'?

its very name evokes age, unchanging permanence and natural beauty of the Orkneys.[10]

The Old Man of Hoy on the south-west coast of the island of Hoy in the Orkney Islands is an icon. It is hardly surprising that the erect sandstone monolith, atop a basal plinth of basalt, at 137 metres, the highest sea stack in Britain, is believed by many to be a symbol of manhood. However, nothing could be further from the truth. When it was named, this spectacular 'man' had two legs with a natural arch between them. The beam of the arch has since collapsed leaving rock rubble strewn on the shore between the stack and the 'mainland'. But how old is the old man? A map of the area produced in 1750 by McKenzie shows a headland protruding into the sea but no stack present.[11] The British landscape artist, engraver and writer William Daniell visited Hoy as part of his epic voyage round the coast of Scotland and the adjacent islands from 1815 to 1822.[12] His magnificent 1815 sketch of the Old Man of Hoy shows the two legs that gave him his name originally (Plate 69). The arch between these and the cleft between the landward leg and the 'mainland' had thus been eroded by the sea during the intervening six to seven decades. Daniell's sketch also depicts several cones of fallen rocky debris at the edge of the 'mainland' along with larger dislodged blocks of rock, poised to tumble. A severe storm in the early nineteenth century was to lay claim to the leg closest to the land leaving just one leg standing to this day. It, too, is in danger of collapse as the sea continues its relentless pounding and fractures within the rock mass are opening up due to weathering. The 'old' man in geological terms is really quite young, a mere boy of a few hundred years of age at the most.

'SOFT' CLIFFS AND COASTAL LANDSLIDES

Soft rock cliffs can be no less impressive than those carved out of hard materials. At the base of the long promontory of Filey Brigg, on the Yorkshire coast, a thin sequence of Jurassic limestone beds is exposed. The wave-cut notch at the base of the cliff and the adjacent, extensive wave-cut platform, over which a walkway has been concreted, is a stark reminder that the promontory is shrinking. The lower rocks are overlain by a thick pile of brown, clay-rich till laid down in the Pleistocene glaciation. Largely above the level of wave attack, these unconsolidated deposits are, however, particularly vulnerable to the weather – especially to the impact of rain-wash. The protective cover of vegetation is scant at best. As a result, they have become sculpted into spectacular gullies and ridges (Plate 70) that are perhaps more akin to the arid badlands of Arizona than to features one might associate with the spray-lashed Yorkshire coast.

Landslides are natural phenomena along our coasts where cliffs are present, but the magnitude and frequency vary according to the local geological conditions. Landslides are movements of masses of rock, earth or debris down a slope of any kind.[13] They remove materials from hillsides, mountain slopes and, specifically, coastlines, gradually lowering and flattening the topography of the land surface. Their principal driver is the down-slope pulling force of gravity; when this exceeds the inherent resistance of the materials involved, a landslide will take place. At the coast, such failures are triggered mainly by wave erosion undercutting the base of a cliff. However, infiltration of rain water from above can also play an important role in cliff destabilisation, as can ground motion caused by earthquakes.

The stability of rocky cliffs is not only a function of the rock type or types present but, importantly, the spacing between and the orientations of the various planes of weakness – bedding planes, joints and faults; collectively known as discontinuities – that subdivide the rock mass. When the discontinuities are very closely spaced waves readily attack the rocks, plucking out fragments directly and undercutting others thereby enhancing their potential to fall. The converse is usually the case when the discontinuities are, say, metres apart and tightly closed with little or no gape. At Nash Point, the centimetre-scale limestone beds are more or less horizontal. In a situation when such beds are inclined at an angle and the so-called angle of dip (the angle made with the horizontal) is towards the cliff face, then there is the strong potential for what is called a translational landslide or plane failure to take place along one or more of the inclined planes and by such means large masses of rock can become displaced onto a beach or wave-cut platform. A fine example of such a failure took place in the early to mid eighteenth century at An Scriodan, located at the northern tip of the Isle of Arran (Plate 71). Here, the cliffs are formed of coarse-grained sedimentary rocks, sandstones and breccias, of Permian age that are inclined approximately northwards, that is towards the sea, at around 20 degrees from the horizontal. The slide has taken place along one such plane strewing large blocks of rock debris over the contemporary beach, a raised beach and the lower slopes of the cliff for almost 650 metres along the shore. So dramatic was this landslide that it was alleged to have been accompanied 'with a concussion that shook the earth and was heard in Bute and Argyllshire'.[14] Deep, dank, wide and gaping, shore-parallel chasms at the top of the cliff denote the uppermost part of the failed rock mass.

By contrast, if the rocks are inclined in the opposite direction, that is landwards, a cliff face will be much more stable. However, there is still the potential for toppling, forward rotation or over-balancing, of masses of rock. This is a common mode of failure when rock beds are near to vertically inclined, as wave attack undercuts the base of a cliff and rock units tip over and crash to the beach below (Plate 72). In soft cliffs of till and clay that lack well-defined systems of discontinuities, the mode of failure is typically on a concave upwards, curving surface; this results in what is known as a rotational landslide that may develop into a slump or debris flow onto the beach at the foot (Plate 73). The appearance of cracks that are actively opening up at the cliff top, roughly parallel with the coastline, or the formation of a displacement, in other words a step down in the ground-surface level at the seaward edge, offer some forewarning that such a failure is imminent (Plate 74). The final trigger may perhaps be a heavy fall of rain that saturates and increases the weight of the material above the slip face or undercutting by wave attack at the toe or indeed a combination of these.

In one such infamous example, the tell tale signs of movement were seen six weeks before the main failure, when cracks developed in the tarmac surfaces of footpaths across the cliffs. These could not, however, foretell that, at the beginning of June 1993, the media spotlight would be directed with such focus onto the Yorkshire town of Scarborough. Early on the fourth of the month, a large portion of the resort's South Cliff collapsed into the sea reducing the length of the panoramic cliff-top lawn and rose garden of the Holbeck Hall Hotel from around 60 to just 15 metres. Soon, cracks were to appear in the walls of the hotel building itself, leading to a dramatic evacuation of its guests, without injury, during their breakfast. Over the following three days, during which heavy rain fell at times, the building became undermined as the cliff receded by a further 35 metres – thus, this famous hotel toppled bit by bit over the cliff, the jumble of ugly debris strewn forlornly down the bare slope; the remnants had to be demolished. Thousands gathered to watch the spectacle.[15]

This area has a long history of instability; for instance, in 1737, an acre of the South Cliff collapsed onto the beach.[16] The cliff materials comprise soft, clay-rich till laid down during the Pleistocene glaciation resting upon Jurassic sedimentary rocks at the base – much like the sequence exposed at Filey Brigg. The instability is quite natural and the Holbeck Hall Hotel failure was a spectacular example of a rotational landslide that led to a debris flow downslope. Hereabouts, the landslides are triggered principally due to drainage problems in the till and not to direct erosion by the sea at the toe. Indeed, the sea wall at the foot of the failed cliff, whilst buried by debris, was undamaged. However, the June 1993 event delivered a very substantial amount of sediment onto the beach at Scarborough's South Bay, which immediately became subject to longshore transport in a southward direction (Plate 75). When it came to rest, the final dimensions of the land slip were 270 metres from head to toe, 120 metres in width and involved the movement of approximately 1 million tonnes of sediment.[17] Had this rather spectacularly introduced, but quite natural and rather plentiful, supply of sediment to the coastal system been left undisturbed, it would have all been removed, albeit relatively slowly, and transported by wave-induced currents, providing a buffer to erosion at sites elsewhere in that direction. Needless to say, it was regarded as a hazard, an eyesore on the beach, and the slipped deposit was taken away quickly by the author-ities before natural processes could really get to work on it.

The land between the perimeter of the Holbeck Hall Hotel's grounds and the shore beneath was owned by the local authority, Scarborough Borough Council. It is perhaps not surprising that, a few years after the landslide, the owners of the hotel sued the Council for damages in what was to become an important case in English civil law. The allegation was that, as owners of the shoreline, the Council had not taken all measures necessary to prevent the landslide's occurrence, claiming that it was in breach of its obligation to support the adjoining land. This claim succeeded in the first instance, but subsequently the Court of Appeal rejected it, ruling that the landslide was a *natural* coastal phenomenon and the Council could not be held responsible for causing it to occur; the hazard was not a result of the Council's actions.[18]

Immediately to the south of Scarborough at the Knipe Point Estate, overlooking Cayton Bay, a landslide similar to that at Holbeck Hall, but smaller in extent, took place in April 2008. This occurred on a slope which has a very long history of failures.[19] Again the event received much media attention because residents had to be evacuated; two bungalows were rendered unsafe and had to be demolished, whilst dozens of other properties were placed under threat along with the main Scarborough to Filey road.[20] Needless to say, there is ongoing concern for the remaining residents in this locality and the outcome of the Court of Appeal in the Holbeck Hall Hotel case offers them cold comfort, at best. However, Scarborough Borough Council is exploring the potential for relocation (see Chapter 7) by undertaking a project with the Knipe Point community to allocate land where properties lost to coastal erosion and landsliding can be rebuilt. Waveney District Council is exploring similar schemes in Suffolk.[21]

Landsliding is a very important, natural and indeed to be an anticipated characteristic of the geological fabric of many parts of the English Channel coast, most notably on the southern shores of the Isle of Wight and along the fringes of east Devon and Dorset.

> Although some three hectares of coastal land are lost each year from the Isle of Wight through the natural processes of weathering, lands-liding and erosion, this has not promoted a 'fortress mentality' in terms of coastal defence. Residents recognize the importance of coastal erosion as a contribution to the sediment budget which helps to maintain the island's beaches.[22]

In the 1920s, cinema goers were given a unique opportunity to witness the wastage of part of Britain in the form of two unique pieces of silent newsreel footage. These British Pathé films were shot in 1926 and 1928. The first, 'Big Landslide in the Isle of Wight: serious collapse on the

Undercliffe (*sic*) – one of the beauty spots of the island – holds up vehicular traffic',[23] was followed by, 'Great Landslide: downfall of 140,000 tons of rock sweeps away all in its path on its way to the sea.'[24] These are remarkable movie records of the collapse and damage caused by two major landslides that occurred between Blackgang and Ventnor on the south coast of the Isle of Wight.

This English isle, itself once part of the British mainland, prior to rising relative sea level at the end of the Pleistocene glaciation, is no stranger to landslide activity and coastal instability over the centuries, especially along its southern fringes between Blackgang and Ventnor, along the so-called Undercliff.[25] Indeed this part of the island, around 12 kilometres in length and 0.5 kilometre in width, plays host to the largest urban landslide complex in north-western Europe.[26] As Beckles Willson remarked:

> In the district known as the Undercliff a great deal of territory has been lost within the past century. A landslip which occurred in 1810 at East End destroyed 30 acres of ground; another in 1818, above 50 acres; and there have been several since of great severity. The débris of many may be seen, especially of those most recent, on the shore. The most extensive of the modern landslips took place at Niton, in February, 1799, when a small farm-house and about 100 acres of land were destroyed.[27]

Since it was developed and promoted as an amusement park in the mid nineteenth century and one of the island's main tourist attractions, the population of Blackgang has reduced owing to the progressive destruction of houses and infrastructure as the coastal cliffs have retreated due to continual landsliding.[28] The Blackgang Chine Theme Park ('chine' is a word used in southern England and principally in the Isle of Wight to refer to a steep-sided river valley or ravine that has been incised downwards through soft cliffs towards the sea; in some places they are up to 45 metres in depth)[29] has thus had to adapt to this instability by continually relocating its attractions; indeed the chine itself has now been destroyed by landsliding. In January 1994, for instance, following a period of exceptional winter rainfall, a landslide at Blackgang destroyed two cottages, several cars and caravans, a large section of coastal footpath and necessitated the evacuation of some twelve homes within the area of collapse.[30]

The geology of the Isle of Wight is complex, its sedimentary formations having been deformed, folded, faulted and uplifted over geological time. The southern half of the island comprises sequences of sedimentary rocks of Cretaceous age which, in the Blackgang to Ventnor coastal area, are inclined at low angles of one or two degrees to the south, which is towards the English Channel. Hereabouts, in broad terms, relatively permeable sandstone and chalk beds rest upon relatively impermeable clay layers. Rain water, percolating downwards through the sandstone and chalk beds, becomes soaked up by the very porous, yet largely impermeable clay layers, which act in much the same way as a large sponge soaks up bathwater. Once the water reaches the underlying clays, it can infiltrate no further so it accumulates in these 'sponges' and typically seeps out as a series of springs where the upper surfaces of the seaward-inclined clay layers crop out of the cliffs. Following prolonged periods of heavy rainfall, often during the winter and early spring months, this build up of groundwater increases the weight of the rocks forming the cliff and reduces the friction between rock layers. The bedding planes between clay and overlying beds thus act as slip surfaces which, when lubricated by water, can induce seawards mass movements so that sliding failure, often accompanied by back-tilting rotation of the slipped mass, takes place – sometimes to dramatic effect. Termed the Gault Clay Formation, this material is locally referred to as 'blue slipper' – a telling term. Undercutting at the toe by wave erosion of what are essentially soft rock types exacerbates the likelihood of landsliding and collapse in such terrain. Indeed, coastal erosion is often a key triggering event for landslides in this part of the island. Hence, this is an area of quite extreme landsliding instability, which is likely to become even more so as relative sea level rises.

Ventnor itself is situated in an unusual location; the whole town is located within a complex zone of ancient landslides. Its Town Council remarks wryly that this 'makes it quite distinctive as a resort'.[31] Around 200 occurrences of ground movement were documented in the period 1855 to 1989 alone and over the last century at least fifty buildings have had to be demolished due to landsliding.[32] This is a legacy of a coastal town having been developed *ab initio* in the wrong location. The numerous landslides had, over time, created stunning and varied coastal scenery that was a magnet to Victorian holidaymakers; as is so often the case at the coast, the heart triumphed over the head. The geological foundation conditions were ignored not least because:

The advantages of this reach of the Island have stood the test of too many searching years of medical annotation to need any fresh impetus. The existence and success of the National Hospital for Consumption is alone sufficient evidence of the healing airs of the Undercliff. In fact, Ventnor is a sun-box, and the east and north winds would have to confess that they have not even a visiting acquaintance with her.[33]

On a much smaller and potentially far less dramatic scale, it is not unlike the development of San Francisco in California, astride the splendid scenery created by the San Andreas Fault system. With a resident population of around 7,000, the resort of Ventnor has now grown to such an extent that, in common with Lyme Regis in Dorset in a similar geological situation, 'total avoidance or abandonment are out of the question as is recourse to large-scale and inordinately expensive engineering solutions'.[34] A Landslide Management Strategy for the Isle of Wight has thus been developed to assist those communities at risk, which is designed to:

- reduce the likelihood of future movements by controlling the factors (both natural and man-made) that cause ground movement;
- limit the impact of future ground movement through the adoption of appropriate planning and building controls.[35]

The Local Authority maintains an extensive network of sensors that monitor ground movement at many locations throughout the Undercliff, as well as weather stations that provide valuable rainfall data that can be used to evaluate groundwater levels; an important factor in slope instability. Whilst the whole of this part of the island is inherently unstable and this strategy is in effect merely 'buying time', it is noteworthy that the most serious destabilising factor associated with the development of the Undercliff has been leakage to groundwater from septic tanks, household water pipes, drains, sewers and swimming pools.[36] Human beings, it would seem, are often their own worst enemies.

At Lyme Regis, in Dorsetshire, the 'Church Cliffs' as they are called, one hundred feet in height, gradually fell away between 1800 to 1829, at the rate of one yard a year. A singular landslip occurred in 1839, on the coast of Devonshire, between Lyme Regis and

Axmouth, carrying away a tract three-quarters of a mile long and
240 feet broad.[37]

Lyme Regis is, on closer view, a sober, drab town, lodged in a gorge
or cleft which opens upon the Channel. The houses, like the
Gadarene swine, appear to be running down a steep place into the
sea. At the end of the street they are only prevented from tumbling
into the ocean by a sudden sea-wall, over which they hang
unsteadily. Just a few escape and wander along the beach.[38]

In common with the south coast of the Isle of Wight, the coastal stretch
between Axmouth in east Devon and Lyme Regis in Dorset, part of the
Jurassic Coast UNESCO World Heritage Site, is also called the Undercliff,
and for much the same reason as this is also an area renowned for its landsliding. Indeed some of the most extensive and finest landslides in Britain
have developed along this section of the English Channel coast,[39] a
paradise for fossil hunters and noted especially for its reptilian remains.
Here, yet again, is the classic landsliding combination of gently seaward-
dipping permeable beds of Jurassic and Cretaceous sedimentary rocks
overlying relatively impermeable clay and shale layers. By contrast with the
Blackgang to Ventnor coast, however, the complex of ancient landslides
that comprise this mainland Undercliff are undeveloped and densely
vegetated, and the beaches below it are relatively remote.

The area is perhaps most famous for the massive landslide that took
place at Bindon Manor in 1839. Six and a half hectares of land slipped
seawards between Axmouth and Lyme Regis[40] in what is thought to be
the first landslide that was recorded in systematic scientific detail in both
words and illustrations.[41] The catastrophic event attracted thousands of
onlookers and national publicity, though some were too afraid to visit the
scene. It is even said that Queen Victoria viewed the sight from the Royal
Yacht. Such was the fame of the landslide that it became the inspiration
for a piece of dance music, 'The Landslip Quadrille', composed by
Ricardo Linter, the front cover sheet of which bore an engraving of the
spectacle.[42] Numerous prints were published to illustrate the detailed
written accounts of the event. Essentially, as the land slid towards the sea,
a vast chasm was created in its wake, 200 metres in width, 100 metres in
depth and with a length of 1.5 kilometres. Between the chasm and
theshore there remained an isolated block of displaced land that had

The 'Lyme Volcano' and the hand of man

In 1908 a series of landslides occurred on the eastern side of Lyme Regis, the largest in June without warning involving the collapse of large quantities of shale; 'a portion of the cliff suddenly gave way, and the large mass, weighing many thousand tons, fell forward on to the beach with a loud rustling and rumbling noise, which was plainly heard in the town, while a cloud of sulphurous smoke issued from the burning mound'.[43] The so-called burning mound had formed in a previous, smaller cliff collapse in January of that year and the emergence of smoke from the rocky rubble on a cliff terrace fuelled stories in the press that a volcano had erupted in the area, thus it soon became a tourist attraction. The later landslide occurred from the cliffs beneath the burning mound with the result that it split in half to reveal a burnt interior.[44] Hereabouts, the shale is rich in iron sulphide, the mineral pyrite, commonly referred to as fool's gold owing to its golden lustre. When suddenly exposed to the atmosphere, pyrite reacts with oxygen and, in so doing, energy in the form of heat is released and spontaneous combustion takes place. To boost visitor appeal, the mythical 'Lyme Volcano' was rumoured to have been enhanced by the periodic application of paraffin.[45] The major landslide had followed a period of heavy rain, so often an important trigger. However, this was not the sole cause. Extraction of limestone from the shore below had undermined the stability of the cliff, which, even at the time, was sharply criticised: 'This harmful practice of getting stone from the shore ought to have been forbidden long ago. Stone was formerly taken from below Church Cliffs; but this has been disallowed for many years, and the Lyme people will do well to put a stop to it everywhere.'[46] As almost ever at the coast; the hand of man is seldom far away.

moved seawards creating what was to become known as Goat Island;[47] offshore a short-lived reef was created.[48] Before the landslide took place, 'Goat Island' had been sown with wheat; in August 1840 when the crop had grown and matured to ripeness it was harvested by local damsels dressed as handmaidens in a ceremony dedicated to the Goddess Ceres.[49]

The cause of the Bindon event was disputed in theory and counter-theory by eminent geologists of the day and clergy alike, including its possible initiation by an earthquake or by a volcanic eruption. One preacher is said to have denounced the geologists as infidels, by no means in agreement with the spontaneous combustion of pyrite to account for the sulphurous smells that accompanied the catastrophe.[50] Today the landslide is interpreted as a translational blockslide – a plane failure like that at An Scriodan on the Isle of Arran, but even more impressive in scale – the huge mass of displaced rock moving along the seaward dipping bedding planes, leaving a chasm, or graben, behind.[51] Failure at the base of the slope, almost certainly the work of wave attack, weakened the support at the toe and triggered the dramatic event.

With the exception of the Bindon landslide, it was noted in 1973, following over thirty years of observations in the Lyme Regis area, that there had been a substantial increase in both the rate and scale of landsliding.[52] This trend appears to have continued to the present day. On 6 May 2008, a landslide described as the biggest landslide seen in Britain for a century[53] took place between Lyme Regis and Charmouth, displacing rock materials along a 400 metre reach. Like so many such events, it occurred following a particularly wet winter and spring. Fortunately, it took place in the evening at high tide when the beach was inaccessible to the public. Had it happened earlier in the day (a Bank Holiday) at low water, there could have been catastrophic loss of life.[54] Newspapers reported that giant chunks of land 'the size of cars' were seen cascading into the sea.[55] One reputable news report even stated that this event had 'destroyed' more than 400 metres of Dorset's World Heritage Jurassic Coast,[56] its author failing to appreciate that this is a natural process in the area. Indeed, without such events and without coastal erosion, the Heritage Coast would not have evolved to its present state of such dramatic scenic splendour. Moreover, if it were not for frequent landslides supplying new debris to the beaches and to the longshore transport system, not only would the fossil collector be left wanting but our knowledge of the evolution of life on Earth would be the poorer. Notices might suggest to the public that, over time, the land will 'settle' and landslide activity cease (Plate 76), but time is no healer in landslide-prone terrain. Engineering solutions might offer some valuable respite, even temporary remission, but they cannot provide a 'cure' for such natural geological processes that play a vital role in ensuring that our beaches receive their rightful supply of sediment.

EPILOGUE

The geology of Britain, or any country for that matter, may be thought of like a giant pack of playing cards with many suits. Nature has dealt these to large numbers of players in the game of coastal zone management, each with a stake – politicians, landowners, fishermen, tourists, local residents, local government officials, port operators, scientists, business people, developers, planners, conservationists, to name but a few – who have a range of experiences and abilities, preconceptions and attitudes. Around the table are the cautious, the impetuous, the wise and the foolish, the domineering and the timid; those who have been in the game for a long time and those who are new to it. To complicate matters, the rules can vary from place to place; the game can be played in many ways, in teams of differing sizes or as singles. Moreover, the actions of one player or team are very much determined by previous events, previous actions and reactions. It is a game that has been around for centuries, so some knowledge and experience of how best to play it must surely have been handed down? Where are we in that game in twenty-first century Britain; have we been playing it long enough to learn? This will be explored in the following chapter.

6

LESSONS FROM THE PAST: WHAT CAN WE LEARN THAT WILL HELP COASTAL ZONE MANAGEMENT?

Here lies a fair fat land;
But now its townships, kirks, graveyards
Beneath bald hills of sand
Lie buried deep as Babylonian shards.
But gales may blow again;
And like a sand-glass turned about
The hills in a dry rain
Will flow away and the old land look out;
And where now hedgehog delves
And conies [rabbits] *hollow their long caves*
Houses will build themselves
And tombstones rewrite names on dead men's graves.

Andrew Young, 'Culbin Sands', *Collected Poems*, 1936

COASTAL ZONE MANAGEMENT IS NOTHING NEW

'History repeats itself' and 'we fail to learn from past mistakes' are commonly used clichés. However, are they true with respect to the coast of Britain and to the ways in which it is managed? First of all though, do we have an appropriate historical record from which to learn? The answer to the last question is an unequivocal 'yes'. It is a misconception that what is today referred to as 'coastal zone management' is a new phenomenon. When and where it began is impossible to ascertain. However, each of the three component countries of Britain has a strong claim to the title as will be explored below. First, Scotland has well over three centuries of appreciation of adverse human impacts in the coastal zone along with what must surely be one of the earliest pieces of common sense coastal legislation prohibiting specific damaging activities.

The late nineteenth-century *Ordnance Gazetteer of Scotland: A Survey of Scottish Topography, Statistical, Biographical and Historical* encapsulates a historical perspective of the Culbin Sands on the southern shores of the Moray Firth (Figure 6.1). The desertification of this once fertile coastal estate has been attributed to the uprooting of bent, juniper and broom bushes; bent being another name for marram grass. These materials, especially marram, make excellent roofing and so were sought after and harvested by the local people. Marram is an incredibly strong grass with sharp leaves. Its root system spreads rapidly like a mat through sand dunes and thus it, along with juniper and broom bushes, has a powerful stabilising effect. So destabilising was the continual removal of these plants that a storm in 1694 was the culmination of a gradual degradation process that created Scotland's Sahara burying the Culbin estate and its dwellings. So great was the devastation that the following year, 1695, an Act of Parliament was passed prohibiting the uprooting of shrub vegetation from the dunes (referred to at the time as 'sand-hills') in order not to destabilise the accumulated sand, thereby preventing it from being eroded by wind and thus blown inland 'ruining' nearby agricultural land and meadows:

Our sovereign lord, considering that many lands, meadows and pasturages lying on the sea coasts have been ruined and overspread

Culbin, a sandy desert on the southern coast of the Moray Firth, extending across the entire breadth of Dyke and Moy parish, Elginshire, into Kinloss parish, Elginshire, and Auldearn parish, Nairnshire. Comprising some 9500 acres of what was once the very garden of Moray, it began to be overwhelmed with sand as far back as 1100, according to Boece; but the barony itself of Culbin was not destroyed till 1670-95, 'the which was mainly occasioned by the pulling up by the roots of bent, juniper, and broom bushes, which did loose and break the surface and scroof of the sand-hills.' Now all is covered with sand or sand-hills, to a depth in places of 100 feet. The worst parts lie immediately west of the lagoon and mouth of the Findhorn river, and these underwent so great a change as to shift the river's mouth nearly 2 miles eastward, and to overwhelm the ancient town and harbour of Findhorn.—*Ord. Sur.*, shs. 84, 94, 1876-78. See vol. iii., pp. 119, 120, of Chambers's *Domestic Annals of Scotland* (1861).

Figure 6.1 The entry for Culbin in the Ordnance Gazetteer of Scotland (1884). *A Survey of Scottish Topography, Statistical, Biographical and Historical*, Volume 2.

in many places of this kingdom by sand driven from adjacent sand-hills, the which has been mainly occasioned by the pulling up by the root of bent, juniper and broom bushes which did loosen and break the surface and skin of the said hills. And particularly considering that the barony of Culbin and house and yards thereof, lying within the sheriffdom of Elgin, is quite ruined and overspread with sand, the which was occasioned by the foresaid bad practice of pulling the bent and juniper, therefore, his majesty, with advice and consent of the estates of parliament, for preventing of the like prejudices in time coming, does strictly prohibit and discharge the pulling of bent, broom or juniper of sand-hills for hereafter, either by the proprietors themselves, or any other whomsoever, the same being the natural fences of the adjacent countries to the said hills; certifying such as shall contravene this act, they shall not only be liable to the damages that shall then ensue, but shall likewise be liable in the sum of £10 of penalty, the one half thereof to belong to the informer, and the other half to the judge within whose jurisdiction the said contravention shall be committed.[1]

The very steep £10 penalty for violating this 1695 Act is a striking reflection of just how seriously this malpractice was regarded at the time; in 2010 this amount would have equated with an enormous fine of around £17,000. This is quite possibly the earliest piece of coastal zone management legislation in Britain. It was not until the acquisition of Culbin Sands by the Forestry Commission in the early 1920s that much of the area was stabilised by the planting of trees and their associated undergrowth.[2]

England, however, can perhaps lay claim to a slightly longer appreciation of the need for coastal management. For instance, dune erosion along the Irish Sea coastal borough of Sefton in Merseyside, once part of Lancashire, was regarded as a problem from at least the early seventeenth century.[3] At that time, attempts were made to stabilise the sand by planting marram grass, also known at the time as star grass. The need for such stabilisation was taken so seriously that in the 1630s so-called 'Hawslookers' were appointed by local the Manors of Ainsdale and Birkdale to watch over the dunes to ensure that the marram grass, once planted, was protected.[4] It would appear that their vigilance was not in vain as in 1637 three inhabitants of Ainsdale and Birkdale were each fined one shilling[5] (five pence) for gathering marram; a material ideally suited to mat making, besom production and roof thatching, so there was much incentive to obtain it. It is apparent that by the early eighteenth century, the introduction of further measures to prevent erosion of the dunes had become necessary. Furthermore, the punishment for any person convicted of cutting or removing marram grass was, however, to become increasingly severe. In 1711 it was legislated that, as a service to the lords of the manors, the planting of star grass was compulsory for those tenants who leased areas of dune land.[6] The marram planters were known as 'star-setters'. Local landowner Nicholas Blundell, Lord of the Manor of Little Crosby, is noted for his prolific diary writings on the life of the gentry in early eighteenth century England. These also record many of his observations of star-setting in the Sefton dune lands. Indeed, he even appears to have taken an active role in the planting himself. Blundell's entry for 20 April 1722, however, has a sinister air as he records that: 'I gave Mr Peters Orders to get a Warant for Ann Ballard for Cutting the Starr.'[7] Within the week, his orders had clearly been acted upon as, in his account for 26 April, Blundell reported that: 'Robert Lunt the Cunstable of Ince brought Richard Ballards Wife a Prisoner to me, he took her yesterday with a Warant for cutting Starr in my Warant.'[8] One can but speculate what happened thereafter to the unfortunate Mrs Ballard as a record of her fate was not consigned to posterity in the pages of Blundell's diaries. Clearly, star cutting was a real problem that could well have contributed to the events some two years previously, in December 1720, that are referred to in Blundells' diary entry of 20 June 1722:

> Parson Acton, Mr Syer and Mr Byron the Church-Wardens &c were here abeging upon Account of the Great Losses sustained in Lancashire in Dec: An: Do: 172/0/ by the violent overflowing of ye Sea; the Sea had overflowed 6600 Aikers of Land, had washed down 157 Houses, and damnifyed 200 more, the whole loss was computed to be more than £10,227.[9]

Even the combined powers of 'Star Lookers' to prevent marram cutting and legislation to make its planting mandatory were unable to prevent very severe erosion in 1739 when a great storm blew vast amounts of sand up to a mile inland from the coastline. This single sandstorm event buried completely the village of Ravenmeols;[10] meols is the Old Norse word for

Blundell's diaries and 'the greatest storm'

Daniel Defoe's account of the late November 1703 storm (see Chapter 1) noted that it induced tidal surges, 'that with such unusual violence, brought up the sea raging in such a manner, that in some parts of England it was incredible, the water rising 6 or 8 feet higher than it was ever known to do in the memory of man; by which ships were fleeted up upon the firm land several rods off from the banks, and an incredible number of cattle and people drowned; as in the pursuit of this story will appear.'[11] Nicholas Blundell's diary entries, however, help to play an important role in determining the northern extent of the devastation in Britain. Had this event impacted upon the shores of Blundell's Lancashire estate at Crosby, it is most unlikely that his sole entry for the 26 of the month would have read: 'Lord Biss: Smith of Callipolis in Asia and Mr. Martin, came to Lodg here.' An additional note explained: 'Right Rev. James Smith, Bishop of Callipolis, V.A. of Northern District May 13 1688. Died May 13, 1711, aged 66. He confirmed 110 at Crosby.'[12] It seems more than improbable that record of even the visit of the vicar apostolic would have taken priority over death or destruction, thus providing important indirect evidence that the effects of this tempestuous storm were confined to the southern parts of the country.

sand dunes. Such was the encroachment of sand that only a farmhouse and a rabbit warren remained. Today Ravenmeols survives but in the name of a lane only. Moreover, reminiscent of the Quendale story in Shetland, this same storm caused extreme damage to Formby Chapel and its graveyard, and thus a decision was taken to relocate the place of worship further inland.[13] A nearby freshwater lake, known as Kirklake, was also infilled by the blown sand.[14] Formby's Kirklake Road is a reminder of its former existence.

The perceived requirement for additional legislation to protect the marram grass thereby preventing dune erosion resulted in a further Act of Parliament being passed in 1742; 'For the more effectual preventing of the cutting up of Starr [sic] or Bent':

Whereas it has been found by experience that the best way to
preserve the said hills from being blown away, is to plant them with
a certain rush or shrub called Starr or Bent . . . And whereas many
idle and disorderly persons residing near the said coasts do unlaw-
fully and maliciously in the night time as well as in the day, cut, pull
up, and carry away the Starr or Bent . . . And instead of working in
an honest manner for the maintenance and support of their families,
do privately sell the said Starr or Bent for making mats, brushes and
brooms or besoms . . . it shall be lawful for His Majesty's justices of
the peace, to issue warrants to apprehend the persons . . . And being
thereof convicted, they shall pay the sum of twenty shillings, one
moiety to the informer, and the other to the lord or owner of such
Starr or sandhills, or to commit the person to the house of
correction for the space of three months, and for a second offence
one year in jail, there to be whipt and kept to hard labour . . . And
if any Starr or Bent shall be found in the custody or possession of
anyone within five miles of the sandhills they shall be convicted and
pay twenty shillings.[15]

Although the fine for possession or custody of star grass, 20 shillings or £1,
is a mere one tenth of that imposed by the Culbin Sands Act of 1695, the
penalties of imprisonment, whipping and hard labour for selling it are
powerful deterrents that underpin the Lancashire coastal zone
management strategy of the day. The requirement of lessees of land to plant
marram grass was taken very seriously. Two such tenants in the Manors of
Birkdale and Ainsdale were, in 1763, each fined the sum of one shilling
(five pence today) for sending boys to 'set starr', a task so important that it
was regarded as man's work.[16] Starr Lookers were appointed by Formby
Court to determine whereabouts marram grass should be planted and, to
ensure that this was indeed carried out, the tenants were levied a rate
according to the area of land that they leased. Those who refused to pay
this were faced with a fine of £1 19s 6d;[17] a rather hefty sum that amounts
to over £3,350 at 2010 rates. The controlled planting of marram grass
continued well into the nineteenth century as did prosecutions for
harvesting it. Notices were erected at several places along the coast,
Birkdale, Ainsdale and Formby, to remind the public of the very severe
penalties for removing marram as laid out in the 1742 Act of Parliament.[18]
Today the main threat to the dunes at Formby comes not from marram-

stealers but from the sea itself. For the last century or so, the beach has been eroding at an average rate of about 4 metres per year and severe storms can cause recession of the dunes by as much as 12 to 15 metres in just one event.[19] Although there is usually some recovery as wind-driven accretion follows erosion, the net trend, with rising relative sea level, is for the dunes to be progressively eaten away. This is something even Hawslookers cannot prevent.

Removal of marram grass still continues but for very different reasons

On 28 April 2010, newspapers and television news programmes reported that more than 1,000 square metres of marram grass had been ripped out of the dunes on the Menie Estate, near Balmedie north of Aberdeen.[20] This area lies within the Sands of Forvie, a spectacular dune system that is a Site of Special Scientific Interest. Along with vandalism to fences and machinery on the site, this act was certainly not carried out with the intention of manufacturing matting, besoms or tablemats. Rather, it was a protest against the construction of United States tycoon Donald Trump's highly controversial £1 billion golf resort and complex, due for completion in 2012. What is certain, however, is that the perpetrators, if indeed they are apprehended, will be spared the sentence of hard labour.

In other parts of Britain, legislation was not so enlightened. For instance, in 1609 an Act of Parliament was passed, 'for the taking, loading of sea sand for the bettering of the ground and for the increase of corn and tillage within the counties of Devon and Cornwall'.[21] Along the north coast of Cornwall this practice of fertilising the land with shell-rich sands led to the removal of vast quantities of material from local beaches. Sands from Bude were one great source of supply; 4,000 horse-drawn loads are known to have been removed in a single day. In 1839 it was calculated that of the order of 5,600,000 cubic feet of sand were taken from the coast annually.[22] Sand extraction has now ceased in most areas, although it was still continuing on a small scale at some sites as recently as 2007.[23] This is

Plate 62 The pinnacles of the 'Stacks of Death' at Duncansby Head in the Devonian age sandstones of Caithness are being eroded by wave action at their bases whilst disintegrating in their upper parts due to freeze–thaw action (photo R.W. Duck).

Plate 63 Marsden Rock off the South Shields coast, Tyne and Wear (photo R.W. Duck).

Plate 64 The arch of Thirl Door near Duncansby Head, Caithness – soon to collapse to form a stack like Gibb's Craig in the distance (photo R.W. Duck).

Plate 65 Caves, incipient geos and reefs eroded out of Torridonian Sandstones at Enard Bay, Wester Ross (photo R.W. Duck).

Plate 66 The cliffs, wave-cut platform and punctured stack of Trow Point near South Shields, Tyne and Wear, eroded out of sedimentary sequences of Permian age (photo R.W. Duck).

Plate 67 Nash Point on the Glamorgan Heritage Coast of South Wales. Recession of the Jurassic limestone cliff is indicated by the extensive wave-cut platform (photo R.W. Duck).

Plate 68 Exposed at low tide, a nest of near-spherical limestone pebbles on the rocky platform beneath Nash Point (photo R.W. Duck).

Plate 69 William Daniell's 1815 sketch of the Old Man of Hoy showing its then two 'legs' with a natural arch between (reproduced by courtesy of The National Library of Scotland).

Plate 70 The 'badlands' of Filey Brigg – spectacular ridges and gullies developed in till layers due to rain erosion (photo R.W. Duck).

Plate 71 Part of the rock fall from the extensive translational landslide at An Scriodan, Isle of Arran. The large block to the left of the field of view (approximately due north) has come to rest at approximately the same angle of inclination as when *in situ* (photo R.W. Duck).

Plate 72 Toppling failure of slabs of near-to-vertically bedded sandstones of Lower Devonian age, near Cowie, Kincardineshire (photo R.W. Duck).

Plate 73 Landsliding of clay-rich till onto the beach near Robin Hood's Bay (photo R.W. Duck).

Plate 74 A step down in the ground-surface level at the seaward edge of a cliff offers some forewarning that a rotational landslide is imminent at Aldbrough, Holderness (photo R.W. Duck).

Plate 75 The Holbeck Hall Hotel landslide, Scarborough, of June 1993 seen from the air. In the foreground is the now closed and infilled South Bay swimming pool (photo courtesy of The Lighthouse for Learning, North East Lincolnshire Council).

Plate 76 Notice at Saltburn-by-the-Sea, North Yorkshire, suggesting that a landslide-prone cliff will 'settle' or eventually become stable. The length of time this has been in place, as witnessed by its degree of deterioration, is telling (photo R.W. Duck).

Plate 77 Coastal interpretation notices today no longer refer to hefty fines or the penalty of hard labour for the cutting of marram grass (photo R.W. Duck).

Plate 78 Controlled access through the dunes to the West Sands of St Andrews, Fife (photo R.W. Duck).

Plate 79 Churchill Barrier No. 4 and the beach-dune system of the Ayre of Cara (photo R.W. Duck).

Plate 80 The curving sweep of the stepped Earth Sculpture, Llanelli, showing protective rock armour defences installed since its construction together with clear evidence of recent erosion along the back edge of the sandy beach (photo courtesy of V. Powell).

Plate 81 The path to nowhere – erosion damage to the Millennium Coastal Path near Llanelli as a result of the severe storm in March 2007 (photo courtesy of V. Powell).

Plate 82 Erosion damage at Anstruther, Fife, caused by the storm of 30 March 2010. Repairs to the sea wall have begun (photo R.W. Duck).

Plate 83 The foundations and brick fireplace are all that remains of a house, demolished before the sea could do its work at Aldbrough in Holderness (photo R.W. Duck).

Plate 84 The forlorn state of the beach, cliffs and remains of houses at Happisburgh in the summer of 2008 (photo courtesy of L. Booth).

Plate 85 Oblique aerial view over the village of Happisburgh showing recession of the soft cliff that threatens the houses immediately to landward of the old, partially breached, sea defences of rock armour and timber revetments. A large erosional bight is present beyond the southern end of the defences in the foreground (photo taken 25 January 2007, Copyright Mike Page: www.mike-page.co.uk)

Plate 86 The dramatic fragility of the narrow neck of the heavily developed and much defended Sandbanks spit is revealed in this Light Detection and Ranging (LIDAR) image from 2008 (image courtesy of the Channel Coastal Observatory).

ironic given that beaches and dunes are so important to the region's tourist industry, and it will come as no surprise to find that the long ongoing activity has led to accelerated erosion of nearby cliffs in many areas of south-west England.[24]

The vast expanse of rolling hills that form the Merthyr Mawr dunes near Bridgend in South Wales, the highest in Britain, was probably at one time the largest dune complex in Europe. Legend has it that the landward encroachment of the sands engulfed the now lost village of Treganllaw much in the same way that nearby Kenfig was buried. So desolate and desert-like are these dunes that they were used as the perfect location to film scenes in David Lean's 1962 direction of the epic *Lawrence of Arabia*. In AD 1119, local church-goers found that large amounts of windblown sands had accumulated around the church door.[25] Since that time, vegetation like sea buckthorn has been planted to stabilise the mobile sands and pine trees have been planted, in much the same way as at Culbin, at the back of the dunes in an effort to promote their stabilisation and prevent such encroachment. Planting vegetation to stabilise sand dunes is often thought of as a modern form of soft engineering, but, as along the Sefton and latterly the Culbin coast, it was being practised in this part of Wales centuries ago. It is also interesting to note that myxomatosis, the deadly virus that spread through Britain in the 1950s,[26] led to a remarkable increase in the area of stable sand dunes at Merthyr Mawr.[27] This is a measure of the immense burrowing impact of these fast-breeding warren dwellers, but also an epitome of Shakespeare's metaphor in *Henry VI*, Part 3; 'Ill blows the wind that profits nobody.'

Today we still erect notices along dune coasts but for different reasons. Times have changed though; marram is no longer such a coveted commodity. It is no longer a raw ingredient of the amenities of contemporary living. In many parts of Britain, dunes and beaches require protection from us and our leisure pursuits. Humans, their animals, their vehicles and their toys can collectively have a huge erosive impact on the coast caused by trampling and driving. Large animals, like horses, ponies and donkeys, can be particularly harmful. Sheep and cattle grazing also cause damage in certain areas as does the inappropriate use of motorbikes, cars, mountain bikes, sand buggies, quad bikes and other all-terrain vehicles. This is especially the case in areas of high visitor numbers like the popular Cornish coast. Visitor management is therefore aimed at reducing this damaging effect, the principal objective being to keep people, their

Objectives of the Sefton Coast Partnership Research Strategy

Today's coastal management strategies are rather different, due in large measure to the co-operative work of voluntary, non-statutory Local Coastal Partnerships such as the Sefton Coast Partnership whose research strategy aims:

- To set the Sefton Coast in its regional, national and international context and to encourage links with other sites
- To encourage multi-disciplinary studies to look at complex issues (for example, the implications of climatic change)
- To encourage studies that look at the whole of the dune system and the wider coastal system
- To enable the managing agencies to generate and support research work
- To maintain a register of research or monitoring projects suitable for school, undergraduate and postgraduate studies
- To encourage research areas in proportion to their capacity to help achieve management objectives
- To disseminate information about research and monitoring activities being undertaken in and around the Sefton Coast.[28]

vehicles and their pets away from the areas they are likely to damage. So today's notices, by and large, are designed with the aid of high quality maps and photographs to help coastal zone management by informing the public as to what to look for in terms of natural processes, landforms, plants and animals, how best to enjoy the environment, where and where not to go, what and what not to do; the threat of hard labour no longer gets a mention (Plate 77).

In especially fragile areas, where excess trampling might damage vegetation or destabilise dunes and stimulate erosion above the natural norm, specially constructed wooden walkways, beneath and through which wind blown sand can pass freely, are now the usual means by which to guide the passage of the footfall and perhaps even the hoof fall to and from the beach (Plate 78). It is noteworthy that, as long ago as 1953, the eminent coastal geographer, the late Professor Alfred Steers, wrote: 'It is difficult to convince people who only visit the coast for a summer holiday that the making of tracks through dunes may be a very real danger.'[29] Steers even went so far as to suggest on the basis of survey work that trampled dunes may well have aided the attack of the sea along parts of the Lincolnshire coast during the 1953 storm surge disaster. So the damage that we are capable of doing to dunes should by no means be underestimated.[30] Rocky coasts that attract large numbers of visitors like the Jurassic Coast World Heritage Site of Dorset and East Devon also require management[31] to prevent inappropriate fossil and rock specimen collecting, footpath erosion and other ill-informed tourist activities.

On Chesil Beach

From hence the shore winding in and out shooteth far into the Sea, and a banke caled Chesil of sands heaped up thick together (with a narrow firth betweene) lieth in length for nine miles, which the South-wind when it is up commonly cutteth in sunder and disperseth, but the Northren wind bindeth and hardneth againe. By this Bank or Sand-ridge Portland, sometime an Iland, is now adjoined to the mainland.[32]

In 1842 a storm burst over the Chesil Bank with great fury, and the village of Chesilton, built upon its southern extremity, was overwhelmed, with many of its inhabitants.[33]

Approaching 30 kilometres in length, Chesil Beach in Dorset (see also Chapter 3) is without doubt one of the most famous landforms on the British coast[34] and 'indeed probably the most extensive and extraordinary accumulation of shingle in the world'.[35] It was originally an offshore gravel bank but, as ice melted and relative sea level rose after the Pleistocene glaciation, it became pushed landward by wave and current action. Along about half of its length it encloses the Fleet, which is the largest tidal lagoon in Britain – as such it is known as a barrier beach. It links the 'island' of Portland in the east to the Dorset mainland in the west (Figure 6.2) and the dominant longshore transport direction is from west to east. A fragile, endangered environment, Site of Special Scientific Interest and part of the UNESCO Jurassic Coast World Heritage Site, its natural supply of sediment is now limited. Commercial extraction of an estimated two per cent of its materials between the 1930s and the late 1970s is believed to have exacerbated the threat of erosion and the flooding of villages, such as Chiswell, to landward.[36] Today a by-law exists, enforced by Weymouth and Portland Borough Council, that prohibits the removal of even a handful of pebbles, such is the perceived vulnerability of the landform. Little did famous author and Man Booker Prize winner Ian McEwan suspect that he was in violation of this legislation when, in 2007, he was facing a fine of £2,000 for removing a handful of pebbles from Chesil Beach,[37] whilst researching the setting for his forthcoming romantic novel.[38] The 'stolen' pebbles were duly returned by McEwan at the request of the Council and thus payment of an embarrassing fine was avoided.[39]

Figure 6.2 Map of Chesil Beach, Dorset (reproduced from Avebury, The Right Hon. Lord (1902) *The Scenery of England and the Causes to Which it is Due*. The Macmillan Company, London).

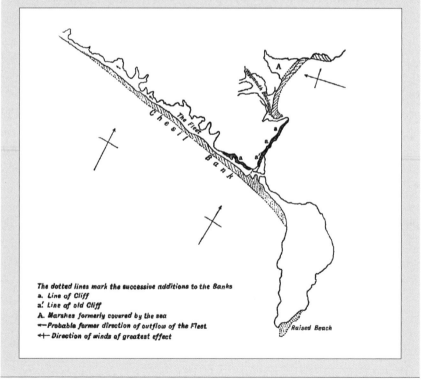

The dotted lines mark the successive additions to the Banks
a. *Line of Cliff*
a.' *Line of old Cliff*
A. *Marshes formerly covered by the sea*
←—*Probable former direction of outflow of the Fleet*
+|—*Direction of winds of greatest effect*

Raised Beach

Offshore leisure activities can also have harmful effects. As well as creating noise pollution, fast power boats and other vessels create wakes that can cause wash erosion along soft coasts, especially if such craft are navigated for bravado or thrill-seeking at high speeds inappropriately close to the shore. This can cause sediment to be stirred up and transported offshore. In fact, boat wakes can be the dominant source of energy impinging on a shoreline during otherwise calm weather conditions. Allied to this is the impact of larger vessels on shores. For instance, increased erosion along the shores of the embayment of Loch Ryan in south-west Scotland, at the head of which is the port of Stranraer, has been attributed to the wash created by the new breed of fast ferries that are now deployed on the route to Northern Ireland.[40] Some opinions have blamed ship wake for enhancing coastal erosion along beaches near the major port of Felixstowe in Suffolk.

Visitors to the coast and local people alike quite understandably enjoy clean, litter-free beaches. To this end, to encourage an influx of visitors to their coastal resorts, local authorities in many parts of Britain expend considerable sums on keeping their beaches clean, often as part of achieving or maintaining 'Blue Flag' or 'Seaside Award' status. At one time, items of litter and dead seaweed were cleared by hand, but today the tendency is increasingly to clean beaches mechanically, sometimes on a daily basis in summer, using specially manufactured rakes being towed behind tractors. Whilst this is aesthetically pleasing for beach users, the clearing of seaweed debris and mats actually removes a natural protection against erosion, an absorber of wave energy. Furthermore, mechanical raking or combing, although a much speedier process than hand picking, has the added drawback of disturbing and decompacting beach sands, rendering them far more susceptible to erosion and removal from a beach face during storms. Conservation volunteers and residents of Cramond, a village suburb on the southern shores of the Forth Estuary close to Edinburgh, were convinced that tractors used to clean the beach by the local authority were responsible for ongoing erosion resulting in a steady reduction in its size. Before mechanical cleaning, when litter and seaweed were cleared by hand, erosion was not a problem. The campaign for reduced mechanical cleaning at the site has been successful and this has resulted in an immediate measureable success; a return to stable conditions.[41] Similar problems are evident elsewhere around Britain's shores as regular mechanical cleaning of beach debris is increasing in popularity.

Winston Churchill inadvertently does his bit to stop Britain shrinking

The Ayre of Cara is one of the most rapidly accreting beach–dune systems in Britain and is the only such site in the Orkney Islands where all other beaches are, by and large, eroding. Colonisation by marram grass, lyme grass and other species has stabilised much of the dunes. The area is popular for recreational use as it is readily accessible and the local authority has provided a car park, toilets and interpretation boards. In addition, it has granted a licence for the commercial extraction of sand from part of this site. However, the

Figure 6.3 Location map of the Churchill Barriers in the Orkney Islands (drawing by T. Dixon).

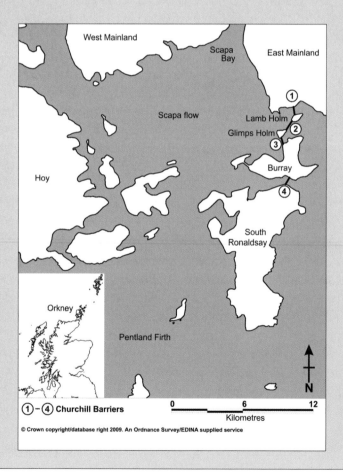

amenity should not be where it is located; its origin is entirely due to relatively recent human intervention. A causeway, known as Churchill Barrier No. 4, one of four constructed in the 1940s on the orders of then Prime Minister Winston Churchill, to protect the British naval fleet in Scapa Flow from enemy attack, has completely cut off the natural east-to-west sediment transport in Water Sound between the islands of Burray and South Ronaldsay (Figure 6.3 and Plate 79). With an average lateral rate of advance of 1 to 6 metres per year, depending upon the location along the length of the barrier, the Ayre of Cara is the unintentional consequence of this action.[42] The sand has not been permitted to travel to where nature intended and this raises the question, who owns it? It is quite possible that the local authority do not, despite the granting of an extraction licence to an adjacent property owner. The Ayre of Cara has even been accorded Site of Special Scientific Interest (SSSI) status, so here is a real conundrum for coastal zone management. But whoever does own the sand, beach users, for whatever purpose, at this popular location have none other than Winston Churchill to thank for their enjoyment.

THE LESSON OF HALLSANDS: A VILLAGE BETRAYED

At one site in Britain, the link between coastal erosion, storm wave activity and excessive gravel extraction is unequivocal. On 26 January 1917, a violent storm devastated the fishing village of Hallsands, located near to Start Point at the south-western end of Start Bay in South Devon. Several buildings had been lost or damaged in earlier storms in 1903 and 1904, but the 1917 event was notoriously catastrophic. Most of the houses in the village were destroyed and those few that remained standing were rendered uninhabitable; surprisingly, no lives were lost. The village had been built on a rock platform cut into schist of Lower Devonian age at a level of about 1 to 2 metres above the shingle beach. Without any consultation with the local people, especially the fishermen, extraction of gravel by dredging from the intertidal zone between high and low water, commenced directly in front of the village in 1897. This operation was sanctioned by the government of the day, in the guise of the then Board of Trade, to provide construction aggregate for the expansion of the nearby Devonport naval dockyard. It continued until 1902. Over the five-year period of dredging an estimated 97 per cent of the beach materials were removed, thereby causing a large lowering of the beach level by up to 6 metres in places. This reckless, uncontrolled extraction thus permitted high storm waves to break directly onto the shore and the dwellings; the beach and the degree of natural protection that it once afforded had all but gone. The ensuing Hallsands disaster was, without any doubt, due to a critical combination of 40-foot storm waves, high spring tides, north-easterly gales and the irresponsible dredging of gravel.[43]

Hallsands has been described as 'a village betrayed' by historian Steve Melia,[44] a reference to the concealment of this scandal by the government at the time. No-one will ever know just how long Hallsands would have remained intact had the dredging not taken place, since it was located in a place that is naturally vulnerable to wave attack. As a result of persistent pressure from the local Member of Parliament, an inquiry into the disaster was set up by the Board of Trade, chaired by Sir Maurice Fitzmaurice, but the details of the findings, the undeniable link between the dredging and the tragedy, were carefully suppressed. The local people who had lost everything, their homes and possessions, never knew its contents. Eventually, the villagers were offered the sum of £6,000 as full and final settlement in compensation for their losses, far less than they deserved. In 2002, Melia wrote to the Secretary of State for Trade and Industry, enclosing a copy of the Fitzmaurice report, requesting that the government revisit the question of compensation to families and for the loss of all communal facilities at Hallsands, such as the village's Reading Room, which were never replaced. Today, as Melia points out, a payphone and a posting box are the only public facilities that exist in Hallsands for a population of over fifty people. A response to his request is still awaited.[45] While the full impact of offshore dredging around our coasts might still not yet be known, the Royal Commission's century-old report of 1911 noted perceptively that, 'The removal of materials from many parts of the shores of the Kingdom and the dredging of material from below low water mark, have resulted in much erosion on neighbouring parts of the coast . . .'[46] Perhaps this was a prophetic forewarning of the infamous Hallsands catastrophe that was to take place a mere six years after its publication?

Human thoughtlessness at the coast:
a salutary lesson from the eighteenth century

The loss of Hallsands to the sea is no one-off. Moreover, it was by no means due to the actions of the villagers themselves; they were innocent victims. Whilst the demise of the small village of Mathers on the east coast of Scotland south of Aberdeen has similarities, it has one very important difference; it was self-inflicted. The human activity at this location might best be described as human thoughtlessness fuelled by greed and is exemplified in the description by the pre-eminent geologist Sir Charles Lyell:

> On the coast of Kincardineshire an illustration was afforded, at the close of last century [the eighteenth], of the effect of promontories in protecting a line of low shore. The village of Mathers, two miles south of Johnshaven, was built on an ancient shingle beach, protected by a projecting ledge of limestone rock. This was quarried for lime to such an extent that the sea broke through, and in 1795 carried away the whole village in one night, and penetrated one hundred and fifty yards inland, where it has maintained its ground ever since, the new village having been built further inland on the new shore.[47]

WHAT ARE OUR OPTIONS?

So, what are the broad policy alternatives available to those who are responsible for managing and defending our coasts? Within the context of shoreline management planning in Britain, the Department of Environment, Food and Rural Affairs (Defra) has defined succinctly the four options, in no particular order, as:

- hold the existing line;
- advance the existing line;
- managed realignment, or managed retreat;
- no active intervention, or do nothing.

Shoreline Management Plans[48] were first conceived and introduced in England and Wales in 1993 by the Ministry of Agriculture, Fisheries and Food, the forerunner to Defra. Their aim is to provide a strategic framework for decision making along the coast, especially with respect to defence, taking account of the natural coastal processes, human and other environmental influences and needs.[49] Now the whole length of the English and Welsh coast is covered by such plans, some in their second generation, together with several parts of Scotland, such as Angus, Fife and Dumfries and Galloway. They are non-statutory plans, living documents that will be updated from time to time, which are intended to inform and in turn be supported by the statutory planning process. Their purpose is to give a large-scale assessment of the risks associated with natural coastal processes and to develop a policy framework that reduces these risks to people and the natural, developed and historical environment in a sustainable way. Each plan evaluates the natural processes that are acting on a length of shoreline and predicts, as far as possible, the way in which it will evolve into the future. The principal issues of concern relating to coastal erosion and flooding are determined, along with the ways in which the natural processes are managed and identification of coastal assets that may be affected by erosion or the current management practices. As such, each plan must take account of the potential impact of present and future coastal defence schemes, hard or soft engineered, on the natural environment and the likely environmental, financial and social costs involved.[50]

In England, Shoreline Management Plans are nested within the overarching Defra strategy of 'Making Space for Water',[51] according to some, a rather insensitively named document. Isn't its title just a euphemism for allowing coastal flooding; for letting the sea 'win'? The strategy aims to take a holistic management approach to all forms of flooding, both river and coastal, and to reduce the risks to people, property and the environment from flooding and coastal erosion. First introduced for consultation in 2004, it communicates an unambiguous message to both the public and responsible authorities; 'The Government proposals for flood management and coastal erosion that work with natural processes to make *more space for water* (Defra's italics) should be identified and pursued wherever possible.'[52]

The four coastal policies of hold the line, advance the line, managed realignment and no active intervention, should not necessarily be thought of in isolation. Each has implications for the future that may result in coast-lines becoming very different in character from those with which we are presently familiar and the policy adopted for a particular stretch of coast may change through time. A policy change from hold the line to no active intervention can be particularly contentious. *Hold the existing line* refers to the policy of continuing to maintain or even to upgrade, especially in areas of rising relative sea level and increased storminess, the degree of protection afforded by coastal defences. This might involve not only strengthening a sea wall but also raising it in height to reflect greater wave heights. *Advance the existing line*, however, is the much less common course of action that involves constructing new defences seaward of existing ones; as, for instance, where existing defences are deemed essential on socioeco-nomic grounds, but they are no longer fit for purpose having been permitted to fall into such a poor, potentially dangerous state of repair that new, adjacent structures are the only viable option. Alternatively, a delib-erate decision might be taken, but very rarely and virtually unheard of in Britain today, to claim some intertidal land or near shore seabed in an area that is likely to be naturally accreting. *Managed realignment* allows the controlled or managed landward retreat of a shoreline, making space for water, as in the site-specific breaching of land claim embankments or other defences. This is an option favoured in England by the 'Coastal Futures Project', a partnership of the Royal Society for the Protection of Birds, the Environment Agency, Natural England and Defra. This project aims to support those communities dealing with coastal change and relative sea level rise with the premise that coastal flood risk management cannot continue in the way that it has done historically and that managed realignment can be the most sustainable way of adaptation. 'By giving a little land to the sea, we have a better chance of protecting ourselves from much greater damage from climate change.'[53] As an example, the Shoreline Management Plan for the Humber Estuary incorporates the use of managed retreat in some locations, including Paull Holme Strays referred to in Chapter 4, within an overall strategy that provides for a continuing line of defence around the water body.[54] It is perhaps of little surprise that public perception of managed realignment schemes is variable.[55]

No active intervention is the do nothing approach or laissez faire; to let nature take its course and permit a coast to erode or accrete, in other words to evolve and change naturally without the provision of or investment in new defences. Contentiously, this policy could also lead to

The impact of the Black Death on medieval coastal defence

The Thames Estuary has a long history of flooding, especially associated with tidal storm surges generated in the North Sea, which culminated in the 1953 catastrophe and was the stimulus to the construction of the Thames Barrier. Historical research has shown that during the later Middle Ages, in the two centuries from around 1250 until 1450 when the Thames Estuary was one of the most economically developed parts of medieval Britain, the resources of coastal communities in the area were put under increasing pressure as a result of the increasing frequency of such events. This is reflected in amounts expended on sea walls, embankments and other forms of coastal defences. However, when the Black Death arrived in Britain in around 1349 the population was decimated. As a consequence of labour shortages, the defences of some of the marshlands around the Thames Estuary that had been claimed from the sea were abandoned – an early form of managed retreat.[56] Nothing, it would seem, is new.

a decision by a responsible authority like a local council not to continue to invest in the maintenance of any existing coastal defences in a particular area, allowing them to fall into disrepair and even their ultimate destruction by the sea. This is, without doubt, the preferred and indeed common sense policy for all natural and semi-natural coastal areas remote from habitation, where there will never have been any form of significant human intervention. The natural repetitive, seasonal cycle of creation and destruction of landforms at these sites is part of their charm, their beauty, their intrinsic value and, from the perspective of landscape conservation, it should be allowed to proceed without impediment. No active intervention is thus the option that is appropriate for both undeveloped hard, rocky coasts of Britain, such as those of the west of Scotland, and similarly soft, sandy coasts with extensive dune fields. Even though the latter areas might be experiencing extreme and even widespread erosion, which might be accelerating as a consequence of a rise in relative sea level, it must be remembered that they are the natural suppliers of sediment, sources from which sediment is being transported to other locations. Even though they might be National Nature Reserves or Areas of Outstanding Natural Beauty or under the umbrella of any number of a host of other potential designations, nature should be allowed to take her course unimpeded in such remote locations. Erosion *is* after all, first and foremost, a natural process.

WILL WE EVER LEARN?

Without any doubt, we have learned a lot from our past mistakes at the coast; of course, so many of them we cannot undo. Whilst there should never be repeats of the Hallsands disaster or the Mathers fiasco in Britain, we do still make mistakes and indeed large ones even in the twenty-first century – as illustrated both unequivocally and powerfully by this example from the coast of South Wales. Following the decline of traditional industries and associated docklands, much of this coastline is undergoing regeneration and the sea frontage is the focus for development. Towards the end of the twentieth century, Llanelli on the Loughor Estuary had become a town of high unemployment and an unattractive prospect for future employers. Its docks had fallen into disrepair and much of the nearby land was unusable due to the high levels of contaminants, a legacy of past coal and lead mining together with former tin, copper, iron and steel industries. An enormously ambitious project, the construction of the Millennium Coastal Park, the Millennium Coastal Path and the so-called Earth Sculpture, was set in place to stimulate a commercial and development strategy in the area. Funding was obtained from the Millennium Commission, the National Lottery, Carmarthenshire County Council and the Welsh Assembly Government. The project has, however, been an unmitigated failure since it took place without due consideration of coastal processes and location.

The Earth Sculpture, so named 'Walking with the Sea', a large artificial hill protruding into the sea and moulded into a series of spirals on the site of the ash tip of the old Carmarthen Bay Power Station, was designed to be seen from land, sea and air. With sustainability at its heart, the structure was built from compacted pulverised fuel ash (PFA), a by-product of coal-fired power stations that would otherwise have been disposed of in landfill. A veneer of silt, dredged from the nearby Burry Port Harbour, together with sewage sludge, facilitated rapid natural revegetation. The Earth

Sculpture was built in a location that made it vulnerable to westward flowing river and eastward marine currents which, together with storm waves, soon set to work cutting away at its toe (Plate 80). Indeed, the potential for erosion was enhanced because the particle sizes of the PFA used for construction were rather smaller than those that characterise the natural sediments of this coast. Within three years of completion of the various components of the project, the signs of erosion were readily apparent. In a severe storm event in March 2007, 10 metres of retreat were recorded and a section of the coastal path suffered catastrophic failure (Plate 81). Subsequent storms added to the erosion of the path and Earth Sculpture, and significant damage became apparent on many newly constructed homes. Existing sea walls were undermined and necessitated rock armour protection. Furthermore, their ability to protect recent developments is now in question.[57] What went wrong? Causes and effects included the inappropriate location of infrastructure, building out the Earth Sculpture into the sea without due consideration of coastal processes and the relocation of nearshore river channels. To make matters worse, inappropriate dredging practices in the area are encouraging further erosion by removing sediment from the system. A catalogue of errors indeed; quite simply, lessons had not been learned following similar construction patterns elsewhere. Ironically, the Millennium Commission's contribution to the funding of the Millennium Coastal Park was made subject to a condition that the coastal path must be maintained and must remain in place for seventy-five years.[58] If the path is lost, reconstruction costs would have to be repaid – a potentially high-cost mistake indeed as recent estimates to repair the defences adjacent to the section of the path between Llanelli and Burry Port to the south are in the range of £15 million to £20 million.[59]

CONFLICT AT THE COAST:
DIFFERING REACTIONS TO COASTAL EROSION

Coastal erosion can sometimes be a highly emotive issue and public opinion can influence coastal zone management strongly. The freshwater lake of Slapton Ley National Nature Reserve in Devon, to the north of the remains of the tragic village of Hallsands, is separated from Start Bay by a narrow ridge of shingle that is around 4 kilometres in length (Figure

6.4). To the seaward side are the Slapton Sands. A main road, the A379, takes a precarious but more or less straight-line route along the top of the ridge and forms an important local thoroughfare known as 'Slapton Line'. In early January 2001, waves generated by storm force easterly winds, coupled with high spring tides, caused major damage to the gravel barrier and the road link was severed, impassable to vehicles along a length of well over 200 metres.[60] Erosion of the road's foundations was accompanied by wave wash over of gravel onto the carriageway. The local authority had to remove some 500 tonnes of debris and after a period of complete closure an emergency single lane diversionary route was constructed. From the consequences of the erosion breach, two somewhat predictable, distinct and passionate schools of thought emerged. On the one hand, the inability to drive along the coast road angered many local people and it was seen as detrimental to the local economy. On the other hand, potential threats to unique habitats and to natural processes were seen as a priority. The sea was variously a powerful enemy that had to be tamed or that its natural processes should be allowed to take their course. For those who wished the road to be repaired, the option of managed retreat was dismissed out of hand as an idea 'straight out of the Polytechnic guidebook'.[61] Others recognised that, even though the road had been in place since 1850, it was inappropriately routed along the crest line of a highly vulnerable and naturally dynamic coastal feature. So tempers flared. A survey of local residents determined that 90 per cent favoured reinstatement and protection of the road whereas just 5 per cent believed that it should be abandoned and rerouted around the opposite side of Slapton Ley. Of those in favour of protection, over two-thirds wanted the installation of a sea wall or sheet steel piling to hold the sea back – a familiar story. A little under one third believed that protection could best be achieved by beach nourishment using imported gravel. As a short-term expedient, the local authority, Devon County Council, who have statutory authority to maintain the roadway, installed rock armour on the seaward side to protect what remained of it. English Nature, however, who have responsibility for maintaining the natural state of the gravel ridge, had the protective boulders removed to 'preserve the integrity of natural processes'.[62] The local Member of Parliament sided with the majority view in the survey and favoured realignment of the road. Thus, the temporary diversion was eventually opened about three months after the storm breach and the following year, 2002, the damaged section of the road was realigned a few

metres to landward. Was this a mistake? Whether this was the right course
of action in the longer term still remains to be challenged by the power
of the sea. In this case, popular opinion was upheld. That, unfortunately,
cannot always be the situation around our coasts, as the final chapter of this
book unfolds. So, what indeed might the future hold in Britain; is my
house safe? Chapter 7 provides some suggestions.

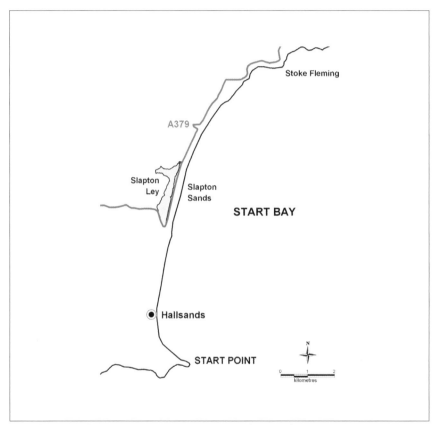

Figure 6.4 Map of Start Bay in Devon showing the route of the A379 coast road along the shingle
barrier that impounds Slapton Ley. Also shown is the location of the nearby remains of the village
of Hallsands (drawing by T. Dixon).

7
IS MY HOUSE WITH ITS SEA VIEW SAFE: WHAT DOES THE FUTURE HOLD?

Civilization exists by geological consent, subject to change without notice
Will Durant

INTRODUCTION

On Wednesday 31 March 2010, the *Dundee Courier and Advertiser* proclaimed boldly in its principal morning headline, 'Gales, Snow and Ice see Spring Postponed'. This and similar stories in other newspapers and on television news programmes were referring to the events of the previous day when much of Scotland was taken by surprise, besieged by a combination of snow, heavy rain, high tides and gale-force winds, causing havoc to householders and motorists alike. Captured on video, the spring tides coupled with unprecedented high winds and surging waves breached the outer harbour at North Berwick in East Lothian.[1] Many boats were damaged, trees were uprooted across the country and there was extensive coastal flooding with damage to promenades. At Kinghorn in Fife the doors of the lifeboat house were damaged so badly that they could not be opened and the vessel had to be taken off station. In Anstruther, the largest of the villages on the coast of the East Neuk of Fife, disaster struck. Large portions of a sea wall and two corner walls of a house above, built from the local Carboniferous sandstones, were ripped asunder by the force of the waves (Plate 82). Battered by the waves and sprayed by their surf for at least 200 years, probably since the late eighteenth century,[2] these structures had hitherto remained intact. But this event was the final straw. Anstruther is no stranger to attack from the sea; for instance, its harbour walls and nearby cottages were extensively damaged in a big storm in December 1655. Elsewhere in eastern Scotland that same event sank twenty-eight vessels in the harbour at Dysart and thirty in Crail and smashed piers at St

Andrews, Crail, Wemyss and Leith.[3] Along the Fife and Lothian coasts, salt pans were 'wronged' by the force of the waves.[4] However, damage to long standing coastal properties, such as those in Anstruther in March 2010, are becoming more frequent occurrences around Britain's shores. There is no doubt that coastal zone managers in parts of Britain, and indeed elsewhere around the world, are going to have to make some very tough, difficult, even unpalatable and unpopular decisions in the future – and that is in the foreseeable future. What might that future hold in store?

Tsunami risk: could the Storegga Slide occur again?

One of the principal reasons why the Storegga Slide has been so comprehensively studied is that a major natural gas field, known as Ormen Lange, the largest on the Norwegian continental shelf, is located within its scar. Hence the risk of another similar event was something that required critical evaluation. Although it was most probably triggered by an earthquake, the slide took place due to the very rapid accumulation of sediment during the Pleistocene glaciation. It is therefore believed that a new glacial period would be a prerequisite for the same preconditions to be generated once again, that is to produce a sufficient thickness of sediments.[5] This may be thought of in much the same way as a snow avalanche which will be triggered only when the snow pile has attained a great enough thickness. In the present conditions of global warming this, therefore, seems unlikely. However, on the scale of geological time, albeit potentially remote, it is a very distant possibility. In other situations, climate change, in particular global warming, might increase the possibility of a tsunami striking Britain's shores. Around the margins of the Atlantic Ocean are deposits of solid methane within the sediments. As ocean temperatures rise, these so-called gas hydrates could start to break down, potentially inducing instability or even failure of the surrounding deposits and potentially resulting in a tsunami[6] that could strike Britain's shores much like the 1607 catastrophe (see Chapter 1). It is possible that the greatest threat, however, comes from Cumbre Veija, a large volcano on La Palma in the Canary Islands. Geological evidence suggests that during a future eruption this may experience a catastrophic failure of its unstable western flank, which would induce a tsunami as hundreds of cubic kilometres of rock fall into the Atlantic Ocean. Modelling suggests that the coastlines of south-west England would experience waves of 5 to 7 metres in height within around three hours of such a collapse.[7] Controversy surrounds the probability of this occurrence. Some scientists believe that the likelihood is small[8] whilst others see the collapse from Cumbre Veija as 'inevitable' and with devastating consequences around the Atlantic shores, but note that it is impossible to predict when it might happen.[9] Since the mid eighteenth century there have been many reports of abnormal sea surface fluctuations and associated coastal floods in south-west England, several of which events have been attributed to historical tsunami.[10] Other studies suggest tsunami have struck the fringes of southern England further back in history, perhaps even to the eleventh century.[11] It is unlikely that these Atlantic shores of Britain have seen their last tsunami, the small, low-lying remnants of Lyonesse being particularly susceptible to future inundation.

NO ACTIVE INTERVENTION

There is an increasing realisation in Britain that the do nothing approach, embracing natural coastal processes rather than working against them, is the only realistic management solution suited to many areas of developed coast, in addition to those that are natural and essentially undeveloped. Of course, this policy becomes very much more controversial when coastal properties, homes, gardens, industrial sites, agricultural land, roads, railway lines and so on, are to be left to the ravages of the hungry sea. Should this even be considered as an option when peoples' homes could be lost and residents would, as a consequence, have to be relocated to other dwellings elsewhere? This is clearly an emotive issue, not least for those whose properties, which could have been held by the same families for generations, might be under threat in the immediate future or in a few years' time. There is inevitably a point of view held by some people that their human rights are infringed should a responsible authority such as a local council, decide not to defend their property from erosion by the sea. However, we have to accept that we simply cannot continue to defend the coasts of Britain at all costs; we must, in certain areas, work with nature rather than against it and learn from the past and our past mistakes.[12]

As described elsewhere in this book, areas of Britain developed out of soft, sometimes unconsolidated rock types are particularly vulnerable to erosion and to landsliding. Had these areas not been developed and defended through time, they would have served naturally as sources, the suppliers of sediment to the coastal system. The soft clay and till coasts of eastern England to the south of the chalk cliffs of Flamborough Head in East Yorkshire; Holderness, Lincolnshire, Norfolk, Suffolk, Essex and North Kent are especially susceptible to attack by the sea. So too are the landslide-prone areas of the south in east Devon, Dorset and the Isle of Wight. In parts of the eastern counties, in particular, there is a chronic erosion problem (Plate 83), amongst the most acute in Europe, where the policy of no active intervention will inevitably and without any shadow of doubt have to be applied eventually. The lessons from the historical record are unambiguous.

The small village of Happisburgh is located on the North Norfolk coast. It is certainly no stranger to attack by the sea. In 1844 it was observed that, 'At Hasborough [an alternative spelling of that day], the sea has encroached upwards of one hundred and seventy yards during the last sixty years, and it is calculated the church will be engulphed [*sic*] in the Ocean before the middle of the ensuing century.'[13] The fifteenth century church of St Mary still stands, however, but now very close to the shoreline; the calculation could not account for the slowing-down effect of the installation of defences in the interim. The village is said to have inspired Charles Dickens and the writing of at least one of the Sherlock Holmes stories by Sir Arthur Conan Doyle who stayed at a local hotel.[14] Today it has become infamous thanks to frequent press articles[15] and television coverage of the erosion problem that its residents face. Noted also for its striking red and white striped lighthouse, the only independently operated lighthouse in Britain, part of the village is under imminent threat of loss to the sea. Around thirty houses have been lost over the past two decades alone and many more are close to destruction. Forlorn, desolate and derelict from the beach, dramatic from the air, Happisburgh is a sad sight. The remains of old defences, themselves eroded, lumps of rocks, concrete and twisted, rusting metal bestrew the beach and cliff (Plate

84). The sea defences date back largely to the late 1950s and early 1960s and were constructed as a response to the devastating 1953 North Sea storm surge that had resulted in so much loss of life in eastern England (see Chapter 1). These defences principally take the form of timber and steel revetments and wooden groynes built on the beach beneath the soft eroding cliff line but they have been allowed to fall into disrepair due to progressive damage by storm waves (Plate 85). The Shoreline Management Plan for the wider area of North East Norfolk and East Suffolk, a coastal defence management document that presents a vision of the region's coastline over the next 100 years, and now in its second iteration, has concluded that it would not be appropriate to continue to defend Happisburgh. Indeed the Plan advocates no active intervention or managed realignment along much of the coastline in the area.[16] The long term strategy to hold the existing coastline applies only to those locations of key economic, commercial and residential importance; towns such as Sheringham, Cromer, Great Yarmouth, Gorleston-on-Sea and Lowestoft.

Although there are serious implications, the loss to erosion of homes, gardens and amenities, these are not seen as sufficient to justify on economic grounds the construction of new defences along the Happisburgh sea frontage and elsewhere. One understandable reaction from local residents has been to set up the 'Buy a Rock for Happisburgh' campaign on the Internet, with the aim of raising enough money to buy and install their own sea defences.[17] This is not a solution, a sadly futile scheme; the continued protection of the village is deemed to be unsustainable in the long term. North Norfolk District Council has adopted the Shoreline Management Plan conditionally at the time of writing. Full adoption will take place only when the conditions have been met that the Government puts in place acceptable measures. These include financial support to mitigate the effects of coastal change in the area and a requirement for a wider economic analysis to be undertaken of those sea frontages where it is proposed that the defence policy is to change from hold the line to that of no active intervention.[18]

Whilst human life must be protected from coastal erosion and flooding at all costs, there are areas of Britain, as exemplified by the village of Happisburgh, where some property assets will quite plainly and bluntly, but sadly, have to be sacrificed, where there are *no* alternatives but to permit houses and gardens to be lost to the sea as has happened over the centuries in many parts of eastern England. This is especially so where the

installation of any form of defence, either hard or soft, would be uneco-
nomically viable, environmentally unsustainable or indeed detrimental to
other areas, typically those in downdrift locations. There is no viable alternative but a shift in thinking, an about-turn from the ad-hoc protectionist
approach as such sites.[19] This is, however, far easier said than done. It will
be more than an uphill struggle to convince those people whose homes
and land are at risk that they will have to relocate further inland sooner
rather than later. A point to ponder is this; how many times over the
centuries must the same concerns as those of the Happisburgh residents
today have been exercising the minds of those living in the now lost towns
of Holderness, in nearby Dunwich and elsewhere in East Anglia? To
implement such a policy of no further intervention and relocation inland
with any success will depend on increasing greatly, and with thoughtful
sensitivity, the public's awareness of the impacts of past and future coastal
changes; increasing the level of environmental education with respect to
improved understanding of how coasts actually work.[20]

It is an instinctive reaction to expect protection to be provided against
coastal erosion, but necessity now compels that individuals and indeed
whole communities will have to adapt to and accept change. This is reality
at its harshest and, furthermore, it is reality that cannot be denied ostrich-
like. However, there will have to be a simultaneous change in UK
Government policy to take account of the not insignificant issues of social
justice or human rights associated with the policy of no active intervention at the coast.[21] There is an argument that it is iniquitous that
current Government legislation is such that compensation is not payable
to owners of properties that are lost to the sea, a belief that this is socially
unjust and necessity compels urgent rectification. It is particularly unfair
to those who inhabit vulnerable coastal areas where there has been a
policy change by the responsible authority from one of hold the line to
one of no active intervention, as a result of a new or revised cost–benefit
analysis. Communities in these locations, where there has been such a shift
in coastal management policy, albeit inevitable, feel let down, betrayed and
ignored by the Government.[22] Salt is rubbed further into wounds in the
knowledge that most other EU member states operate a far more socially
just system than that which currently exists in island Britain.[23] France, for
instance, pays compensation in appropriate circumstances, when total
property loss is suffered. Payment is made from what is called the
'Solidarity Fund' at a rate of 100 per cent of the property market without

the coastal erosion problem.[24] Remote sensing observations by satellite of the southern part of the North Sea have revealed during stormy winter months a turbid, plume-like feature of high fine-grained suspended sediment concentration. This extends from the source area, the soft till cliffs of north-east Norfolk from which the material is eroded, out in a north-easterly direction right across the North Sea towards the island of Texel in the Netherlands.[25] In view of this observation that fine sediment particles make their way from East Anglia across the North Sea's waters to the Netherlands, there is even an argument in support of a Europe-wide fund for compensation.

Location, location, location: where not to build a millionaires' paradise

And the rain descended, and the floods came, and the winds blew, and beat upon that house; and it fell not: for it was founded upon a rock.

And everyone that heareth these sayings of mine, and doeth them not, shall be likened unto a foolish man, which built his house upon the sand:

And the rain descended, and the floods came, and the winds blew, and beat upon that house; and it fell: and great was the fall of it.

Matthew 7:25–27.

It may come as a surprise to find that what is believed to be the fourth most expensive piece of real estate in the world is located not in Monte Carlo or in Beverley Hills but on the English Channel coast of Dorset. A narrow peninsula, 600 metres wide and 1 kilometre long, a spit of land projecting as a barrier beach at the mouth of Poole Harbour, the aptly but unoriginally named Sandbanks was, a century ago, little more than a collection of a few beach huts in the sand along with a row of coastguards' cottages. In 1894, the Board of Trade secured approval to defend the peninsula from erosion, envisaging that land sales for housing development would fund the coastal protection and by the start of the First World War

numerous fashionable villas had been constructed. Following the
Second World War, land values began to rise on Sandbanks, as
demand grew for seaside accommodation close to public beaches.
In 1965, John Lennon bought a bungalow for his Aunt Mimi and
from then on property values began to climb sharply.[26] Today,
Panorama Road is fringed with some of the most desirable water-
front residences in the country, home to the rich and the very rich.[27]
The feature of a 2008 ITV documentary series presented by Piers
Morgan, this fragile bit of land, heavily defended with rock armour
and groynes, is described as the British Monte Carlo, one of the
most expensive places to live in the world and the most glamorous
place to live in Britain (Plate 86).[28] A sensational land of futuristic
concept houses with spectacular sea views and the Riviera lifestyle,
here the average house prices are over £600,000 but the most
prestigious properties can cost £7 million and more. The few
original small houses and beach huts that remained among the
dunes have long been demolished and the dunes flattened. Here
there is a 'don't worry about tomorrow' attitude. But could the
dream become a nightmare in the future? For some, this is sadly but
predictably inevitable. It is telling that plans to erect a landmark
white spire on the Sandbanks spit, Skywalk Tower, at a cost of £7
million in 2006, which would have given visitors a bird's eye view
of Poole Harbour from an observation pod 39 metres in height,[29]
have not come to fruition, the application having been withdrawn.[30]

MANAGED RELOCATION

Intriguingly, Derek McGlashan[31] has drawn attention to the possibility of
managed relocation as a coastal management option, a process that
involves the relocation of buildings in one unit, rather than demolition of
buildings and reconstruction. This might seem far fetched, but a hotel in
the Brooklyn area of New York and a number of large buildings in North
Carolina, USA, have in the past been relocated bodily from eroding coasts.
It might come as a surprise to find that this technique has also been
employed in Britain. In March 1999, the Belle Tout Lighthouse, which had

stood on the top of the 100-metres-high chalk cliffs at Beachy Head near Eastbourne in East Sussex since 1834, was moved 17 metres further inland from the cliff edge. When it was originally constructed, the lighthouse was 35 metres from the cliff edge, but natural erosion over the years had seen the cliff recede, thereby rendering the listed building under threat. It was thus replaced, decommissioned as a light and sold off as a private dwelling, with the purchasers fully aware of its vulnerability. The move of the former lighthouse inland was an elaborate technical engineering feat, involving underpinning of the foundations, the construction of new foundations and the installation of slide rails to allow its movement by pushing jacks. It attracted much press publicity at the time and was even the focus of a BBC Television *Tomorrow's World* Special in 1999.[32] The cost of the operation was estimated to be somewhere in the range of £200,000 to £300,000, rather more than the £285 1s 9d that was expended in relocating the

Relocation, relocation, relocation

Built in 1830, Clavell Tower was to become the inspiration for P.D. James's mystery *The Black Tower* in which a desolate cliff-top retreat is witness to a series of bizarre and inexplicable deaths – a real cliffhanger. Much earlier, in 1898, it was the frontispiece for Thomas Hardy's *Wessex Poems and Other Verses*; but, as the twenty-first century dawned, it had become under imminent threat of being lost to the sea. Perched conspicuously on the very edge of the cliffs of the Jurassic Coast World Heritage Site at the wide sweep of Kimmeridge Bay in Dorset, Clavell Tower looked set to very soon fall victim to coastal erosion. Derelict since it was gutted by a fire in the 1930s, an emergency appeal was launched in 2004. A subsequent study commissioned to by the Landmark Trust, which ensured that the views of local people were listened to, came to the conclusion that the only feasible option to make the folly safe for at least the next 125 years was to relocate it.[33] Thus, piece by piece, it was dismantled and systematically rebuilt 25 metres inland from the cliff edge. Time has been bought; this Dorset coastal icon is today restored fully and run by the Landmark Trust as an unusual holiday let.

Buddon Lighthouse on the Tay Estuary to the east of Dundee in 1884,[34] but much less than the sum that would be required to stabilise the naturally eroding, vertical chalk cliffs of Beachy Head.

However, this will probably never be a technique that will be of widespread economic viability. It is very costly and in the present day will be technically feasible only in very particular cases where isolated, historically important or high-value buildings are at threat of loss to coastal erosion or to landsliding. However, managed relocation could potentially become a much more viable companion to the policy of no active intervention at Britain's most rapidly eroding sites were we prepared or able to build houses that have the capability of being moved readily either as modules or as whole units. Of course, this process would be viable only in locations where there is sufficient space available to accommodate the progressive relocation of buildings inland.

COASTAL PLANNING FOR THE FUTURE: BE REALISTIC, BE VERY REALISTIC

There needs to be vastly improved dialogue among coastal scientists, developers and planners. Science and scientific understanding of coastal processes and the rates at which these processes are taking place must be expressed in such a way that they inform coastal management and decision-making processes, with a view to the future over the next fifty to a hundred years. Models for coastal planning will have to be developed that characteristically subdivide coastal areas into a series of shore-parallel zones, strips defined on the basis of the risk of land and property loss to the sea within each.[35] Thus the highest risk zone will be that closest to the shoreline and that with least risk will be furthest inland. But, how far inland, is the question? This is a question to which scientific knowledge and understanding are paramount. No new developments or property improvements will be allowed in the highest risk zone; some properties might well have been lost to erosion already and the occupants of others will need progressively to be relocated to the zone of least risk or beyond. Between these two zones there are likely to be others in which no new developments are allowed with perhaps only minor alterations permitted to existing properties. New housing developments will be permitted only in the zone of least risk and further inland. Thus, the locations of new properties and the inhabitants are set back progressively from the coastal edge through time, but the owners must be compensated for their losses. As one zone and all the property within it becomes lost to the sea, the others become redesignated in terms of erosion risk and so the cycle of set back or roll back continues, a practice that is applied readily to holiday caravan and mobile home sites. It is imperative that new houses are not built in inappropriate areas at the coast, areas of unacceptably high risk, in just the same way that the widespread, post-Second World War bad practice of building houses on the flood plains of rivers in Britain has been shown, at enormous cost to both home owners and the insurance industry, to be utter folly.[36]

The seriousness of the situation is amplified starkly at the time of writing by the five word lead headline on the front page of *The Independent* newspaper which asserts with candour, 'Abandon homes to the sea'.[37] For many people this will be a potentially bleak prospect but this is a realistic take-home message, the key soundbite emphasised by the Right Honourable Lord Chris Smith of Finsbury in his first press interview since taking office three months earlier as the Chairman of the Environment Agency of England and Wales. As described in this chapter and elsewhere in the book, parts of north-east Norfolk and Suffolk are most immediately at risk. Hard choices will have to be made as to which areas of the coast to protect and which to allow the sea to consume; 'We are almost certainly not going to be able to defend absolutely every bit of coast – it would simply be an impossible task, both in financial and engineering terms.' With specific reference to coastal erosion and the additional threat of rising sea levels in low-lying areas, Lord Smith asserts, 'This is the most difficult issue we are going to face as an agency', an unequivocal statement that demonstrates an appreciation of the seriousness of the problem. Furthermore, he contends that the Government cannot continue to rely on insurance companies to cover families whose homes are lost to the sea (indeed many in the most vulnerable settlements have been unable to obtain buildings insurance cover for several years), putting renewed pressure on the Government to instigate with urgency a policy of rehousing those families and individuals affected at the taxpayers' expense.

The protection of important coastal archaeological clusters, World Heritage Sites like the Neolithic Skara Brae village, poses a thorny dilemma to coastal management. One school of thought is that such remarkable ancient monuments, even though there is no associated threat

**Assistance for adaptation – as opposed to compensation –
in the East Riding of Yorkshire: the Coastal Change Pathfinder**

A funding package of £1.2 million, to be spent in a period of a little over one year ending in March 2011, was recently secured by the East Riding of Yorkshire Council from the Defra Coastal Change Pathfinder.[38] In effect, this is a pilot scheme, one of several under consideration, to help coastal communities adapt to erosion. It aims to provide incentives to those residents of Holderness living with immediate threat of loss of their properties to relocate to safer inland areas. However, the local authority emphasises that this scheme 'does not seek to provide compensation for loss, but rather provide assistance to those who are seeking to adapt to the impacts of coastal change'.[39] For those living permanently in houses deemed to be in the most imminent threat to coastal erosion, the types of assistance that might be considered under this scheme are:

- Costs of demolition of the property and restoration of the site
- Relocation costs
- A small hardship payment
- Payment of up to 50 per cent of a twelve-month tenancy
- Payment of management or agent fees
- Provision of essential second-hand furnishings and white goods for a new dwelling.[40]

Where the level of erosion risk is high but less than imminent, typically where homes are likely to be lost over the next fifteen years or so, other options might be available. In particular, the Pathfinder scheme would permit, in such circumstances, the Local Authority to purchase properties and lease them back to their owners, giving them some financial leeway to plan for a future relocation and potentially to relieve some of the worry. Although warmly welcomed by residents in the local press,[41] it is, overall, too early to assess the success or otherwise of this pilot but a prediction is made here that similar adaptation schemes will become inevitable in several, similarly vulnerable parts of Britain within the foreseeable future.

Immediately prior to going to press, this has come true but has been met with much less enthusiasm than in the East Riding of Yorkshire. At Happisburgh, North Norfolk District Council has agreed a plan to purchase the ten homes that are in the greatest danger along the village's Beach Road having obtained funding from the Pathfinder scheme. The proposal is that the homeowners be offered 40–50 per cent of the values of their properties, calculated on the basis that these are located inland and therefore not at risk from erosion. This deal, which is not compulsory, has been branded as 'insulting' by the residents, but the local council maintains it is all that it can afford.[42] Along with atmospheric temperatures, the social justice debate is heating up.

to human life, should be defended from the ravages of the sea at all costs. Skara Brae is unique and, therefore, it should not be permitted to be either damaged or destroyed by the sea. The counter view is laissez faire; there must surely be other 'Skara Braes' hidden elsewhere, buried for millennia under sand dunes, that are waiting to be exhumed by storm wave activity. But what if Skara Brae is truly unique and there are no remaining similar ancient monuments in undefended coastal locations waiting to be exposed by coastal erosion? If this is true, and that is indeed a very real possibility, then defend at all costs, by whatever is determined to be the most appropriate means, must surely be the preferred management option if future generations are to appreciate and learn from such important sites.

But is this just – especially if houses elsewhere in Britain, communities, gardens and indeed memories are to be committed to the sea as a direct result of a policy shift to one of no active intervention in an area that had formerly been defended from erosion? From the perspective of a resident of, for example, Happisburgh, presently one of the settlements most vulnerable to coastal erosion in England, the importance of protecting Skara Brae whilst they receive no or, perhaps, limited compensation for loss of their homes must seem more than incongruous. This, however, begs further questions; should those individuals who stand to lose so much to coastal erosion have been aware of this threat when they purchased their properties; the historical record of lost towns and villages in eastern and southern England is, after all, well known? Or, should they have been informed of the level of risk by their local authority? Many homeowners claim that they were misinformed or misled by local authorities about the rate of coastal retreat and were given to believe that their houses would be safe far into the future. Some, however, bought in full knowledge of the rate of encroachment by the sea. For them, the magnetic allure of the coast was more forceful than reality and they have been living in complete denial of the severity of the erosion problem, putting it to the backs of their minds.

With regard to compensation on an eroding coast, it has been suggested that there is a strong argument that it is socially unjust that those who lose homes and land are not compensated. However, turning the same argument on its head, is it fair that those who gain land on an accreting coast, as can indeed happen in Britain, should pay for that privilege? They do not, of course, do so. Given the *caveat emptor*, 'let the buyer beware' principle of property law, it would appear strange not to place at least some burden on the purchaser to make their own enquiries into the mobility, vulnerability and stability of any coastal land they intended to purchase.[43] But what of those local families and individuals who live in houses that have been passed down, inherited through the generations? When these houses were acquired originally, they were likely to have been far inland from the sea, like the Easington gas terminal (see Chapter 3), and under no threat of erosion for the foreseeable future. Are such homeowners somehow more worthy of compensation than those who bought their clifftop homes a year or so ago on a coast that is receding at say 5 metres per year whether or not they were in full knowledge of that fact at the time of purchase? There are therefore some very complex, thorny legal and social justice questions, together with not inconsiderable administrative obstacles, underpinning the compensation of landowners and homeowners on eroding coasts that will need to be addressed, and without delay, before more homes are lost to the sea. Reality, however, dictates that relocation of people to inland sites is the only environmentally sustainable response to the rapid coastal erosion being experienced in many parts of eastern England. Whilst they might make people feel safe and secure, more and bigger sea walls or ever-expanding masses of rock armour are unequivocally not the solution.

APOCALYPSE NO, CATASTROPHES YES

As documented earlier in this book, around our coastline throughout history we have seen devastation, fiasco, defeat by the sea, ruin and disaster. Is there a coastal apocalypse in prospect, a Wagnerian Götterdämmerung or twilight of the Gods – the end of the world as we know it? This country has seen innumerable catastrophes at the coast in the past; from storm surge in eastern England to tsunami in Shetland, the post-glacial submergence of Doggerland, Lyonnesse and so many other areas, from landslides in the Isle of Wight and Dorset to the erosion-ravaged lost towns of Holderness. There is no expectation of a single apocalypse – but catastrophes will continue to be a fact of life around the British coast and beyond. Journalist Richard Girling in his provocative book *Sea Change: Britain's Coastal Catastrophe* states that: 'Whereas it is a truism that not every inch of coast can be defended, it is equally true that we can protect anything we really want to.'[44] However, this misses the point. We cannot 'protect' anything or anywhere we want to at all. What we can do is to *install protection measures* or defences wherever we want to – but that is far from the same thing. That is not learning from history, not learning from our past mistakes – but merely perpetrating the vicious cycle of coastal problems that we have to be bold enough to step aside from. It is the same kind of attitude as that of the man in the old Russian tale of the big iron stove who, without thinking of the consequences of his actions, burned, as if with blinkers on, all his furniture and ultimately his wooden home itself just to feed the insatiable roaring fire. We simply cannot preserve all of Britain's coasts in a time-lapse cocoon. It is tough, very tough, and cruel even, but we must work with nature rather than against it. We have to accept the natural dynamism of coastal processes, concede that change is inevitable and strive to avoid or, at worst, minimise inappropriate interventions. One person's catastrophe is another person's beach – the list of Britain's lost coastal towns is unfinished business.

Two powerful and thought provoking quotations distil into a nutshell the take-home message of this book. As long ago as 1998, the House of Commons Select Committee on Agriculture reflected thus:

> our nation's history is one of continual intervention in coastal and riverine processes, punctuated by occasional awesome reminders of the power of the sea. It is not surprising that our lexicon for

describing the relationship between the land and the sea is dominated by militaristic terminology: we speak of flood and coastal 'defence', of 'reclaiming' or 'winning' land from the sea – even of the sea 'invading' the land. Hard-engineered defences remain essential to protect many vital national assets, especially in urban areas. But, overall, we believe that it is time to declare an end to the centuries-old war with the sea and to seek a peaceful accommodation with our former enemy. It is far better to anticipate and plan a policy of managed realignment than to suffer the consequences of a deluded belief that we can maintain indefinitely an unbreachable Maginot Line of towering sea walls and flood defences.[45]

These words are even more acutely pertinent today. It is, moreover, imperative as we enter the second decade of the twenty-first century that we also recognise that:

In the future, the most profound changes affecting the UK coastal zone will be driven by climate change, particularly by rising sea level. The rate and level of sea level rise are expected to be substantial, although predictions are surrounded by differing degrees of uncertainty. Pressures on land use will be many. Many major challenges will have to be confronted if we are to successfully and equitably manage and adapt to the consequences of climate change and the competing human demands on coastal land.[56]

It is all too easy to attribute all of today's coastal problems to the most recent phase of climate change, to jump onto the global warming bandwagon. Climate change, whether or not exacerbated by human activities, is certainly an important contributory factor but it is geology, natural processes and man's inappropriate developments and interactions with these over the centuries that are to 'blame'. Even if we could somehow magically halt human-induced climate change, stop global warming, Britain would still, as it has since the end of the Pleistocene glaciation, be in many places a shrinking land subject to flooding, erosion and landsliding at its coastal edges. We have to learn to *adapt* to and manage climate change, recognise that we cannot fight every battle with the sea in every location and we really *must* learn from the past – and that past extends back not only through historical timescales but also through geological time as recorded in the very rocks and earth materials that make up the wonderfully varied fabric of island Britain. There will inevitably be some winners and some losers as climate change continues, as relative sea level rises and as Britain shrinks around its fringes through coastal flooding and erosion. That is the price we pay for being an island nation.

NOTES

Preface

1. Farnhill, B. (1966) *Robin Hood's Bay: The Story of a Yorkshire Community*. Dalesman Publishing Company Ltd., Clapham, Yorkshire.
2. Walmsley, L. (1948) *Phantom Lobster*. Penguin Books, Harmondsworth, Middlesex.
3. Jecock, M. (2009) A fading memory: the North Yorkshire coastal alum industry in the light of recent analytical field survey by English Heritage. *Industrial Archaeology Review*, 31, 54–73.
4. Forbes, D. (1961) *British Fossils*. Adam and Charles Black, London.
5. Whatley, C.A. (1987) *The Scottish Salt Industry 1570–1850: An Economic and Social History*. Aberdeen University Press, Aberdeen.
6. Pilkey, O.H. and Cooper, J.A.G. (2004) Society and sea level rise. *Science*, 303, 1781–1782.
7. Jones, O.T. and Pugh, W.J. (1949) An early Ordovician shore-line in Radnorshire, near Builth Wells. *Quarterly Journal of the Geological Society of London*, 105, 65–99.
8. Rolfe, W.D.I. (1980) *Geological Howlers*. Geological Society of Glasgow, Glasgow.

Chapter 1

1. Smith, D.E., Shi, S., Cullingford, R.A., Dawson, S., Firth, C.R., Foster, I.D.L., Fretwell, P.T., Haggart, B.A., Holloway, L.K. and Long, D. (2004) The Holocene Storegga Slide tsunami in the United Kingdom. *Quaternary Science Reviews*, 23, 2291–2321.
2. Bondevik, J., Mangerud, J., Dawson, S., Dawson, A. and Lohne, Ø. (2005) Evidence for three North Sea tsunamis at the Shetland Islands between 8000 and 1500 years ago. *Quaternary Science Reviews*, 24, 1757–1775.
3. Bryant, E. (2008) *Tsunami: The Underrated Hazard* (2nd edn), Springer Praxis Books, Dordrecht, The Netherlands.
4. Bryant, E.A. and Haslett, S.K. (2007) Catastrophic wave erosion, Bristol Channel, United Kingdom. Impact of tsunami? *Journal of Geology*, 115, 253–269.
5. Haslett, S.K. and Bryant, E.A. (2004) The AD 1607 coastal flood in the Bristol Channel and Severn Estuary: historical records from Devon and Cornwall. *Archaeology in the Severn Estuary*, 15, 81–89.
6. Bryant, E.A. and Haslett, S.K. (2002) Was the AD 1607 coastal flooding event in the Severn Estuary and Bristol Channel (UK) due to a tsunami? *Archaeology in the Severn Estuary*, 13, 163–167.
7. British Geological Survey (2005) *The Threat Posed by Tsunami to the UK*. Study Commissioned by Defra Flood Management.
8. Bryant and Haslett, Was the AD 1607 coastal flooding event in the Severn Estuary and Bristol Channel (UK) due to a tsunami?, 163–167.

9. British Library Manuscript No. 1103.e.62.

10. Clow, D.G. (1988) Daniel Defoe's account of the storm of 1703. *Weather*, 140–141.

11. Brayne, E. (2005) *The Greatest Storm: Britain's Night of Destruction*. Cambridge University Press, Cambridge.

12. Haslett, S.K. and Bryant, E.A. (2007) Reconnaissance of historic (post-AD 1000) high-energy deposits along the Atlantic coasts of southwest Britain, Ireland and Brittany, France. *Marine Geology*, 242, 207–220.

13. Defoe, D. (1704) *The Storm: or, a Collection of the Most Remarkable Casualties and Disasters which Happen'd in the Late Dreadful Tempest, both by Sea and Land*. G. Sawbridge, London.

14. Defoe, *The Storm*, pp. 251–421.

15. Met Office. *Saturday 31 January (East Coast Floods)*. http://www.metoffice. gov.uk/corporate/library/dws/east_coast_floods_31_January_1953.pdf.

16. Vega-Leinert, A. C. de la and Nicholls, R.J. (2008) Potential implications of sea-level rise for Great Britain. *Journal of Coastal Research*, 24, 342–357; Canvey Island Town Council. *History*. http://www.canveyisland-tc.gov.uk/history.htm.

17. Steers, J.A. (1953) The east coast floods. *The Geographical Journal*, 119, 280–295.

18. Grieve, H. (1959) *The Great Tide: The Story of the 1953 Flood Disaster in Essex*. The County Council of Essex, Chelmsford.

19. White, D.J.B. (1961) Some observations on the vegetation of Blakeney Point, Norfolk, following the disappearance of the rabbits in 1954. *Journal of Ecology*, 49, 113–118.

20. White, Some observations on the vegetation of Blakeney Point, Norfolk, 113–118; Bartrip, P.W.J. (2008) Myxomatosis in 1950s Britain. *Twentieth Century British History*, 19, 83–105.

21. Steers, J.A., Stoddart, D.R., Bayliss-Smith, T.P., Spencer, T. and Durbidge, P.M. (1979) The storm surge of 11 January 1978 on the east coast of England. *The Geographical Journal*, 145, 192–205.

22. National Piers Society (2010) *Celebrating Seaside Piers*. http://www.piers.org.uk/.

23. Steers *et al.*, The storm surge of 11 January 1978, 192–205.

24. Arnott, K. (2000) *Hunstanton: The Story of a Small Norfolk Seaside Resort*. Witley Press, Hunstanton.

25. Steers *et al.*, The storm surge of 11 January 1978, 192–205.

26. National Piers Society, *Celebrating Seaside Piers*.

27. Steers *et al.*, The storm surge of 11 January 1978, 192–205.

28. BBC On this day, 31 January 1953: 130 die in Ferry Disaster. http://news.bbc.co.uk/ onthisday/hi/dates/stories/january/31/newsid_2505000/2505913.stm.

29. Hickey, K.R. (2001) The storm of 31 January to 1 February 1953 and its impact on Scotland. *Scottish Geographical Journal*, 117, 283–295.

30. Met Office. *Saturday 31 January (East Coast Floods)*; Anonymous (1953) *The Battle of the Floods: Holland in February 1953*. Netherlands Booksellers and Publishers Association, Amsterdam.

31. Moffat, A. (2005) *Before Scotland*. Thames and Hudson, London.

32. Gaffney, V., Thomson, K. and Finch, S. (2007). *Mapping Doggerland: The Mesolithic Landscapes of the Southern North Sea*. Archaeopress, Oxford.

33. Weninger, B., Schulting, R., Bradtmöller, Clare, L., Collard, M., Edinborough, K., Hilpert, J., Jöris, O., Niekus, M., Rohling, E.J. and Wagner, B. (2008) The catastrophic final flooding of Doggerland by the Storegga Slide tsunami. *Documenta Praehistorica*, XXXV, 1–24.

34. Dawson, S. and Wickham-Jones, C.R. (2007) Sea level change and the prehistory of Orkney. *Antiquity*, 312.

35. Bell, M. (2007) *Prehistoric Coastal Communities: The Mesolithic in Western Britain*. Research Report, 149, Council for British Archaeology, York.

36. Bell, M., Caseldine, A. and Neumann, H. (2000) *Prehistoric Intertidal Archaeology in the Welsh Severn Estuary*. Research Report, 120, Council for British Archaeology, York.

37. Allen, J.R.L., Bell, M.G. and Scales, R.R.L (2004) Animal and human footprint tracks in archaeology: description and significance. *Archaeology in the Severn Estuary*, 14, 55–68.

38. Bell, *Prehistoric Coastal Communities*.

39. Bell, *Prehistoric Coastal Communities*.

40. National Trust. *UK Top 10 Coastal Hotspots*. http://www.nationaltrust.org.uk/main/w-global/w-news/w-latest_news/w-news-holiday_hotspots.htm.

41. Chapple, W. (1785) *A review of Risdon's survey of the County of Devon, & of the City & County of Exeter: with corrections, additions, annotation, &c*. Gale ECCO, National Library of Scotland, Edinburgh.

42. Adams, J. (1876) *The Lady of Lyonesse*.

43. Ingram, J. (trans.) (1912) *The Anglo-Saxon Chronicle*, Everyman Press Edition, London.

44. Borlase, W. (1753) An account of the great alterations which the Islands of Sylley have undergone since the Time of the Ancients, who mention them, as to their number, extent and position: in a letter to the Rev. Thomas Birch. *Philosophical Transactions of the Royal Society*, 48, 55–69.

45. Shaw, W. (1995) *Spying in Guru Land: Inside Britain's Cults*. Fourth Estate Ltd., London.

46. Swithin, A. (1990–1993) *The Perilous Quest for Lyonesse* (series of four novels), Fontana/Collins, London.

47. Hitchen, K. (1999) What's in a name? *The Edinburgh Geologist*, 32, 15–19.

48. Torrey Canyon. Hansard, 4 April 1967.

49. BBC On this day, 18 March 1967: Supertanker Torrey Canyon hits rocks. http://news.bbc.co.uk/onthisday/hi/dates/stories/march/18/newsid_4242000/4242709.stm.

50. Tacitus. The Roman Attack on Anglesey and the British Druids. *Annals* XIV, xxix. http://resourcesforhistory.com/celtic_druids.htm.

51. *Mona Insula, Ynys Môn, Last Outpost of the Druids*. http://www.roman-britain.org/places/mona.htm.

52. Tacitus. *Agricola*, 18.3–5 http://www.roman-britain.org/places/mona.htm.

53. Roberts, M., Scourse, J., Bennell, J., Huws, D., Jago, C. and Long, B. (2010) Devensian, late glacial and Holocene relative sea-level change in North Wales, UK. *Sea-level Changes: The Science of a Changing World*. Quaternary Research Association Annual Discussion Meeting, University of Durham (Abstract).

54. Pennick, N. (1987) *Lost Lands and Sunken Cities*. Fortean Tomes, London.

55. Jones, C. (1983) Walls in the sea: the goradau of Menai. Some marine antiquities of the Menai Straits. *The International Journal of Nautical Archaeology and Underwater Exploration*, 12, 27–40.

56. Ashton, W. (1920) *The Evolution of a Coast-line: Barrow to Aberystwyth and the Isle of Man, with notes on Lost Towns, Submarine Discoveries etc*. Edward Stanford Ltd., London.

57. Pennick, *Lost Lands and Sunken Cities*.

58. Ashton, *The Evolution of a Coast-line*.

59. Ashton, *The Evolution of a Coast-line*.

60. The Monthly Record (1940) Llys Helig. *The Geographical Journal*, 96, 298–299.

61. The Monthly Record, Llys Helig.

62. Ashton, *The Evolution of a Coast-line*.

63. Cooper, S. (1977) *Silver on the Tree*. Scholastic Inc., New York.

64. Ashton, *The Evolution of a Coast-line*.

65. Willson, B. (1902) *The Story of Lost England*. George Newnes Ltd., London; Pennick, *Lost Lands and Sunken Cities*.

66. Edwards, Rev. G. (1849) *The Inundation of Cantre 'R Gwaelod; or, The Lowland Hundred*. Reprinted from The Archaeologia Cambrensis, No. XV, W. Pickering, London.

67. Edwards, *The Inundation of Cantre 'R Gwaelod*.

68. Willson, *The Story of Lost England*.

69. Chandler, J. (1809) The New Seaman's Guide and Coaster's Companion, *Part 1, Directions for the North Side of the British Channel*, 16th edn. P. Mason, London.

70. Reid, C. (1913) *Submerged Forests*. Cambridge University Press, Cambridge.

71. Reid, *Submerged Forests*.

72. Archaeological Research Services Ltd (2008) *North East Rapid Coastal Zone Assessment (NERCZA) Report*, No. 2008/81.

73. Innes, J.B. and Frank, R.M. (1988) Palynological evidence for Late Flandrian coastal changes at Druridge Bay, Northumberland. *Scottish Geographical Magazine*, 104, 14–23.

74. Sheahan, J.J. and Whellan, T. (1857) *History and Topography of the City of York; The East Riding of Yorkshire; and a Portion of the West Riding; Embracing A General Review of the Early History of Great Britain, and a General History and Description of the County of York. Volume II*. John Green, Beverley.

75. Momber, G. (2000) Drowned and deserted: a submerged prehistoric landscape in the Solent, England. *The International Journal of Nautical Archaeology*, 29, 86–99.

76. French, C.N. (1999) The 'submerged' forest palaeosols of Cornwall. *Geoscience in South-West England*, 9, 365–369.

77. Ashton, *The Evolution of a Coast-line*.

78. Willson, *The Story of Lost England*.

79. Willson, *The Story of Lost England*.

80. Fleming, J. (1822) On a submarine forest in the Frith of Tay, with observations on the formation of submarine forests in general. *Transactions of the Royal Society of Edinburgh*, 9, 419–431.

81. Fleming, Rev. Dr. (1830) Notice of a submarine forest in Largo Bay in the Frith of Forth. *The Quarterly Journal of Science, Literature and Art*, 29, 21–29.

82. Reid, *Submerged Forests*.

83. Willson, *The Story of Lost England*.

84. Willson, *The Story of Lost England*.

85. Young, H.E. (1909) *A Perambulation of the Hundred of Wirral in the County Of Chester with an Account of the Principal Highways and Byways, Old Halls, Ancient Churches, and Interesting Villages Situated Between the Rivers Mersey and Dee*. Henry Young & Sons, Liverpool.

86. Raglan, Lord. (1960) Canute and the waves. *Man*, 60, 7–8.

87. Drayton, M. (1612 [2005]) *The Complete Works of Michael Drayton: Volume 1. Poly-Olbion*. Adamant Media Corporation, Boston, USA.

88. Drayton, *Poly-Olbion*.

89. Evans, A.L. (1991) *Lost Lancashire: The Story of Lancashire-beyond-the-Sands*. Cicerone Press, Milnthorpe, Cumbria.

90. Lyell, C. (1830) *Principles of Geology*. John Murray, London.

91. BBC News (27 April 2009) Naturists lose battle for beach. http://news.bbc.co.uk/1/hi/england/suffolk/8020424.stm.

Chapter 2

1. Price, R.J. (1983) *Scotland's Environment during the Last 30,000 Years.* Scottish Academic Press, Edinburgh.
2. Boulton, G and Hagdorn, M. (2006) Glaciology of the British Isles Ice Sheet during the last glacial cycle: form, flow, streams and lobes. *Quaternary Science Reviews,* 25, 3359–3390.
3. Koster, E.A. (2005) *The Physical Geography of Western Europe.* Oxford University Press, Oxford.
4. Candow, R. (1989) *Prehistoric Morton: The Story of Mesolithic Discoveries at Morton Farm on Tentsmuir in North East Fife.* David Winter & Son Ltd., Dundee.
5. Candow, *Prehistoric Morton.*
6. Natural Environment Research Council: Planet Earth Online (2009) *Pine Island Glacier May Disappear Within 100 Years.* http://planetearth.nerc.ac.uk/news/story. aspx?id=505.
7. National Oceanic and Atmospheric Administration National Climatic Data Center (undated) Global Warming, Frequently Asked Questions. http://www.ncdc.noaa.gov/oa/climate/globalwarming.html.
8. Crutzen, P. J., and Stoermer, E.F. (2000) The 'Anthropocene'. *Global Change Newsletter* 41, 17–18.
9. IPCC (2007) *Fourth Assessment Report: Climate Change* (AR4). Contribution of Working Group I to the Fourth Assessment Report of the Intergovernmental Panel on Climate Change. Solomon, S., Qin, D., Manning, M., Chen, Z., Marquis, M., Averyt, K.B., Tignor, M. and Miller, H.L. (eds). Cambridge University Press, Cambridge.
10. IPCC (2005) *Second Assessment Report: Climate Change* (SAR).
11. UK Climate Impacts Programme (undated) *The Climate is Changing: What's the Outlook for You?* http://www.ukcip.org.uk.
12. Met Office (16 December 2008) *2008 Global Temperature.* http://www.metoffice.gov.uk/corporate/pressoffice/2008/pr20081216.html.
13. Met Office Hadley Centre (1659–2011) *Monthly Mean Central England Temperatures.* http://hadobs.metoffice.com/hadcet/cetml1659on.dat.
14. IPCC (2007) *Fourth Assessment Report: Climate Change* (AR4).
15. Ball, T., Werritty, A., Duck, R. W., Edwards, A., Booth, L. and Black, A.R. (2008). *Coastal Flooding in Scotland: A Scoping Study.* Report for Scotland and Northern Ireland Forum for Environmental Research (SNIFFER).
16. Defra (2009) *UK Climate Projections.* http://ukclimateprojections.defra.gov.uk/.
17. Smith, D.B. (1981) *Curling: An Illustrated History.* John Donald, Edinburgh.
18. The Royal Caledonian Curling Club (2010) *Grand Match.* http://www.royalcaledonian curlingclub.org/rccc/index.cfm/about-rccc/origin-history/grand-match/.
19. The Royal Caledonian Curling Club, *Grand Match.*
20. Kays of Scotland. http://www.kaysofscotland.co.uk/about.cfm.
21. Extract from the poem: *The Wreck of the Titanic While on Her Way to America in April 1912* that has been attributed to Dundee poet and tragedian William Topaz McGonagall. However, McGonagall died in 1902.
22. McKean, C. (2006) *Battle for the North: The Tay and Forth Bridges and the 19th-Century Railway Wars.* Granta Books, London.
23. Duck, R.W. and McGlashan, D.J. (2010) The Lighthouse Stevensons and the first Tay Railway Bridge: discovery of an original manuscript: Unpublished article.
24. Hutton, G. (1995) *Old Perth.* Stenlake Publishing, Catrine, Ayrshire.
25. Gilvear, D.J. and Black, A.R. (1999) Flood-induced embankment failures on the River Tay: implications of climatically induced hydrological change in Scotland. *Hydrological Sciences Journal,* 44, 345–362.

26. Duck, R.W. (2011) The physical development of the Tay Estuary in the twentieth century and its impact. In: Tomlinson, J. and Whatley, C.A. (eds). *Jute No More: Transforming Dundee*, Dundee University Press, Dundee, pp. 52–69.

27. Defra (2009) *UK Climate Projections: Key Findings for Sea Level Rise*. http://ukclimateprojections.defra.gov.uk/content/view/2145/499/.

28. Gray, R. (2000). How Scotland is bouncing back: after 6,000 years, Ice Age phenomenon is keeping rising tides at bay. *Daily Mail*, Wednesday 12 April, 2000, p. 31.

29. BBC News (13 January 2005) Community shock over storm deaths. http://news.bbc.co.uk/1/hi/scotland/4170621.stm.

30. Scottish Natural Heritage (undated). *Monach Isles National Nature Reserve*. http://www.snh.org.uk/pubs/detail.asp?id=522.

31. Scottish Natural Heritage, *Monach Isles National Nature Reserve*.

32. The Spalding Club (1846) Miscellany of the Spalding Club, Volume Third. Printed for the Club, Aberdeen; Macaulay, M. (2010) *The Prisoner of St Kilda: The True Story of the Unfortunate Lady Grange*. Luath Press Ltd, Edinburgh.

33. Dawson, A. (2009) *So Foul and Fair a Day: A History of Scotland's Weather and Climate*. Birlinn, Edinburgh.

34. Northern Lighthouse Board (2009) *Monach*. http://www.nlb.org.uk/ourlights/history/monach.htm.

35. Scottish Natural Heritage, *Monach Isles National Nature Reserve*.

36. Love, J.A. (2009) Oh dear! What can the machair be? *The Glasgow Naturalist*, 25, Supplement, Machair Conservation: Successes and Challenges, 3–10.

37. *Sunday Times* (19 March 2000) Global Warming to Sink Scots Isles.

38. Defra/Environment Agency Flood and Coastal Defence R&D Programme. (2002) *Soft Cliffs: Prediction of Recession Rates and Erosion Control Techniques*. R&D Project FD2403/1302.

39. Jennings, J.N. (1952) The origin of the Broads. *Royal Geographical Society Research Memoir*, 2.

40. Jennings, J.N. and Lambert, J.M. (1953) The origin of the Broads. *The Geographical Journal*, 119, 91; Lambert, J.M., Jennings, J.N., Smith, C.T., Green, C. and Hutchinson, J.N. (1960). The making of the Broads: a reconsideration in the light of new evidence. *Royal Geographical Society Research Memoir*, 3.

41. Smith, C.T. (1966) Dutch peat digging and the origin of the Norfolk Broads. *The Geographical Journal*, 132, 69–72.

42. Darby, H.C. (1940) The draining of the Fens. *Cambridge Studies in Economic History*.

43. Chisholm, M. (2006) Navigation and the seventeenth-century draining of the Fens. *Journal of Historical Geography*, 32, 731–751.

44. Fowler, Major G. (1933) Shrinkage of the peat-covered Fenlands. *The Geographical Journal*, 81, 149–150.

45. Fowler, Shrinkage of the peat-covered Fenlands.

46. Waltham, T. (2000) Peat subsidence at the Holme Post. *Mercian Geologist*, 15, 49–51.

47. Dawson, Q., Kechavarzi, C., Leeds-Harrison, P.B. and Burton, R.G.O. (2010) Subsidence and degradation of agricultural peatlands in the Fenlands of Norfolk, UK. *Geoderma*, 154, 181–187.

48. BBC News (29 November 2002) UK's lowest spot is getting lower. http://news.bbc.co.uk/1/hi/england/2529365.stm.

49. Darby, The draining of the Fens.

50. Bevis, T. (2001) *Flooded Fens: Floods and the Stoical Determinedness of the Fen and March People and the Hazardous nature of their Work*. March, Cambridgeshire.

51. Steers, The east coast floods.

52. Williams, S. and Worth, D. (2003) Planning for flood risk in the Fens. *Water and Environment Journal*, 17, 226–231.
53. Defoe, *The Storm*, pp. 251–421.
54. Williams, M. (1970) *The Draining of the Somerset Levels*. Cambridge University Press, Cambridge.
55. Steers, J.A. (1967) Geomorphology and coastal processes. In: Lauff, G.H. (ed.), *Estuaries*, American Association for the Advancement of Science Publication No. 83, Washington, pp. 100–107.
56. Environment Agency. *The Thames Barrier*. http://www.environment-agency.gov.uk/homeandleisure/floods/38353.aspx; Environment Agency (2008) *The Thames Barrier Project Pack*. http://www.environment-agency.gov.uk/static/documents/Leisure/Thames_Barrier_2010_project_pack.pdf; Kendrick, M. (1988) The Thames Barrier. *Landscape and Urban Planning*, 16, 57–68.
57. Crichton, D. (2007) What can cities do to increase resilience? *Philosophical Transactions of the Royal Society A: Mathematical, Physical and Engineering Sciences*, 365, 2731–2739.
58. Defra *UK Climate Projections: The Climate of the UK and Recent Trends: 1.6*. http://ukclimateprojections.defra.gov.uk/content/view/756/9/.
59. Zong, Y. and Tooley, M.J. (2003) A historical record of coastal floods in Britain: Frequencies and associated storm tracks. *Natural Hazards*, 29, 13–36.
60. Zong and Tooley, A historical record of coastal floods in Britain.
61. Ball *et al. Coastal Flooding in Scotland: A Scoping Study*.
62. Smits, A., Klein Tank, A.M.G. and Können, G.P. (2005) Trends in storminess over The Netherlands, 1962–2002. *International Journal of Climatology*, 25, 1331–1344.
63. Owens, J.S. and Case, G.O. (1908) *Coast Erosion and Foreshore Protection*. The St Bride's Press Ltd, London.

Chapter 3

1. Bathurst, B. (1999) *The Lighthouse Stevensons*. Flamingo, London.
2. Reid, C. (1906) Coast erosion. *The Geographical Journal*, 28, 487–495.
3. Walcott, M.E.C. (1861) *The East Coast of England from the Thames to the Tweed Descriptive of Natural Scenery, Historical, Archaeological and Legendary*. Edward Stanford, London.
4. De Boer, G. (1964) Spurn Head: its history and evolution. *Transactions and Papers (Institute of British Geographers)*, 34, 71–89.
5. De Boer, Spurn Head: its history and evolution.
6. Reid, C. (1906) Coast erosion. *The Geographical Journal*, 28, 487–495.
7. Ward, E.M. (1922) *English Coastal Evolution*. Methuen & Co., London.
8. Willson, B. (1902) *The Story of Lost England*. George Newnes Ltd., London.
9. Sheppard, T. (1912) *The Lost Towns of the Yorkshire Coast*. A. Brown & Sons, London.
10 Sheppard, *The Lost Towns of the Yorkshire Coast*.
11. Willson, *The Story of Lost England*.
12. Sheppard, *The Lost Towns of the Yorkshire Coast*; Pennick, *Lost Lands and Sunken Cities*.
13. Sheppard, *The Lost Towns of the Yorkshire Coast*.
14. Nicholson, J. (1890) *Folk Lore of East Yorkshire*. Simpkin, Hamilton, Marshal, Kent and Co., London.
15. Sheppard, *The Lost Towns of the Yorkshire Coast*.
16. Nicholson, *Folk Lore of East Yorkshire*; Sheppard, *The Lost Towns of the Yorkshire Coast*.
17. Sheppard, *The Lost Towns of the Yorkshire Coast*.
18. Sheppard, *The Lost Towns of the Yorkshire Coast*.

19. Ostler, G. (undated) Coastal erosion and the lost towns of Holderness. *Humberside Geologist*, No. 14. http://www.hullgeolsoc.org.uk/gordon.htm.

20. EUROSION (2007) Case Study: Holderness Coast (United Kingdom). http://copranet.projects.eucc-d.de/files/000164_EUROSION_Holderness_ coast.pdf.

21. EUROSION Case Study: Holderness Coast (United Kingdom).

22. Mathison, P. (2008) *The Spurn Gravel Trade*. Dead Good Publications, Newport, East Yorkshire.

23. Mathison, *The Spurn Gravel Trade*.

24. Hayward, J. (2001). *The Bodies on the Beach: Sealion, Shingle Street and the Burning Sea Myth of 1940*. CD41 Publishing, Norfolk.

25. Furneé, B. (2009) Lines of Defence, East Lane, Bawdsey. http://www.youtube.com/watch?v=ukcuw0c6kho.

26. Strickland, A. in Wake, R. (ed.) (1839) *Southwold and its Vicinity, Ancient and Modern*. F. Skill, Yarmouth.

27. Curran, *Lost Lands*.

28. Walters, C. (1901) Cities beneath the sea. In: Walters, C. (ed.) *Bygone Suffolk: Its History, Romance, Legend, Folk-Lore &c.* A. Brown and Sons, London.

29. Defoe, D. (1762) *A Tour Thro' the Whole Island of Great Britain Divided into Circuits or Journeys*, 6th edn, London.

30. Walters, Cities beneath the sea.

31. Stamp, L.D. (1969) *Britain's Structure and Scenery*. The Fontana New Naturalist (6th Impression), London.

32. Bacon, J. and Bacon, S. (1979) *The Search for Dunwich: City Under the Sea*. Segment Publications, Colchester.

33. Bacon and Bacon, *The Search for Dunwich*.

34. Bacon and Bacon, *The Search for Dunwich*; Willson, *The Story of Lost England*.

35. Bacon and Bacon, *The Search for Dunwich*.

36. Lyell, *Principles of Geology*.

37. Bacon and Bacon, *The Search for Dunwich*.

38. Walters, Cities beneath the sea.

39. Ward, *English Coastal Evolution*.

40. Suffolk Cards. http://www.suffolkcards.co.uk/turner_dunwich.html.

41. Lyell, *Principles of Geology*.

42. Gattie, G.B. (1904) *Memorials of the Goodwin Sands, and their Surroundings, Legendary and Historical*. J.J. Keliher and Co. Ltd., London.

43. Gattie, *Memorials of the Goodwin Sands*.

44. Willson, *The Story of Lost England*.

45. Halcrow Group Ltd. (2003). *Review of Goodwin Sands Airport Proposal*. http://webarchive.nationalarchives.gov.uk/+/http://www.dft.gov.uk/about/ strategy/whitepapers/air/responses/ewofgoodwinsandsairportp5685.pdf.

46. Airport Environment Federation (2009) *Thames Estuary Airport: AEF Position Paper*. http://www.aef.org.uk/uploads/Thames_Estuary_Airport_proposal___ AEF_position_paper.pdf.

47. Walcott, *The East Coast of England from the Thames to the Tweed*.

48. Ward, *English Coastal Evolution*.

49. May, V.J. (1971) The retreat of chalk cliffs. *The Geographical Journal*, 137, 203–206; McGlashan, D.J., Duck, R.W. and Reid, C.T. (2008). Unstable boundaries on a cliffed coast: geomorphology and British laws. *Journal of Coastal Research*, 24, 181–188.

50. Dornbusch, U. (2002) *BERM Final Report - Technical Report*. http://www.geog. sussex.ac.uk/BERM/BERM-final-report-UK.pdf.

51. BBC (2007) Seahenge comes home to Norfolk. http://www.bbc.co.uk/norfolk/content/articles/2007/08/23/feature_seahenge_display_20070823_feature.shtml.

52. BBC, Seahenge comes home to Norfolk.

53. BBC, Seahenge comes home to Norfolk.

54. Miller, H. (1834) *Scenes and Legends of the North of Scotland or the Traditional History of Cromarty*. Adam and Charles Black, Edinburgh.

55. Reid, *Submerged Forests*.

56. Fotheringham, Rev. W. (1907) Notes on the old Crosskirk at Quendale in Dunrossness, Shetland, and its monumental stones. *Proceedings of the Society of Antiquaries of Scotland*, 41, 173–180.

57. Evans, A.L. (c.1960) *The Story of Kenfig*. Evans, Port Talbot.

58. Professor Allan Williams (2008) Personal communication.

59. Crawford, R.M.M. and Wishart, D. (1966) A multivariate analysis of the development of dune slack vegetation in relation to coastal accretion at Tentsmuir, Fife. *Journal of Ecology*, 54, 729–743.

60. Wal, A. and McManus, J. (1993) Wind regime and sand transport on a coastal beach-dune complex, Tentsmuir, eastern Scotland. In: Pye, K. (ed.), *The Dynamics and Environmental Context of Aeolian Sedimentary Systems: Geological Society Special Publication*, 72, 159–161; Whittington, G. (1996) *Fragile Environments: The Use and Management of Tentsmuir National Nature Reserve*. Scottish Cultural Press, Dalkeith.

61. Wal and McManus, Wind regime and sand transport on a coastal beach-dune complex, Tentsmuir, eastern Scotland.

62. Great Northern Railway Poster (1908) *Skegness 'It's so Bracing'*.

63. Walcott, *The East Coast of England from the Thames to the Tweed*.

64. Skegness Town Council (2009) Jolly Fisherman 1908 to the Present Day. http://www.skegness.gov.uk/pages/jollyfisherman.htm.

65. Wake, R. (1839) *Southwold and its Vicinity, Ancient and Modern*. F. Skill, Yarmouth.

66. Wake, *Southwold and its Vicinity, Ancient and Modern*.

67. Hudson, W.H. (1909) *Afoot in England*. Hutchinson, London.

68. Be beside the seaside, *Daily Telegraph* (11 August 2008).

69. Quick, R.H. (1888) *Positions: by Richard Mulcaster*. Longmans, Green and Co., London.

70. Hewitt, W. (1844) *An Essay on the Encroachments of the German Ocean along the Norfolk Coast, with a Design to Arrest its Further Depredations; Dedicated to the Right Honourable the Lords Commissioners of the Admiralty*. Matchett, Stevenson and Matchett, Norwich.

71. North, D. and Smith, M.H. (2004) *Elements of the North Norfolk Coast: Wildlife, Villages, History, Myths, Legends*. Birdseyeview Books, Thurgarton, Norwich.

72. Cromer Parish Church with St Martin's (2011) A brief history. http://www.cromer-church.org.uk/.

73. Girling, R. (2008) *Sea Change: Britain's Coastal Catastrophe*. Eden Project Books, London.

74. 'A Naturalist' (1855) *Rambles among the Channel Islands*. The Society for Promoting Christian Knowledge, London.

75. Plees, W. (1817) *An Account of the Island of Jersey; Containing a Compendium of its Ecclesiastical, Civil, and Military, History: A Statement of its Polity, Laws, Privileges, Commerce, Population and Produce: A Survey of the Public Buildings, Antiquities, and Natural History: Together with Some Detail Respecting the Manners & Customs of the Inhabitants*. T. Baker, Southampton.

76. The National Trust for Jersey (2003) La Mare au Seigneur. http://www.nationaltrustjersey.org.je/showcase/lamareauseigneur.asp.

77. Plees, *An Account of the Island of Jersey*.

78. Cooper, N.J. and Pethick, J.S. (2005) Sediment budget approach to addressing coastal erosion problems in St Ouen's Bay, Jersey, Channel Islands. *Journal of Coastal Research*, 21, 112–122.

79. Cooper and Pethick, Sediment budget approach to addressing coastal erosion problems in St Ouen's Bay.

Chapter 4

1. Royal Commission on Coast Erosion and Afforestation (1911) *Report of the Royal Commission Appointed to Inquire into and to Report on Certain Questions Affecting Coast Erosion, the Reclamation of Tidal Lands, and Afforestation in the United Kingdom.* HM Stationery Office, London, 3 vols.

2. Lessons from Dunwich, *The Independent* (18 August 2008).

3. Burbrigde, P (2005) *Land-Ocean Interactions in the Coastal Zone (LOICZ).* Research Seminar, Department of Geography, University of Dundee, 21 February 2005. Unpublished.

4. Galvin, C. (1990) Importance of longshore transport. *Shore and Beach*, 58, 31–32.

5. Walmsley, *Phantom Lobster.*

6. Nordstrom, K.F. (2000) *Beaches and Dunes of Developed Coasts.* Cambridge University Press, Cambridge.

7. Hewitt, W. (1844) *An Essay on the Encroachments of the German Ocean along the Norfolk Coast, with a Design to Arrest its Further Depredations; Dedicated to the Right Honourable the Lords Commissioners of the Admiralty.* Matchett, Stevenson and Matchett, Norwich.

8. Ferguson, J. (1907) *The Law of Water and Water Rights in Scotland*, 2nd edn. Green and Sons, Edinburgh.

9. Royal Commission on Coast Erosion and Afforestation.

10. Ward, E.M. (1922) *English Coastal Evolution.* Methuen & Co., London.

11. Rennie, J. (1845) *Minutes of the Proceedings of the Institution of Civil Engineers*, 4, 24.

12. Saiu, E., McManus, J. and Duck, R.W. (1994) Impact of industrial growth and decline on coastal equilibrium, eastern Scotland. *Coastal Zone Canada '94*, 2205–2219.

13. Conwy Borough Council (2001) Unitary Development Plan: Consultation Draft.

14. Gray, M. (2004) *Geodiversity: Valuing and Conserving Abiotic Nature.* John Wiley & Sons, Ltd, Chichester.

15. Royal Commission on Coast Erosion and Afforestation.

16. Charlier, R.H., De Meyer, C.P. and Decroo, D. (1989) Beach protection and restoration Part II: a perspective of 'soft' methods. *International Journal of Environmental Studies*, 33, 167–191.

17. Charlier, De Meyer and Decroo, Beach protection and restoration.

18. MARINET Campaigning to Protect the Marine Environment. http://www.marinet.org.uk/.

19. *The Morpeth Herald* (22 January 2008) Trees Help the Dunes.

20. Rose, M. (1995). Saving the sands of time. *Surveyor*, 5337, 16–18.

21. EUROSION (2007) Case Study: Essex Estuaries (United Kingdom). http://copranet.projects.eucc-d.de/files/000163_EUROSION_Essex_estuaries.pdf.

22. Williams, A.T., Davies, P. and Ergin, A. (2002) Coastal engineering and erosion along the Glamorgan Heritage Coast, UK. *Proceedings of the 28th International Conference, 'Coastal Engineering 2002'*, World Scientific, 3539-3551.

23. Williams, A.T. and Davies, P. (1980). Man as a geological agent: the sea cliffs of Llantwit Major, Wales, UK. *Zeitschrift fur Geomorphologie, Supplementband*, 34, 129–141.

24. Ward, *English Coastal Evolution*.

25. Hutchinson, J.N. (2002). Chalk flows from the coastal cliffs of northwest Europe. In: Evans, S.G. and DeGraff, J.V. (eds), Catastrophic landslides: effects, occurrence and mechanisms. *Geological Society of America Reviews in Engineering Geology*, 15, 257–302.

26. AggRegain (2003) Use of tyre bales as replacement for shingle in flood defence scheme at Pevensey Beach. http://www.wrap.org.uk/downloads/78-TyreBeach Recharge.0a6e0c23.1096.pdf.

27. HR Wallingford (2005) *Sustainable Re-Use of Tyres in Port, Coastal and River Engineering: Guidance for Planning Implementation and Maintenance.* Report SR 669.

28. Cadell, H.M. (1929) Land reclamation in the Forth Valley. I. Reclamation prior to 1840. *Scottish Geographical Magazine*, 45, 7–22.

29. Cadell, H.M. (1929) Land reclamation in the Forth Valley. II. Later reclamation and the work of the Forth Conservancy Board. *Scottish Geographical Magazine*, 45, 81–100.

30. Young, Rev. G. (1824) *A Picture of Whitby and its Environs*. R. Rodgers, Whitby.

31. Scarborough Borough Council (2004) *Legend of the Penny Hedge*. http://www.discoveryorkshirecoast.com/documents/pdf/factsheets/whitby/the_ legend_of_the_penny_hedge.pdf.

32. British Pathé (1938) Planting the Penalty Hedge at Whitby Video Newsreel Film. http://www.britishpathe.com/record.php?id=17614.

33. Pennick, *Lost Lands and Sunken Cities*.

34. Davidson, N.C., Laffoley, D.d'A., Doody, J.P., Way, L.S., Gordon, J., Key, R., Drake, C.M., Pienkowski, M.W., Mitchell, R. and Duff, K.L. (1991) *Nature Conservation and Estuaries in Great Britain*. Nature Conservancy Council, Peterborough.

35. Davidson, *et al*. *Nature Conservation and Estuaries in Great Britain*.

36. Ogilvie, A.G. (1945) Land reclamation in Scotland. *Scottish Geographical Magazine*, 61, 77–84.

37. Hodd, A.N.L. (1974) *Agricultural Change in the Carse of Gowrie, 1750–1875*. PhD Thesis, University of Dundee; Alizai, S.A.K. and McManus, J. (1980) The significance of reed beds on siltation in the Tay Estuary. *Proceedings of the Royal Society of Edinburgh*, 78B, s1–s13.

38. Brittain, V. (1940) *Testament of Friendship: The Story of Winifred Holtby*. The MacMillan Company, New York.

39. Sheahan and Whellan, *History and Topography of the City of York; The East Riding of Yorkshire; and a Portion of the West Riding*; Ellis, S. and Atherton, J.K. (2003) Properties and development of soils on reclaimed alluvial sediments in the Humber estuary, eastern England. *Catena*, 523, 129–147.

40. Ellis and Atherton, Properties and development of soils on reclaimed alluvial sediments in the Humber estuary.

41. Ellis, S. and Van de Noort, R. (undated). The archaeology of the Humber estuary: proposals for a strategic approach in environmental management and planning. http://www.hull.ac.uk/geog/PDF/WP9808.pdf.

42. Nicholson, *Folk Lore of East Yorkshire*.

43. Ellis and Atherton, Properties and development of soils on reclaimed alluvial sediments in the Humber estuary.

44. Pethick, J.S. (1994) *Humber Estuary and Coast Management Issues*. http://www.hull.ac.uk/iecs/pdfs/he&cman.pdf.

45. Sheppard, *The Lost Towns of the Yorkshire Coast*.

46. Pethick, *Humber Estuary and Coast Management Issues*.

47. Davidson *et al*., *Nature Conservation and Estuaries in Great Britain*.

48. Grant. A. (2009) Restoration and creation of saltmarshes and other intertidal habitats. http://www.uea.ac.uk/~e130/Saltmarsh.htm.

49. Mazik, K., Smith, J.E., Leighton, A. and Elliott, M. (2007) Physical and biological development of a newly breached managed realignment site, Humber estuary, UK. *Marine Pollution Bulletin*, 55, 564–578.

50. ABP Marine Environmental Research Ltd. (2010) *The Online Marine Managed Realignment Guide*. http://www.abpmer.net/omreg/.

51. Wilson, T. (2010) STEP Forth: a unique habitat creation and flood alleviation project on the Forth. *The Geographer*, Summer 2010, 14.

52. Taylor, J.A., Murdock, A.P. and Pontee, N.I. (2004) A macroscale analysis of coastal steepening around the coast of England and Wales. *The Geographical Journal*, 170, 179–188.

Chapter 5

1. Defra (2009) *Charting Progress: Section 3.2 Coastal Defence*. http://chartingprogress. defra.gov.uk/feeder/Section_3.2_Coastal%20Defence.pdf.

2. French, P.W. (1997) *Coastal and Estuarine Management*. Routledge, London.

3. Sunamura, T. 1992) *Geomorphology of Rocky Coasts*. John Wiley and Sons, Chichester.

4. Steers, J.A. (1962) Coastal cliffs: report of a symposium. *The Geographical Journal*, 128, 303–307.

5. Hall, A.M., Hansom, J.D., Williams, D.M. and Jarvis, J. (2006) Distribution, geomorphology and lithofacies of cliff-top storm deposits: Examples from the high-energy coasts of Scotland and Ireland. *Marine Geology*, 232, 131–155; Hansom, J.D., Barltrop, N.D.P. and Hall, A.M. (2008) Modelling the processes of cliff-top erosion and deposition under extreme storm waves. *Marine Geology*, 253, 36–50.

6. Macgregor, M., Herriot, A. and King, B.C. (1972) *Excursion Guide to the Geology of Arran*. The Geological Society of Glasgow, Glasgow.

7. Mackenzie, W.M. (1914) *The Book of Arran, Volume Second, History and Folklore*. The Arran Society of Glasgow, Glasgow.

8. Mackenzie, *The Book of Arran*.

9. Ager, D. (1995) *The New Catastrophism: The Importance of the Rare Event in Geological History*. Cambridge University Press, Cambridge.

10. Hansom, J.D. and Evans, D.J.A. (1995) The Old Man of Hoy. *Scottish Geographical Magazine*, 111, 172–174.

11. Hansom and Evans, The Old Man of Hoy.

12. Daniell, W. (2006 [modern edition with facsimile colour reproductions]) *Daniell's Scotland: A Voyage around the Coast of Scotland and the Adjacent Isles 1815–1822*. Two Volumes. Birlinn, Edinburgh.

13. Cruden, D.M. (1991) A simple definition of a landslide. *Bulletin of Engineering Geology and the Environment*, 43, 27–29.

14. Downie, R.A. (1933). *All About Arran*. Blackie and Son Limited, Glasgow.

15. British Geological Survey. *The Holbeck Hall landslide, Scarborough*. http://www.bgs.ac.uk/science/landUseAndDevelopment/landslides/HolbeckHall. html; West, L.J. (1994) The Scarborough landslide. *Quarterly Journal of Engineering Geology*, 27, 3–6; Clements, M. (1994) The Scarborough experience: Holbeck landslide, 3/4 June 1993. *Proceedings of the Institution of Civil Engineers: Municipal Engineer*, 103, 63–70; May, V. (1993) Tourism and managing the coast: a review of recent meetings. *Tourism Management*, 14, 404–405.

16. GeoNews (1993) Scarborough landslip. *Geoscientist*, 3 (5), 2–3.

17. GeoNews, Scarborough landslip.

18. Holbeck Hall Hotel Ltd and Another v. Scarborough Borough Council. Court of Appeal (Civil Division), 22nd February 2000. http://www.coastlaw.uct.ac.za/iczm/cases/holbeck3.htm; Hopkins, C.A. (2000) Slipping into uncertainty. *The Cambridge Law Journal*, 59. 438–440; Thompson, M.P. (2001) Case comment: coastal erosion and collapsing hotels. *The Conveyancer and Property Lawyer*, March/April, 177–184.

19. Fish, P.R., Moore, R. and Carey, J.M. (2006) Landslide geomorphology of Cayton Bay, North Yorkshire, UK. *Proceedings of the Yorkshire Geological Society*, 56, 5–14.

20. British Geological Survey (2011) *Landslide at Knipe Point, Cayton Bay, North Yorkshire.* http://www.bgs.ac.uk/science/landUseAndDevelopment/landslides/ caytonBay.html.

21. Defra (2010) *Adapting to Coastal Change: Developing a Policy Framework March 2010*, Defra, London.

22. McInnes, R.G., Jewell, S. and Roberts, H. (1998) Coastal management on the Isle of Wight, UK. *The Geographical Journal*, 164, 291–306.

23. British Pathé (1926) Big landslide in the Isle of Wight video newsreel film. http://www.britishpathe.com/record.php?id=24588.

24. British Pathé (1928) Great landslide video newsreel film. http://www.britishpathe.com/record.php?id=16468.

25. Hutchinson, J.H., Brunsden, D. and Lee, E.M. (1991) The geomorphology of the landslide complex at Ventnor, Isle of Wight. *Slope Stability Engineering. Proceedings of an International Conference, Isle of Wight,* 213–218.

26. McInnes *et al.*, Coastal management on the Isle of Wight, UK.

27. Willson, B. (1902) *The Story of Lost England*. George Newnes Ltd., London.

28. Moore, R., Clark, A.R. and Lee, E.M. (1998) Coastal cliff behaviour and management: Blackgang, Isle of Wight. *Geological Society of London, Engineering Geology Special Publications*, 15, 49–59.

29. Norton, T., Leyland, J. and Darby, S. (2006) Modelling flow, erosion and long-term evolution of incising channels: managing hydrology and geomorphology for ecology. *International Association of Hydrological Sciences Publication*, 306, 205–213.

30. Moore *et al.,* Coastal cliff behaviour and management.

31. The Official Ventnor Town Council Website. *The Town of Ventnor.* http://www.ventnortowncouncil.org.uk/.

32. Lee, E.M. and Moore, R. (2001) Land use planning in unstable areas: Ventnor, Isle of Wight. *Geological Society of London, Engineering Geology Special Publications*, 18, 189–192.

33. Ward Lock Guide (1948) *The Isle of Wight.* Ward Lock and Co. Ltd, London.

34. Lee and Moore, Land use planning in unstable areas.

35. Isle of Wight Council. *Landslide Management on the Isle of Wight.* http://www.coastalwight.gov.uk/PDFs/Landslide%20Management.pdf.

36. Lee and Moore, Land use planning in unstable areas.

37. Willson, *The Story of Lost England*.

38. Treves, F. (1906) *Highways and Byways of Dorset*. Macmillan and Co., Ltd., London.

39. Brunsden, D. (1996) Landslides of the Dorset coast: some unresolved questions. *Proceedings of the Ussher Society*, 9, 1–11.

40. Holiday, H. (2009) The Jurassic coast mass movement processes. *Geography Review*, September 2009, 2–5.

41. Allison, R.J. and Brunsden, D. (2008) Chapter 6: Mass movement. In: Burt, T.P., Chorley, R.J., Brunsden, D., Cox, N.J. and Goudie, A.S. (eds), *The History of the Study of Landforms or the Development of Geomorphology, Volume 4, Quaternary and Recent Processes and Forms (1890–1965) and the Mid-Century Revolutions*, Geological Society of London, London, pp. 165–216.

42. Allison and Brunsden, Chapter 6: Mass movement.

43. Jukes-Browne, A.J. (1908) The burning cliff and the landslip at Lyme Regis. *Proceedings of the Dorset Natural History and Antiquarian Field Club*, 29, 153–160.

44. Jukes-Browne, The burning cliff and the landslip at Lyme Regis.

45. Gallois, R.W. (2009) A recent large landslide at The Spittles, Lyme Regis, Dorset and its implications for the stability of the adjacent urban area. *Geoscience in South-West England*, 12, 101–108.

46. Jukes-Browne, The burning cliff and the landslip at Lyme Regis.

47. Pitts, J. (1979) Morphological mapping in the Axmouth-Lyme Regis Undercliffs, Devon. *Quarterly Journal of Engineering* Geology, 12, 205–217.

48. Pitts, J. and Brunsden, D. (1987) A reconsideration of the Bindon Landslide of 1839. *Proceedings of the Geologists' Association*, 98, 1–18.

49. The Parish of Axmouth. http://www.axmouthparishcouncil.co.uk/uploads/axmouthbriefhistory.pdf; Fowles, J. (1989) Foreword. In: Franks, E. (ed.) *The Undercliffe: A Sketchbook of the Axmouth–Lyme Regis Nature Reserve*, J.M. Dent and Sons Ltd., London, pp. 7–9.

50. Allison and Brunsden, Chapter 6: Mass movement.

51. Pitts and Brunsden, A reconsideration of the Bindon Landslide of 1839.

52. Arber, M.A. (1940) The coastal landslips of South-East Devon. *Proceedings of the Geologists' Association*, 51, 257–271; Arber, M.A. (1973) Landslips near Lyme Regis. *Proceedings of the Geologists' Association*, 84, 121–133.

53. *The Independent* (8 May 2008) Huge Landslide Hits Dorset's Jurassic Coast. http://www.independent.co.uk/news/uk/home-news/huge-landslide-hits-dorsets-jurassic-coast-822822.html.

54. Holiday, The Jurassic coast mass movement processes.

55. Huge landslide hits Dorset's Jurassic coast, *The Independent*, 8 May 2008.

56. BBC (7 May 2008) Landslip is 'worst' in 100 years. http://news.bbc.co.uk/1/hi/england/dorset/7386923.stm.

Chapter 6

1. Records of the Parliaments of Scotland (1695) Act for preservation of meadows, lands and pasturages, lying adjacent to sand-hills. Records of the Parliaments of Scotland to 1707, University of St Andrews. www.rps.ac.uk.

2. Ovington, J.D. (1950) The afforestation of the Culbin Sands. *Journal of Ecology*, 38, 303–319.

3. Adams, M. and Harthen, D. (with a contribution by Cowell, R.) (2007) *An Archaeological Assessment of the Sefton Coast, Merseyside: Part 1*. National Museums Liverpool Field Archaeology Unit, Albert Dock, Liverpool.

4. Adams and Harthen (with Cowell) *An Archaeological Assessment of the Sefton Coast*.

5. Harrop, S. (1985) *Old Birkdale and Ainsdale: Life on the South-West Lancashire Coast 1600–1851*. The Birkdale and Ainsdale Historical Research Society, Birkdale, Southport.

6. Smith, P.H. (2009) *The Sands of Time Revisited: An Introduction to the Sand Dunes of the Sefton Coast*. Amberley Publishing, Chalford, Stroud, Gloucestershire.

7. Gibson, Rev. T.E. (1895) *Crosby Records. Blundell's Diary: Comprising Selections from the Diary of Nicholas Blundell Esq., from 1702 to 1728*. Gilbert G. Walmsley, Liverpool.

8. Adams and Harthen (with Cowell) *An Archaeological Assessment of the Sefton Coast*.

9. Gibson, *Crosby Records*.

10. Smith, *The Sands of Time Revisited*.

11. Defoe, *The Storm*, pp. 251–421.

12. Gibson, *Crosby Records*.

13. *Parish Church of St Luke Formby: A Brief History of St Luke's Church*. http://stlukes.merseyside.org/History.htm.

14. Smith, *The Sands of Time Revisited*.

15. Smith, *The Sands of Time Revisited*.

16. Harrop, *Old Birkdale and Ainsdale*.

17. Harrop, *Old Birkdale and Ainsdale*.

18. Harrop, *Old Birkdale and Ainsdale*.

19. National Trust, *UK Top 10 Coastal Hotspots*.

20. Kinney, L. (2010) £50,000 of vandalism at Trump's golf resort. STV News, http://news.stv.tv/scotland/173694-/.

21. Simmonds, A. and Frost, S. (1978) Conservation recommendations for a sand quarry at Gwithian Beach, St. Ives Bay, Cornwall. *Landscape Research*, 3, 1718.

22. Ward, E.M. (1922). *English Coastal Evolution*. Methuen & Co., London.

23. Joint Defra/EA Flood and Coastal Erosion Risk Management R&D Programme (2007) *Sand Dune Processes and Management for Flood and Coastal Defence. Part 4: Techniques for Sand Dune Management*. R&D Technical Report, FD1392/TR.

24. Bird, E. (2005) Coastline changes. In: Schwartz, M.L. (ed.), *Encyclopedia of Coastal Science*. Springer, Dordrecht, pp. 319–323.

25. Williams, A., Davies, P. and Caldwell, N. (1997) *Coastal Processes and Landforms: the Glamorgan Heritage Coast*. The Glamorgan Heritage Coast Centre, Dunraven Park, Southerndown, Vale of Glamorgan.

26. Bartrip, P.W.J. (2008) Myxomatosis in 1950s Britain. *Twentieth Century British History*, 19, 83–105.

27. Williams *et al.*, *Coastal Processes and Landforms*.

28. Ball, I. (2006) *Coastal Partnerships and Research Strategy Development: A Review*. Marine and Coastal Environment (MACE) Research Group, Cardiff University; Stojanovic, T.A., Ball, I., Ballinger, R.C., Lymbery, G. and Dodds, W. (2009) The role of research networks for science-policy collaboration in coastal areas. *Marine Policy*, 33, 901–911.

29. Steers, The east coast floods.

30. Ritchie, W. (1993) Coastal sand dunes: Natural stability and artificial stabilisation. In: Dawson, A.H., Jones, H.R., Small, A. and Soulsby, J.A. (eds) *Scottish Geographical Studies*, Universities of Dundee and St Andrews, Scotland, pp. 73–87.

31. Dorset and East Devon Coast World Heritage Site Management Plan (2009–2014) http://www.jurassiccoast.com/downloads/WHS%20Management/jurassic_coast _plan_lowres.pdf.

32. Camden, W. (1607 [2004]) *Britannia*. Holland, P. (trans.). Hypertext Critical Edition by Sutton, D.F. The Philological Museum, University of Birmingham. http://www.philological.bham.ac.uk/cambrit/.

33. Willson, *The Story of Lost England*.

34. Bennett, M.R., Cassidy, N.J. and Pile, J. (2009) Internal structure of a barrier beach as revealed by ground penetrating radar (GPR): Chesil beach, UK. *Geomorphology*, 104, 218–229.

35. Avebury, The Right Hon. Lord (1902) *The Scenery of England and the Causes to Which it is Due*. The Macmillan Company.

36. Carr, A.P. (1983) Chesil Beach: environmental, economic and sociological pressures. *The Geographical Journal*, 149, 53–62; Lewis, J. (1983) Change, and vulnerability to natural hazard: Chiswell, Dorset. *The Environmentalist*, 3, 277–287.

37. *Mail Online* (2 April 2007) Author faces £2,000 fine after taking 'a handful' of pebbles from the beach. http://www.dailymail.co.uk/news/article-446256/ Author-faces-2-000-fine-taking-handful-pebbles-beach.html.

38. McEwan, I. (2007) *On Chesil Beach*. Vintage Books, London.

39. *Times Online* (6 April 2007) Author returns 'stolen' stones. http://entertainment. timesonline.co.uk/tol/arts_and_entertainment/books/article1621108.ece.

40. Bell, A., Elsaesser, B., and Whittaker, T. (undated). Environmental impact of fast ferry wash in shallow water. http://www.qub.ac.uk/waves/fastferry/reference/EnvImpact1.pdf.

41. *Strandline* (2008) The Marine Conservation Society Adopt-a-Beach Newsletter, Issue 36, Autumn 2008.

42. McGlashan, D.J. and Duck, R.W. (2011) Who owns the sand? The Ayre of Cara, Orkney Islands, Scotland. *The Geographical Journal*, 177, 35–43.

43. Hails, J.R. (1975) Submarine geology, sediment distribution and Quaternary history of Start Bay, Devon. *Journal of the Geological Society*, 131, 1–5.

44. Melia, S. (2004). *Hallsands: A Village Betrayed*. Forest Publishing, Newton Abbott.

45. Melia, *Hallsands*.

46. Royal Commission on Coast Erosion and Afforestation.

47. Lyell, *Principles of Geology*.

48. Ministry of Agriculture, Fisheries and Food; The Welsh Office; Association of District Councils; English Nature; National Rivers Authority (1995). *Shoreline Management Plans: A Guide for Coastal Defence Authorities*.

49. Environment Agency (2011) *Shoreline Management Plans (SMPs)*. http://www.environment-agency.gov.uk/research/planning/104939.aspx.

50. Brooke, J. (2000) Strategic coastal defence planning: the role of the planning system. *Journal of the Chartered Institution of Water and Environmental Management*, 14, 140–142.

51. Defra (2005) *Making Space for Water: Taking Forward a New Government Strategy for Flood and Coastal Erosion Risk Management in England*. http://www.defra.gov.uk/ environment/flooding/documents/policy/strategy/strategy-response1.pdf.

52. Defra (2004) *Making Space for Water: Developing a New Government Strategy for Flood and Coastal Erosion Risk Management in England: a Consultation Exercise*, PB 9792.

53. Coastal Futures (undated) *Don't Bank on it: the Economics of Managed Realignment*. http://coastalfutures.org.uk/pdfs/RSPB%20CF%20Brochure_210_Square.pdf.

54. Winn, P.J.S., Young, R.M. and Edwards, A.M.C. (2003) Planning for the rising tides: the Humber Estuary Shoreline Management Plan. *The Science of the Total Environment*, 314–316, 13–30.

55. Myatt-Bell, L.B., Scrimshaw, M.D., Lester, J.N. and Potts, J.S. (2002) Public perception of managed realignment: Brancaster West Marsh, North Norfolk, UK. *Marine Policy*, 26, 45–57.

56. Galloway, J.A. and Potts, J.S. (2007) Marine flooding in the Thames Estuary and tidal river *c.* 1250-1450: impact and response. *Area*, 39, 370–379.

57. Phillips, M.R., Powell, V.A. and Duck, R.W. (2009) Coastal regeneration at Llanelli, South Wales, UK: lessons not learned. *Journal of Coastal Research*, SI 56, 1276–1280.

58. Phillips *et al.* Coastal regeneration at Llanelli, South Wales, UK.

59. *Wales on Sunday*. (5 December 2004) £20M bill to save walk. http://www.highbeam.com/doc/1G1-125825409.html

60. Chell, K. (2002) Coastline in decay. *Geography Review*, January, 32–36.

61. Trudgill, S. (2009) 'You can't resist the sea': evolving attitudes and responses to coastal erosion at Slapton, South Devon. *Geography*, 94, 48–57.

62. Trudgill, 'You can't resist the sea'.

Chapter 7

1. You Tube (2010) *North Berwick Harbour Dinghy Park Flooding 30 March 2010.*
   http://www.youtube.com/watch?v=cBZWS7sO4Ow

2. Professor Charles McKean (2010). Personal communication.

3. Whittington, G. (1985) The Little Ice Age and Scotland's weather. *Scottish Geographical Magazine*, 101, 174–178.

4. Lamont, J. (1830) *The Diary of Mr John Lamont of Newton, 1649–1671.* James Clark and Co., Edinburgh.

5. Forsberg, C.F. (2010) Geomorphological evidence for the development of the Storegga Slide. *Frontiers of Seismic Geomorphology: A Joint Meeting of the Petroleum Group and the Virtual Seismic Atlas*, 7, Geological Society of London, London.

6. McGuire, B. (2005) Swept away. *New Scientist*, 188 (2522), 38–42.

7. Ward, S.N. and Day, D. (2001) Cumbre Vieja Volcano: potential collapse and tsunami at La Palma, Canary Islands. *Geophysical Research Letters*, 28, 3397–3400.

8. Løvholt, F., Pedersen, G. and Gisler, G. (2008) Oceanic propagation of a potential tsunami from La Palma Island. *Journal of Geophysical Research C: Oceans*, 113, Article No. C09026.

9. McGuire, Swept away; BBC News (10 August 2004) Expert slams wave threat inertia. http://news.bbc.co.uk/1/hi/sci/tech/3553368.stm.

10. Dawson, A.G., Musson, R.M.W., Foster, I.D.L. and Brunsden, D. (2000) Abnormal historic sea-surface fluctuations, SW England. *Marine Geology*, 170, 59–68.

11. Haslett, S.K. and Bryant, E.A. (2008) Historic tsunami in Britain since AD 1000: a review. *Natural Hazards and Earth System Sciences*, 8, 587–601.

12. Pontee, N.I. (2005) Management implications of coastal change in Suffolk, UK. *Proceeding of the Institution of Civil Engineers Maritime Engineering*, 158, 69–83.

13. Hewitt, *An Essay on the Encroachments of the German Ocean along the Norfolk Coast.*

14. Happisburgh Village Website. *The Village as it Was.* http://www.happisburgh.org/history/village/as-it-was; Literary Norfolk. *Happisburgh.* http://www.literarynorfolk.co.uk/happisburgh.htm.

15. *Mail Online* (11 July 2008) Living on the edge: the owners whose homes are going over a cliff. http://www.dailymail.co.uk/femail/article-1034456/Living-edge-The-owners-homes-going-cliff.html; BBC News (13 March 2007) Last rocks arrive to save coast. http://news.bbc.co.uk/1/hi/england/norfolk/6444581.stm.

16. North Norfolk District Council (2007) *Kelling to Lowestoft Ness Shoreline Management Plan First Review.* http://www.north-norfolk.gov.uk/ files/SMP_Aug07.pdf; Brennan, R. (2007) The North Norfolk coastline: a complex legacy. *Coastal Management*, 35, 587–599; North Norfolk Shoreline Management Plan 2 Old Hunstanton to Kelling Hard – Draft (2009) http://www.northnorfolk.org/files/Managing_the_Coast.pdf.

17. Buy a Rock for Happisburgh. http://www.buyarockforhappisburgh.com/.

18. North Norfolk District Council (2009) Environment and Waste: Shoreline Management Plan. http://www.north-norfolk.gov.uk/coastal/810.asp.

19. Pontee, N.I. (2005) Management implications of coastal change in Suffolk, UK; McGlashan, D.J. and Duck, R.W. (2010) The PDMU approach to the integration of coastal management. *Journal of Coastal Research*, 26, 465–469.

20. Fletcher, S., Potts, J.S., Heeps, C. and Pike, K. (2009) Public awareness of marine environmental issues in the UK. *Marine Policy*, 33, 370–375.

21. Stallworthy, M. (2006) Sustainability, coastal erosion and climate change: an environmental justice analysis. *Journal of Environmental Law*, 18, 357–373; Cooper, J.A.G. and McKenna, J. (2008) Social justice in coastal erosion management: the temporal and spatial dimensions.

Geoforum, 39, 294–306; Johnson, C., Penning-Rowsell, E. and Parker, D. (2007) Natural and imposed injustices: the challenges in implementing 'fair' flood risk management policy in England. *The Geographical Journal*, 173, 374–390.

22. Brennan, The North Norfolk coastline.

23. Nowell, D. (21 April 2008) Coastal land is only leased from the sea. *The Guardian*, p. 33.

24. Coastal Concern Action Group. Royal Commission on Environmental Pollution Study on Adapting the UK to Climate Change: A response from Coastal Concern Action Group (CCAG). http://www.rcep.org.uk/reports/28-adaptation/documents/036_ Coastal_Concern_Action_Group.pdf.

25. Dyer, K.R. and Moffat, T.J. (1988) Fluxes of suspended matter in the East Anglian plume. Continental Shelf Research, 18, 1311–1331; HR Wallingford, CEFAS/UEA, Posford Haskoning and D'Olier, B. (2002) Southern North Sea Sediment Transport Study, Phase2: Sediment Transport Report. Report EX 4526 for Great Yarmouth Borough Council.

26. Borough of Poole (2009) *Sandbanks Conservation Area: Character Appraisal and Management Plan*. http://www.boroughofpoole.com/downloads/ assets/Sandbanks_Conservation_Area_Brochure~low_res.pdf.

27. *The Independent* (11 August 2007) Rising sea levels threaten to engulf Millionaires' Row. http://www.independent.co.uk/environment/climate-change/rising- sea-levels-threaten-to-engulf-millionaires-row-461146.html.

28. ITV.com *Sandbanks*. http://www.itv.com/Sandbanks/default.html.

29. BBC News (5 December 2006). Spire Plans for luxury peninsula. http://news.bbc.co.uk/1/hi/england/dorset/6210778.stm.

30. Minutes of the Branksome Park, Canford Cliffs and District Residents' Association (8 October 2008) http://branksomepark.com/227/bpccra-minutes-october-8th-2008/.

31. McGlashan, D.J. (2003) Managed relocation: an assessment of its feasibility as a coastal management option. *The Geographical Journal*, 169, 6–20.

32. BBC News (19 March 1999) Lighthouse megamove complete. http://news.bbc.co.uk/1/hi/sci/tech/specials/set99/298123.stm.

33. The Landmark Trust (2010) New landmarks. http://www.landmarktrust.org.uk/news/ClavellTower.htm.

34. Cunningham, D. (1885) Account of shifting one of the lighthouses at Buddonness near Dundee Harbour. *Minutes of Proceedings of the Institute of Civil Engineers*, 79, 347–350.

35. McInnes, R.G. (2006) Responding to the risks from climate change in coastal zones: a good practice guide. *RESPONSE: European LIFE Environment Project 2003–2006*. Isle of Wight Centre for the Coastal Environment, Isle of Wight, UK.

36. Black, A.R., Werritty, A. and Paine, J. (2006) Financial Costs of Property Damages due to Flooding: the Halifax Dundee Flood Loss Tables 2005. University of Dundee, Scotland, sponsored by Halifax General Insurance Services; Werritty, A. (2006) Sustainable flood management: oxymoron or new paradigm? *Area*, 38, 16–23.

37. *The Independent* (18 August 2008) Stark warning on Britain's shrinking coast: abandon homes to the rising sea warns Britain's new environment chief. http://www.independent.co.uk/news/uk/home-news/stark-warning-on-britains- shrinking-coast-900638.html.

38. Defra (2010) *Adapting to Coastal Change: Developing a Policy Framework March 2010*. Defra, London.

39. East Riding of Yorkshire Council (2011) East Riding Coastal Change Pathfinder. http://www.eastriding.gov.uk/cps/community-and-sustainable-development/ sustainable-development-services/coastal-change-pathfinder/.

40. East Riding of Yorkshire Council: East Riding Coastal Change Pathfinder.

41. This is Hull and East Riding (2010) £1.2M help for erosion-risk homeowners.
    http://www.thisishullandeastriding.co.uk/news/163-1-2m-help-erosion-risk-
    homeowners/article-1798328-detail/article.html.

42. Coastal Concern Action Group (16 October 2010) *Erosion-hit Happisburgh residents criticise
    'insulting' compensation offer.*
    http://www.happisburgh.org.uk/press/edp161010.html.

43. McGlashan, D.J., Duck, R.W. and Reid, C.T. (2009). Legal implications of mobile
    shorelines in Great Britain. *Area*, 41, 149–156.

44. Girling, *Sea Change: Britain's Coastal Catastrophe*.

45. Sixth Report of the House of Commons Select Committee on Agriculture (1998)
    Conclusions and Recommendations, House of Commons, London, Paragraph 115.

46. Hadley, D. (2009) Land use and the coastal zone. *Land Use Policy*, 26 Supplement 1,
    S198–S203.

INDEX